1996

D1599369

Piers Plowman Studies IV

THE CLERKLY MAKER

Piers Plowman Studies

I   THE THEME OF GOVERNMENT IN PIERS PLOWMAN
Anna Baldwin

II   THE FIGURE OF PIERS PLOWMAN
Margaret E. Goldsmith

III   PERSONIFICATION IN PIERS PLOWMAN
Lavinia Griffiths

ISSN 0261–9849

The Clerkly Maker

Langland's Poetic Art

A. V. C. SCHMIDT

Hit bycometh for clerkes Crist for to serue . . .
Somme to synge masses or sitten and wryten
　　　　　(*Piers Plowman* C. V 61, 68)

A Poet is as much to say as a maker
　　　　　(George Puttenham, *The Arte of*
　　　　　English Poesie, I.i)

D. S. BREWER

First published 1987 by D. S. Brewer
240 Hills Road, Cambridge
an imprint of Boydell & Brewer Ltd
PO Box 9, Woodbridge, Suffolk IP12 3DF
and Wolfeboro, New Hampshire 03894–2069, USA

ISBN 0 85991 233 7

British Library Cataloguing in Publication Data

Schmidt, A. V. C.
    The clerkly maker: Langland's poetic art.
    (Piers Plowman studies; 4)
    1. Langland, William. Piers Plowman
    I. Title   II. Series
    821'.1   PR2015
    ISBN 0-85991-233-7

Library of Congress Cataloging-in-Publication Data

Schmidt, A. V. C. (Aubrey Vincent Carlyle)
    The clerkly maker.

    (Piers Plowman studies, ISSN 0261–9849; 4)
    Bibliography: p.
    Includes index.
    1. Langland, William, 1330?–1387? – Versification.
    I. Title.   II. Series.
    PR2018.S36   1987   821'.1   86-26378
    ISBN 0-85991-233-7

Photoset by Rowland Phototypesetting Ltd
Bury St Edmunds, Suffolk
Printed in Great Britain by St Edmundsbury Press Ltd
Bury St Edmunds, Suffolk

Contents

For PIERS, SIMON and ROBIN

Forthi love we as leve children shal, and ech man laughe of oother

Acknowledgements

I am deeply grateful to Prof. John Burrow for reading this book in typescript and for many valuable comments which helped me to eliminate errors and confusions and to express my argument more clearly. He cannot be held responsible for the errors that doubtless remain, but he bears part of the blame for my writing on Langland's art at all, since I first began to think about the subject in a paper given at one of his classes in Oxford nearly twenty-five years ago. The main argument of this study was worked out during lectures given at various intervals since 1979, and I am greatly obliged to Oxford University and to Balliol College for terms of sabbatical leave during this period. Many of the ideas in ch. 4 first emerged in discussions with Mr James Simpson, and the footnotes do scant justice to the degree of my indebtedness to him. My publishers have been very patient with what has been a much-delayed project. Patience itself has found a personification in my wife Judith, whose support during *siknesse and angres* ensured that *The Clerkly Maker* got written at all.

My final thanks are due to the three musicians named in the dedication for reminding me with *murthe of hire mouthes* that there *is* an end to the making of books.

Oxford, 1986   AVCS

ABBREVIATIONS

CSEL	*Corpus Scriptorum Ecclesiasticorum Latinorum*
EC	*Essays in Criticism*
EETS	Early English Text Society
ELH	English Literary History
JEGP	*Journal of English and Germanic Philology*
MÆ	*Medium Ævum*
MED	*Middle English Dictionary*
Med. St.	*Medieval Studies*
NQ	*Notes and Queries*
OED	*Oxford English Dictionary*
PBA	*Proceedings of the British Academy*
PL	*Patrologia Latina*
RES	*Review of English Studies*
Spec.	*Speculum*
ST	*Summa Theologica*

Introduction

Although this book forms part of a series of '*Piers Plowman* Studies', it is written not only for the Langland specialist but for anyone who cares for English poetry, whatever its period or the apparent difficulty of its language and subject-matter. My sub-title indicates a wider range of topics than it is possible to address in a short book. I have in fact concentrated on three main areas of poetic art – versecraft, diction and wordplay. I have largely ignored imagery, a theme on which I have written elsewhere, and one which deserves a full-length study to itself.[1] I have based the book almost entirely on the B-text, the one in which, to quote a passage of Dr Johnson given recent prominence by Christopher Ricks, 'is exerted all the force of poetry, that force which calls new powers into being, which embodies sentiment, and animates matter'.[2] My approach is both analytical and descriptive, with a preponderance of the latter in the chapter on versecraft, where I have tried to be comprehensive. I have aimed as far as possible to avoid unnecessary technical terms, but I am aware that in some places, especially in chapter two, I have had to invent a number of these in order to argue my case that Langland really cared about the technique of alliterative verse. I have attempted throughout to write criticism rather than covert literary biography or historical literary theory. What we know of Langland, even allowing for imperfections in the text of his work, is the poetry, not the man; and we have nothing from his age comparable to the treatises on poetry left by Dante and Boccaccio that might throw additional light on the literary theory of the alliterative poets. The most important assumptions that I make are

---

1 See 'Langland's Structural Imagery', *EC* XXX (1980) 311–25 and 'Elemental Imagery in *PP*' (forthcoming). [All bibliographical references are given in full on their first appearance and thereafter in abbreviated form, except for the standard abbreviations for journals, etc., for which see the list of abbreviations on p. viii].
2 *The Rambler*, No. 168, 26 Oct. 1751; quoted as epigraph by Christopher Ricks, *The Force of Poetry* (Oxford, 1984).

1

embodied in the main title of the book. I believe that they are borne out by this study, but I do not have the space to justify them in detail here.

The expression 'the Clerkly Maker', although modelled upon Put-tenham's famous 'courtly makers', describes what is probably a class of only one member. The makers, the vernacular poets,[3] of the late four-teenth century, included those who wrote in *rym*, like Chaucer, and those who wrote in *lel letteres loken*, like the *Gawain*-poet (who combined the two in *Pearl*). Chaucer was certainly and the *Gawain-Pearl* poet probably a 'courtly maker' in the double sense of writing some at least of their works for a court audience and on courtly themes (*fyn lovyng*, chivalrye, cour-teisie); we do not, of course, know what court the latter belonged to or wrote for. The poet of *Winner and Waster*, too, deplores in his Prologue the decline of aristocratic patronage of makers like himself;[4] the more fortun-ate 'William', author of *William of Palerne*, on the other hand, praises 'þe hende erl of Hereford, Humfray de Boune', because 'He let make þis mater in þis maner speche' (5532–3).[5] Langland, however, says nothing of either the loss or the enjoyment of patronage by himself (though he certainly criticises the decline in aristocratic taste); and this is presumably because he had nothing to say. For those who supported Langland as a maker appear to have done so only indirectly by supporting him as a clerk. They were his family, who paid for his education ('My fader and my frendes foende me to scole' (C. V 36))[6] and those who provided him food in return for his prayers (C. V 48–51). There is evidence from the early ownership of *Piers Plowman* manuscripts that churchmen were interested in Langland's work, but none, within or outside the text, that they actively patronised him as a writer. By calling Langland a 'clerkly maker' I mean, then, not that he belonged to a recognisable category of poet but that he was himself conscious of being a practitioner of the maker's art and a real member of the estate of clergy.

These last two points are explicitly affirmed by Langland, as I shall show in chapter one. But the link between 'clerk' and 'maker' was not merely, in the metaphysical sense, 'accidental', even if, being problem-atic, it receives less than explicit formulation in the poem. In saying this I mean that Langland's poetry, while fully participating in the 'makerly' qualities of the alliterative tradition (from whose heartland he apparently

3 See the Appendix, 'Poet, Maker, Translator, Versifier'.
4 *WW* 19–30, ed. T. Turville-Petre in B. Ford, ed: *Medieval Literature*, I: *Chaucer and the Alliterative Tradition* (Harmondsworth, 1982). See further ch. 1, pp. 6–7 below.
5 Ed. W. W. Skeat, EETS E.S. 1 (1867). T. Turville-Petre, *The Alliterative Revival* (Cambridge, 1977) 41, argues that the poem was written for de Bohun's provincial households, not for the Earl himself.
6 Unless otherwise stated the C-text is quoted from the York Medieval Texts edition by Derek Pearsall (London, 1978).

came),[7] is deeply coloured by his 'clerkly' culture and also, one may believe, by the character of his primary audience. Just as the implied audience of Chaucer's *Troilus* is one of *loveres*, familiar with the language, theory and practice of the art of love, so the implied audience of *Piers Plowman* is one familiar with the Bible, the liturgy, and the moral and spiritual concerns of the poet, not least among them being the state of the English clergy. Such an implied audience would find its real counterpart in the clergy of the metropolis where Langland seems to have composed the poem: the one known contemporary who mentions it, the radical John Ball, was himself a priest,[8] as was the earliest recorded owner of the work, William Palmere, rector of St Alphage, Cripplegate (d. 1400).[9]

The clerical primary audience, however, without whom the Latinity and learnedness of the poem would be hard to explain, was by no means the exclusive audience. Langland, not the less a clerk in this, was also concerned with communicating to the common people; his poem, even more than Gower's *Confessio Amantis*, is 'A bok for Engelondes sake' (Prol 24), his concern for the Church a concern for the whole English people who were its members. If Langland's poetry is difficult, this is not because, like that of the *Pearl*-poet, it uses vocabulary and idioms unfamiliar to 'Southren men', but because it draws so audaciously both upon the wealth of Latin and upon the unexploited resources of the vernacular in its many levels and registers – literary, legal, commercial and demotic. Nor should it be forgotten that Latin itself, though a learned language, was in the Universities at least a living (and remarkably inventive) 'vernacular' of sorts, the vulgar tongue of clerks. The true difficulty of Langland's poetry, however, is that much of the time it *seems* plain, its vocabulary not obviously rare and strange like so much of the alliterative lexicon. But on the basis of a *sermo humilis* like that of the Vulgate Bible, he can build a wide range of artistic effects varying from the sinewy bareness of the Haukyn passage, through the coarse realism of the Glutton scene, to the astonishing fusion of grotesque and sublime in the Harrowing of Hell passus, with its combination of lyric intensity, dazzling macaronics and impassioned rhetorical wordplay.

These qualities, and the very special Langlandian one of combining childlike simplicity with cunning subtlety, invite and reward close

7 See D. Pearsall, 'The Origins of the Alliterative Revival' in B. S. Levy and P. E. Szarmach, *The Alliterative Tradition in the Fourteenth Century* (Kent, Ohio, 1981) 1–17, esp. p. 17.
8 Ball's Letter to the Peasants of Essex is printed in K. Sisam, ed., *Fourteenth Century Verse and Prose* (Oxford, 1955) 160–1.
9 See R. A. Wood, 'A 14th-Century London Owner of *PP*', *MÆ* LIII (1984) 83–90.

examination, for it can hardly be denied that many readers have found 'his termes hard and obscure', as did Puttenham, 'so as in them is little pleasure to be taken'.[10] This book will have failed unless it convinces the reader that Puttenham is largely mistaken. The maker and clerk, the poet and thinker in Langland, have sometimes been thought of almost as separate creatures sharing an uncomfortable *modus vivendi* which is in constant peril of collapse and occasionally gives way altogether. My conviction is not only that he is at his didactically most convincing when he is at his poetically most inventive, but also that we have only begun to understand and appreciate the nature of his art. In this study of the Ricardian Age's Clerkly Maker, I hope that I have succeeded in advancing rather than retarding the enterprise.

10 *The Arte of English Poesie* I xxxi in G. G. Smith, ed., *Elizabethan Critical Essays* II (Oxford, 1904) 65.

Chapter One

Meddling with Making

I. MAKING AND JANGLING

In the course of the B-text, Langland twice considers the nature and moral responsibility of his activity as a maker: in the dialogues with Lewte (XI 84–107) and with Ymaginatif (XII 10–32).[1] These passages, which I discuss at length in the third section of this chapter, provide what may be called the positive or constructive aspect of his treatment of the problem of making, and they deal with it largely in relation to his own position as clerk and maker. But he also offers a negative or critical account of the situation of makers and patrons. This is found in a long speech of Dame Studie (X 30–50) and in a passage of direct authorial comment following the description of Haukyn the minstrel (XIII 409–56). Important themes of both passages are, however, anticipated almost at the outset of the poem (Pr 33–9), so that we are given the negative side of the picture, in relation to others, before the positive and the personal aspect. Accordingly, I examine these, closely related groups of lines, in the second section below. Langland's defence of making and his attack on 'jangling' (false making) thus occur in separation from each other: he does not attack the janglers explicitly *as* a maker (although he comes near to doing so implicitly at one point, XIII 443–5). As I see it, he has disengaged two strands of an argument which are found woven together as a single defence-cum-critique in *Winner and Waster*. This is a work which I believe, notwithstanding Elizabeth Salter's case for a possibly later date, was written in the early 1350's, and was known to Langland.[2] It is the product of a maker of very considerable skill, but not one who appears to have

---

1 All B-text citations are from the 1984 reprint of my edition.
2 'The Timeliness of *Wynnere and Wastoure*', *MÆ* 47 (1978) 40–65; D. Lawton, 'Literary History and Scholarly Fancy . . .' and *ME Alliterative Poetry* (1982) 125–6 also believes *WW* to be later than *PP*, despite the clear statement at 206 that Edward III had reigned for 25 years (which there is no reason to query). My argument is unaffected even if *WW* is the later work.

been a clerk in the sense I have described Langland in the Introduction. Nonetheless, it offered him certain key oppositions – notably those between the verbs *make* and *jangle* and the nouns *myrthes* and *japes*[3] – which he was to turn to his own use in developing a critique of corrupt making from his own distinctive standpoint as a clerk. I therefore begin this chapter with a very brief look at the complaint of Langland's anonymous predecessor.

In the Prologue of *Winner and Waster* the author recalls an unspecified time in the past when things were better for the art of making and its practitioners:

> Whylome were *lordes* in londe that *loved* in thaire hertis
> To here *makers of myrthes* that matirs couthe fynde

and he contrasts it with the present day:

> But now a child appon chere, withowtten chyn-wedys,
> That never wroghte thurgh *witt* three wordes togedire,
> Fro he can *jangle* as a jaye and *japes* telle,
> He shall be levede and *lovede* and lett of a while
> Wele more than the man that made it hymselven.
> But never the lattere at the laste, when ledys bene knawen,
> Werke witnesse will bere who wirche kane beste.
> (WW 19–20, 24–30).[4]

Thorlac Turville-Petre's gloss to line 28 sees the writer as comparing the youth who recites (but lacks talent or skill to compose) with the mature author of the poem he recites; the youth is applauded now, but at the final reckoning (before posterity or, more likely, at the Judgement Day) 'the work itself' will prove whose the skill really is. The passage is not unambiguous, though I think it must mean by *werke* (30) 'the poetic composition, the *makyng*' rather than 'the activity of composing *or* reciting'. However, I question whether line 26 necessarily implies a reciter as opposed to a composer. I see the opposition rather as one between a crude, comic entertainer who has never produced intelligent, artistic poetry ('wroghte thurgh witt') and a creator of original verse. It is not necessary to emend *made it* (28) to *makes* as Gollancz does[5] in order to

---

3 *The* senses 'compose a poem' for *maken* and 'an entertainment, story' for *myrthe* are both found in the C13th (*MED* s.v. 5(a) for both) but *janglere* 'teller of dirty stories' (*MED* s.v. (d)) and *jape* 'rubbishy tale, comic tale' (*MED* s.v. n. 2(a)) are not instanced from a date earlier than *PP* and/or *WW*.

4 Ed. Turville-Petre, in Ford, ed., *Medieval Literature* (Pelican Guide I.1); the italicised words recur in the *PP* passages.

5 In his edition, *Select Early English Poems* III (1920). Ll. 19–28 are discussed by Nicolas Jacobs, who suspects one or more lines to have been lost after 21; see 'The Typology of Debate and the Interpretation of *WW*' *RES* 36 (1985) p. 500.

obtain this sense, since the *it* has no explicit antecedent and may be taken as pleonastic. Turville-Petre's reading, though grammatically possible, yields a rather odd sense; for it is hard to see how a poem like *Winner and Waster*, if recited by an inexperienced youth, could end up sounding like 'jangling' and 'japes'. Is the *Winner*-poet not, instead, setting up a contrast between the reciting of scurrilous pieces (perhaps improvised, with no real distinction of performance from composition) and the skilled fashioning of serious 'matirs'; between jangling and making; 'japes' and 'myrthes'? At the explicit level, the seriousness in question seems primarily one of a craftsmanship that invites critical scrutiny. But the allusion to the Last Judgement at least implicitly attributes moral significance to well-made art, and the *japes* with which the *myrthes* are contrasted have overtones of moral worthlessness,[6] while the substance of the poem that follows the Prologue, a debate on 'matirs' of ethical purport and political urgency, also implies serious themes as the maker's proper concern. Another, probably later alliterative poem, the *Morte Arthure*, which describes the world that the *Winner*-poet initially evokes (lines 1–3), opens with a prayer to God (in a context of man's death and judgement) for guidance

> to werpe owte some worde at this tyme,
> That nothyre voyde be ne vayne, bot wyrchip tille hymeselvyne,
> Plesande and profitabille to the popule that theme heres.

There is more didactic emphasis here, but the address to those 'that liste has to lyth, or luffes for to here, / Off elders of alde tyme' is reminiscent of *Winner and Waster* 19–20, quoted above (*Morte Arthure*, 9–13).[7] The *Morte*-poet, in his own way, is 'in the act of "making" . . . necessarily delivered up to judgement' too[8]. For since he asks God to *gye* himself and his audience 'thorowe vertuous lywynge' (5) and then to *wysse* him in his effort as maker, his terms *nothyre voyde . . . ne vayne* surely entail as complete a rejection of *jangling* and *japes* as that of the *Winner*-poet.

II. CLERKLY CARPING

The attitudes explored above are those of what we may think of as the Maker *tout court*, proud of his title, aware of his responsibility to his art and to God, contemptuous of coarseness and scornful of lack of skill. There is nothing clerkly about either the *Winner* or the *Morte* poet: the

---

6 See *MED mirthe* 2(a) 'the joys of heaven', *jape* 2(b) 'immoral act'.
7 *Morte Arthure*, ed. E. Brock, EETS O.S. 8 (1871).
8 Geoffrey Hill, *The Lords of Limit: Essays on Literature and Ideas* (1984) 14.

earnestness of both is that of pious laymen, just as their subject-matter, though moral, is thoroughly secular by comparison with Langland. Their style, likewise, is free from the Latinity and learnedness characteristic of Langland as a member of the clerical estate, which alone had access to higher education.[9] When we turn from these two Prologues to that of *Piers Plowman*, the initial impression is of being in the same secular world, but an even more courtly one, it would appear, with 'May morwenynge' and 'Fairye'[10] in place of 'Bretayne the brode' (*Morte Arthure*, 4346; cf. *Winner*, 1). But the perspective soon becomes dramatically and explicitly religious; the 'judgement' motif found in different guises in the other two Prologues here presents itself in starkly eschatological form in the 'tour', the 'deep dale' and the 'fair feeld' (Pr 14, 15, 17). When we are shown amongst the Folk some whose task is 'murthes to make as mynstralles konne, / And geten gold with hire glee' (33–4), not only does the b-half of line 34 immediately introduce the problematic issue of their moral status in Christian society – '[gilt]lees, I leeve' –[11] but that of the next line, 35, delivers an unexpectedly ferocious condemnation of a group whose guilt lacks the qualification of 'I leeve' – the 'japeres and jangeleres, Judas children', who 'Feynen hem fantasies, and fooles hem maketh – / And han wit at wille to werken if they wolde' (Pr 36–7).

Although Langland here recalls the *Winner*-poet's opposed terms, he develops a typically more subtle distinction by his paronomasia on *make* and *werken*, a clerkly feature, as I shall argue. The offence of Langland's janglers is a graver one: neither young nor skilless, they perversely quit the 'wit' they have 'at wille', their only 'making' being of themselves into 'fooles'. If *their* 'work' will also bear witness at judgement time, the mention of Judas serves to equate them with the 'deep dale', the dwelling of the arch-liar, rather than with the 'tour', the abode of Truth.

The first of the longer passages of criticism, Dame Studie's speech, also attacks 'japeris and jogelours and jangleris of gestes'[12] who 'feynen hem

---

9 See E. F. Jacob, 'English University Clerks in the Later Middle Ages', in *Essays in the Conciliar Epoch* (1963) 207–39 and J. Dunbabin, 'Careers and Vocations' in J. I. Catto, ed.: *The History of the University of Oxford, I: The Early Oxford Schools* (Oxford, 1984) 565–605.

10 Cf. *Sir Orfeo*, 57, 193 in *Medieval English Romances*, I, ed. A. V. C. Schmidt and N. Jacobs (1980); *Romaunt of the Rose*, 49ff, in F. N. Robinson, ed., *Works of Geoffrey Chaucer* (2nd edn., 1957).

11 I presume *I leeve* to be affirmative, but cf. the dubitative effect of the phrase at VII 177.

12 The context, and the linking with *japeris* and *jangleris*, indicate that Langland has the unfavourable sense of *jogelours* in mind, *MED* s.v. 2(a) 'illusionist' (cf. the low company kept by Jakke the Jogelour at VI 70), and for *geste*, normally a positive term in alliterative poetry, the 'low' sense 'disreputable prank' (*MED* s.v. 2(a), illustrated only from c. 1450, but very aptly).

foolis and with faityng libbeth' (X 31, 38).[13] But these, notwithstanding the closely similar phrasing, are not the same as the 'Judas children' of the Prologue, since

> Thei konne na moore mynstralcie[14] ne musik men to glade
> Than Munde the Millere of *Multa fecit Deus*   (X 43–4).

Of the former class Langland writes that '*Qui loquitur turpiloquium* is Luciferes hyne' (Pr 39); of the latter, that they 'Spitten and spuen and speke foule wordes' (X 40). It would take someone with 'wit at wille', a clerk, no less, simply to understand the charge (in both senses) of line 39a, while even the *lewed* can grasp *foule wordes*. Langland may indeed intend a variety of clerks, *goliardi*,[15] by the first group, whose sin is the more heinous since they 'know' (as their 'father', Judas, knew Jesus yet betrayed him). Yet the end result of both types is the same, and justifies his later joining of them in XIII 454–6, which describe the effect of their 'work' on those who hear and support them:

> . . . flatereres and fooles thorugh hir foule wordes
> Leden tho that loved hem to Luciferis feste
> With *turpiloquio*, a lay of sorwe, and Luciferis fithele.[16]

This effect is the spiritual corruption of the 'lordes and ladies and legates of Holy Chirche' (XIII 421) who patronise them, and also the neglect of the 'lered man' who would aim to 'lere [him] what Oure Lord suffred / For to save [his] soule fram Sathan . . .'. Such a man, clearly, could be the author of Passus XVIII; but this oblique suggestion is the nearest that Langland comes to a plea for patronage. His substantive point is the general collapse of the maker's profession as such:

13 *Feynen* appears in literary uses, but never without negative moral overtones (e.g. Chaucer, *HF* 1478) and its association with *faiten* here is fatal (*faiten* (< OF *faire* 'make', ironically enough) is a term of reproach confined almost entirely to *PP*).
14 The *MED* examples of *mynstralcie* 'music-making, musicianship' are wholly favourable in tone (but cf. next note).
15 Langland calls his *goliardeis, a glotoun of wordes* (Pr 139), playing on the supposed derivation of the name from Latin *gula* 'gluttony' (cf. Robert Mannyng's 'A mynstralle, a gulardous' (*Handlyng Synne* 4701), where the second term, plainly *hostile* in context, is not in the AF original). But this figure is clearly no buffoon like Munde the Millere or Chaucer's *janglere* (*CT*, A 560) and quotes shrewd Latin; for some more elevated associations of the term, see P. G. Walsh, '"Golias" and Goliardic Poetry', *MÆ* 52 (1983) 1–9.
16 This passage echoes the source of Pr 39, Eph 5:3–6, which mentions *turpitudo, aut stultiloquium* (cf. 'fooles'), *aut scurrilitas* ('foule wordes').

> 'Ac murthe and mynstralcie amonges men is nouthe
> Lecherie, losengerye and losels tales'   (X 48–9).[17]

I shall say nothing here of Langland's idiosyncratic allegorisation of the term 'minstrel' at XIII 442ff except to note how it serves to underscore his view of the high moral function of poetry. The 'povere' are consociated with 'a lered man' as *ideal* recipients of the rich man's largesse; in *actuality*, '*if* thei carpen of Crist, thise clerkes and thise lewed' (X 51) it is to speculate blasphemously about the greatest theological mysteries, the Incarnation and the Trinity (X 53–7). The rejection of sound matter is the result of the corrupting alliance between clerks and lay patrons, so that 'murthe . . . is nouthe / Lecherie', in Studie's words, a disaster taken yet further in the passage of direct address by the poet complaining how

> Whan men carpen of Crist, or of clennesse of soule,
> He wexeth wroth and wol noght here but *wordes of murthe*
> > (XIII 416–7).

Even so innocent and 'lele'[18] a word as *murthe*[19] has become tainted – 'voyde' and 'vayne', not 'plesande and profitabille' (in the *Morte Arthure* – poet's terms) but simply *turpiloquium*, 'foule wordes'.

The intensity of Langland's indignation seems due to a sense that life as well as art is being betrayed: that a 'Judas'-like attitude to one's clerkly wit and makerly craft is treachery to one's own soul and to the souls of one's hearers.[20] Langland sees clerks and makers as bearing a special responsibility towards language, the divine gift with which they in particular have been endowed, and which they should use for the glory of God and the good of their fellow men. As early as Wit's speech in Passus IX, misuse of the gift of language is vehemently denounced, and proper cultivation of it figured, with unpremeditated naturalness, as the exercise of sober minstrelsy:

---

17 The decline is of a *craft* (*mynstralcie*) into a form of immoral *conduct* (*lecherie*): neither *losengerye* nor *losels tales* refers primarily (if indeed at all) to types of 'making'.
18 See *MED* s.v. 1(e) 'veracious, trustworthy'. As *lel letteres* properly join alliterative staves, *lele wordes* (XVI 6) are words used with their true, divinely-appointed meanings, *lele speche* (XI 69) an utterance made sincerely and corresponding to reality (cf. also C VII 238). See further my '*Lele Wordes* and *Bele Paroles*', *RES* 34 (1983), esp. 139–41.
19 See *MED* s.v. *mirthe* 3(c) 'sexual dalliance'. The *lele* senses 1a, 2 and 3(a) have collapsed into a speciously *bele* euphemism: in X 48 (see above) *is* = 'means'.
20 Judas, who 'jangles' (protests hypocritically) at XVI 144 and is made by Christ the supreme exemplar of 'Falsnesse . . . in thi faire speche' (cf. Pr 35, discussed above, p. 8) is himself said to have been 'japed' by the 'Fader of falshede' (I 67, 64).

'[Tyn]ynge of tyme, Truthe woot the sothe,
Is *moost yhated* upon erthe of hem that ben in hevene;
And siththe to spille speche, that spire is of grace,
And Goddes gleman and a game of hevene.
Wolde nevere the feithful fader his fithele were untempred,
Ne his gleman a gedelyng,a goere to tavernes'   (IX 99–104).

There is no real subordination intended, I believe, by that *siththe* 'next' in
line 101: Langland virtually identifies sloth (failure to use one's gift) and
waste (misuse or abuse of one's gift), as when the character Sloth himself
confesses his derelictions 'In speche and in sparynge of speche' (V 436).
Whether the instrument is left untuned or used to play the devil's music,
it is failing in its prime purpose, which for Langland means the service of
God.[21] It is hard not to trace the depth of his feelings about the abuse of
language to a sense of his own dual responsibility to it – as clerk and as
maker – a double vocation where failure risks twofold punishment, *double
scathe* (XV 59). However, a negative critique of such severity, if it is to
succeed as correction, necessitates both a *rationale* for his general
approach and an *apologia pro vita sua*, an account of his own stewardship of
the gifts of clerk and maker. It is these two topics that I discuss in the third
section of this chapter.

III.   ALLEGING SOOTH AND MEDDLING WITH MAKING

Of the two passages in which Langland defends the activity of making
and his own involvement in it, one puts the case through Will's interlocu-
tor, the other makes Will himself the defendant. Neither passage is free of
interpretative difficulties, but it is perhaps easier to begin with Lewte's
speech in Passus XI, which is both more general and more explicit. The
context in which it occurs is a crisis in the Dreamer's religious life which
may be somewhat baldly summarised. He has neglected spiritual things
for the world, but eventually approaches the Friars to make his peace with
God through confession. However, because he cannot assure them of his
burial fees (he wishes, once shriven, to be buried in his own parish) they
call him a fool and love him the less for his 'lele speche' (XI 69). This leads

21 His model and example, David, 'patron-saint' of psalter-clerks, is regularly
    evoked as the champion of *truthe* (I 99, II 37, III 241–3, XI 96, 286); as the voice of
    clerkly conscience reminding him to '*sapienter*/Synge' (XI 312–13); and as the
    severe critic of 'flatereris and fooles . . . the fendes disciples' (XIII 429) '*qui
    loquitur iniqua*' (XIII 432a), a phrase here applied to false minstrels and one that
    echoes Pr 39 and is itself echoed at XIII 454–6 (cf. n. 16 above).

him to an outburst against the friars' venality, culminating in an appeal to his clerkly audience for support: 'Loke, ye lettred men, wheither I lye or do noght' (83). But he seems to fear public statement of his grievance (which has so far been voiced only to the unhelpful friar). It is at this point that the character Lewte interposes with his celebrated injunction to Will to rebuke sin fearlessly, provided he is just and disinterested.

The whole of this passage is coloured by the tone of the legal terminology with which it opens. Lewte would take Peter and Paul 'to witnesse' (87); Will fears the friars 'wole aleggen also' and 'by the Gospel preven' (88), where *aleggen* plays on the senses 'claim by way of defence, excuse or justification' and 'appeal to as evidence / cite a law or authority'.[22] The crucial issue is *judgement*: Christ said *Nolite iudicare quemquam* (90; Mt 7:1) and there is no higher authority, plainly. Lewte's way round this obstacle is to see legitimate criticism of vice as possible if the vice is a public, widespread, long-standing abuse, and if the critic is himself free from personal animus (101–6). It is worth observing that he does not say 'if the critic is himself free from fault': it is a deep-held belief of Langland that, as the verse following the one quoted states, 'In quo enim iudicio iudicaveritis, iudicabimini' (Mt 7:2) – no one need fear judgement more, therefore, than the man who presumes to judge others. This is arguably the classic defence of moral satire, and it receives from the authoritative figure of Scripture what sounds like warm approval: 'He seith sooth' (107). Since, then, Will's 'lele speche' has been commended by Lewte and endorsed by Scripture, it comes as somewhat of a surprise that her sermon on the text 'Many are called, but few are chosen' (Mt 22:14) should make Will's heart tremble for *tene* and throw him into a *weer* (both are strong words suggestive of a distraught spiritual state,[23] not the clarity of mind that would seem necessary if he is to 'reden it in retorik to arate dedly synne' (102)).

Although Lewte's injunction to '[l]egge the sothe' (96) is hard to fault, it leaves Will strangely uncertain, still vexed by the question of his own salvation, 'Wheither I were chose or noght chose' (117) – a matter that makes him remember his first vision of Holy Church and his anxious plea to her then 'tel me this ilke – / How I may save my soule' (I 84). This is the dangerous conceit that burns like the mines of sulphur, threatening to corrode any serious attempt to remedy the spiritual ills of society. The clue to what is undoubtedly a puzzling and otherwise perhaps incoherent passage is, I think, to be found in the two appearances of the word *lewed* at 108 and 96. The second of these, which immediately serves to qualify the affirmativeness of Scripture's 'He seith sooth' expresses what can only be

22 See *MED* s.v. 1(a) and 3(a), (b).
23 Cf. VII 115, XVI 86 (*tene*); XVI 3 (*weer*).

described as clerkly *Angst* – an experience from which the lay author of *Winner and Waster* (as I take him to have been) would have been exempt:

> Ac the matere that she meved, if lewed men it knewe,
> The lasse, as I leve, lovyen thei wolde
> The bileve o[f Oure] Lord that lettred men techeth   (109–10).

Langland's dilemma is not just the relatively trivial one of being a clerk attacking the order to which he himself belongs. So were the *goliardi*, and from one viewpoint that fact could strengthen his satire. It is the morally more weighty one of possibly undermining the faith of his hearers. His stated fear here is that if he attacks the friars, the contemporary aspirants to the highest learning and the highest holiness, he may bring into discredit both holiness and learning: the more laymen believe *him*, the less they will *believe*. The immediate referent of *matere* (108) is not, of course, the friars' claims to perfection, but the doctrine of predestination. However, the two are arguably connected: for to undermine the friars' claim to be perfect (they are the 'chosen' *par excellence*)[24] may be also to unsettle the common man's belief in his own possible salvation.

The alternative possibility, raised by the other use of the word *lewed*, by Lewte, is that legitimate criticism of clerical abuse is open to a man if he is a *layman*:

> 'It is *licitum* for lewed men to [l]egge the sothe
> If hem liketh and lest . . .'   (96–7).

Lewte's argument voices what is very much a layman's point of view, and one could be forgiven for catching in it a premonitory whiff of the Reformation as it actually unfolded a century and a half later.[25] There is little comfort here, accordingly, for Will, who is a clerk, even if Langland himself has already put some of the poem's most vigorous criticism of clerical failure into the mouth of the layman Piers (in the Pardon Scene of Passus VII, esp. 131–9). But the situation is not, I would maintain, completely lost for Langland. The seeds of a future possible resolution lie in the injunction 'To reden it in retorik to arate dedly synne' (102), one of the most important lines in *Piers Plowman*. Not only does it evoke the creative triumph of the Confessions of the Seven Deadly Sins in Passus Five, where moral criticism is held in tremulous solution with imaginative sympathy and compassion for weakness; it also hints at a way in which

---

24 Compare Anima (XV 230–2), Conscience (XX 251–2) and the Friars Minor at VIII 118–119.

25 Cf. the remarks of Skelton (himself a clerk) in *Collyn Clout* (*c.* 1523) ll. 75ff. (ed. J. Scattergood, *John Skelton: the Complete English Poems* (Harmondsworth, 1983)).

laymen themselves can become the object as well as the instrument of an effective moral critique. The quasi-diptychal structure of the poem's great Fourth Vision, in which the Doctor of Divinity is set on one side and Haukyn, Minstrel and Active Man on the other, provides a means for Langland to 'locate' himself, in the person of Will,[26] imperfect clerk and aspiring religious maker. That position is one which makes it *licitum* for him to utter 'lele speche' and 'legge the sothe' without fear of falling under the terrible judgement threatened in Mt 7:1–5. The hypocrisy of the Doctor and of Haukyn can be displayed and contemplated, can help without harming, because it is an evil that Langland comes to recognise in himself, a thing of darkness he acknowledges his when Anima, his soul, calls him 'inparfit . . . and oon of Prides knyghtes!' (XV 50).

In the second passage dealing with his activity as a maker, Langland grapples with a more personal and intimate theme – the place of poetry in his own life.[27] This greater intimacy is marked not only by the fact that Will defends *himself*, but by the very nature of his interlocutor, Ymaginatif. The latter is clearly a 'noetic'[28] personification, a power within the Dreamer, whereas Lewte is sufficiently external to him to sound almost like an embodiment of his ideal audience. The two encounters are nonetheless closely related in several ways, of which I mention only two here. One is the shared emphasis on the threat of encroaching old age: 'fele fernyeres are faren, and so fewe to come' (XII 5; cf. '. . . I foryat youthe and yarn into elde', XI 60). This brings with it an urgent need to take stock of one's life and to question the value of one's work (were it not for the bathetic overtones of the phrase, this state of affairs could be seen as a 'mid-life crisis'; cf. XII 7). The second point, linked with the first, is the stress on repentance. As I have said, the Lewte encounter is preceded by a desire to make confession, personal 'amendment', an impulse that is

---

26 Will encounters both (cf. XIII 25, 271); but the Doctor and Haukyn, who embody the extremes of what Will might be or become, do not meet each other. It is the layman Haukyn, whose weeping at XIV 324 recalls 'Wille's' at V 61, who is (perhaps paradoxically) the closer to him: though he can 'telle no gestes' (XIII 230), neither can he 'lye and do men laughe' (XIII 228).

27 I am aware that *PP* is no more 'simple' autobiography (whatever that may be) than the Prologue to Chaucer's *Legend of Good Women*. 'Langland's' awareness, comprehending the viewpoint of Ymaginatif as well as Will, clearly does not find complete expression in Will alone; but I agree with John Burrow that this passage reveals him to be 'in fact sensitive to the moral issues which his poem raised for him, *as its maker*' ('Words, Works and Will', in Hussey, ed: *PP: Critical Approaches* (1969) 118; my italics).

28 See my 'Langland and Scholastic Philosophy', *MÆ* 38 (1969) 134 on this term, which is borrowed from P. Dronke, *Medieval Latin and the Rise of the European Love Lyric* (Oxford, 1965), I, ch. 2.

converted into a move to amend others (encouraged by Lewte's advice). Similarly, the discussion of making here is introduced by Ymaginatif's triple injunction to change his way of life: '. . . amende it in thi myddel age' (7); 'Amende thee while thow myght . . .' (10); 'It is but murthe as for me to amende my soule' (15). In each case the need stressed is Will's own ('thi', 'thee', 'my') not that of some other group of people, but Ymaginatif's tone, unlike that of Will's last interlocutor, Reson, is restrained, one of suasion more than rebuke. Even his term 'murthe' (15) is designed to make Will feel that the vicissitudes of fortune can more easily be borne through adopting a positive attitude to suffering in line with Reson's 'Amende thow it if thow myght, for my tyme is to abide' (XI 377).[29] However, it serves to lead directly on to the topic of the kind of 'murthe' Will actually goes in for (in place of prayerful meditation upon suffering) – that of the maker. The passage is so subtly woven that it needs to be quoted in full:

> 'And thow medlest thee with makynges – and myghtest go seye thi
>   Sauter,
> And bidde for hem that yyveth thee breed; for ther are bokes ynowe
> To telle men what Dowel is, Dobet and Dobest bothe,
> And prechours to preve what it is, of many a peire freres'.
>   I seigh wel he seide me sooth and, somwhat me to excuse,
> Seide, 'Caton conforted his son that, clerk though he were,
> To solacen hym som tyme – a[lso] I do whan I make:
>   *Interpone tuis interdum gaudia curis.*
> 'And of holy men I herde', quod I, 'how thei outherwhile
> Pleyden, the parfiter to ben, in [places manye].
> Ac if ther were any wight that wolde me telle
> What were Dowel and Dobet and Dobest at the laste,
> Wolde I nevere do werk, but wende to holi chirche
> And ther bidde my bedes but whan ich ete or slepe'
>
> $\hspace{6cm}$ (XII 16–28).[30]

The tone of Ymaginatif is, as I said, restrained: *medlest* does not appear to mean 'interfere'[31] so much as 'be concerned with, work at',[32] though admittedly not without some *suggestion* of 'intermixture with'[33] – possibly

29 See XI 375 ff, a passage I discuss in 'The Inner Dreams in *PP*' (*MÆ* 55 (1986)
     34–7).
30 For further discussion of this passage and its revision in C see the 'Con-
     clusion'.
31 See *MED* s.v. 2a. (b). This is the sense at XII 124.
32 *MED* s.v. 2a. (a). This is almost the sense at XI 343, though 2a. (g) 'associate
     with, have to do with' is perhaps closest.
33 Cf. C VI 260 (= *MED* sense 1(a)), where parallel B XIII 361 has *menged*.

including that with which one has 'noght to doone' (XI 376). His criticism is twofold: you *should* pray for those who feed you (implying that Will does not) and you should *not* write unneeded books (the injunction implied by 'ther are bokes ynowe'). Will, in short, leaves undone what he ought to do and does what he ought not to: he fails to use his time rightly and he wastes it, too, (even in 'making') allowing *his* 'fithele' (the psalter) to lie 'untempred' like the *gleman gedelyng* denounced by Wit (IX 103–4; see p. 11 above). Ymaginatif, therefore, seems to be in agreement with Wit earlier that

> 'He dooth best that withdraweth hym by daye and by nyghte
> To spille any speche or any space of tyme' (IX 97–8).

– lines that attach the highest priority to the ideal of unremitting prayer (not excluding study preparatory to meditative prayer) which is the contemplative ideal of *cloistre* and, to some extent, of *scole*. If, as in Clergie's words at X 297–8, *hevene . . . on this erthe* is to be found in those two places if anywhere,[34] and if the *game of hevene* (IX 102) is, as Wit says, to avoid 'spilling speech', it seems that Ymaginatif's criticism boils down to saying that Will is a *clerk* and would be departing from his vocation if he were to spend too much time on his *making*.

Nonetheless, it is worth recalling that Ymaginatif, however we choose to 'define' him (and there is some disagreement among critics about this)[35] is associated in this period with the poetic power and hence with the activity of making. A striking instance of 'imagine' meaning 'represent vividly to oneself'[36] occurs in the Latin notes to a fourteenth-century Marian lyric where the 'doctor' Chrysostom 'ymaginatur de planctu virginis quod beata virgo stat sub cruce' etc.[37] In spite of Will's concurrence, therefore, we should not take 'he seide me sooth' (20) entirely at face value; there is, after all, more than a touch of irony in 'And prechours to preve what it is, of many a peire freres' (19).[38] Ymaginatif may not be

---

34 The phrase 'hevene . . . on this erthe' does not betoken worldly contentment but a spiritually blessed state in which the moral virtues (obedience, love, mutual help) as well as the intellectual ones (study, learning) prevail; *ese* 297 likewise does not bespeak lack of effort but inner tranquillity.

35 The more important recent studies (which include full reference to earlier discussions) are J. S. Wittig, 'Design of the Inward Journey' (*Traditio* 28 (1972) esp. 264–79; B. J. Harwood, 'Imaginative in *PP*' (*MÆ* 44 (1975) 249–63); A. J. Minnis, 'Langland's Ymaginatif and late-medieval theories of imagination' (*Comparative Criticism* 3 (1981) 71–103); H. White, 'Langland's Ymaginatif, Kynde and the *Benjamin Major*' (*MÆ* 55 (1986) 241–8).

36 Wittig, *art. cit.* p. 272.

37 Carleton Brown, *Religious Lyrics of the XIVth Century* (Oxford, 1924), no. 128.

38 This phrase alludes to the pair of Friars Will encounters in VIII 8 and to the pair he is to meet later at XIII 40 (the Doctor's 'man' is presumably a junior brother of his convent-friary).

urging Will to 'make', as is Lewte, with his bold 'wherfore sholdestow spare / To reden it in retorik' (XI 101–2); but neither, I believe, is he enjoining a total 'sparynge of speche' (cf. V 436). Through his *tone* he leaves Will a loophole through which he can pass to establish a case incorporating Ymaginatif's substantive point (a clerk's *prime* work is study and prayer, from which making should not distract him). This is the *sooth* that Will concedes even as he sets out to 'excuse' himself in some degree (*somwhat*); and the wit he shows is something it would take a true clerk to savour, since the procedure is the classical scholastic one of granting part of the opponent's case before going on to restate one's own in duly modified form. This is to demonstrate that one can be a clerk even while acting as a maker!

What Will does is to adduce an authority (Cato) who encouraged his son ('clerk though he were', 21) to amuse or entertain himself occasionally (*som tyme* 22 echoing *somwhat* 20). The Latin word quoted *Interpone* could happily be rendered by *medle*, as *gaudia* could by *murthes*. This takes care of the objection that Will might not be spending enough time in studying the word of God. But of course Ymaginatif's explicit objection is that he is not spending all the time he might *praying* – and in particular praying for those to whom he is obliged for his bodily livelihood. Accordingly he adds to Cato, whose secular 'science' Dame Studie earlier contrasted with sacred wisdom (X 191–99), the example of the saints, 'holy men', who 'outherwhile / Pleyden, the parfiter to ben . . .' (23–4). He thus, in high clerkly style, adduces *two separate and distinct* authorities (which might, as Studie's instance revealed, sometimes contradict one another) and even keeps the more authoritative till the end, crowning his response with the neat 'the *parfiter* to ben', so that what began as *conceding* Ymaginatif's point ends by *confuting* it.[39] This is saying *Contra* 'as a clerc' with a vengeance; but whereas Will's dispute with that first 'peire of freres' (recalled in XII 19) had evinced mere syllogistic prowess (VIII 20–26),[40] this riposte is altogether subtler, yet not less but more persuasive for that. In proving to Ymaginatif that a clerk can be a maker without ceasing to be a clerk, what better way than to use one's imagination?[41]

The cunning of Langland's art in this passage is reflected locally in the handling of syntax and rhythm, especially in lines 23–4. Here the last stressed word of 23 leaves the line syntactically incomplete, and a listener trained in dialectic might have expected the word following the enjambe-

39 Examples of typical disputation-procedure can be found in the *articuli* of the *Summa Theologica* of Aquinas, with their stages of *pro, contra* and *responsum*.
40 See my commentary on VIII 20–6, *ed. cit. ad loc.*
41 Langland's adducing of the sacred *after* the secular authority represents not a strict imitation but an imaginative modification, for rhetorical effect, of the standard procedure (see n. 39 above).

ment to be *maden* 'wrote poetry', thus rigorously strengthening the case by *a fortiori* reasoning: 'if *holy* men could "make", surely *I* can?' But, as I shall argue, Langland has done something more interesting, which seriously suggests the argumentative claims of *retorik* as at least equal to those of pure *logik*. In saying that the saints merely 'played', he has left open to himself the option of claiming that to make poetry, which is more *strenuous* than merely reading it, is to do something more *meritorious* than even the saints do when they are relaxing and not praying. That this *is* what Langland is getting at seems to me clear from line 27, 'Wolde I nevere do *werk*, but wende to holi chirche / And there bidde . . .'. What is this *werk* if not to 'dyngen upon David eche day til eve' (III 312), which is his proper task as a psalter-clerk? The context indicates unequivocally that the *werk* is *in fact* none other than what he does 'whan I make'. Will is affirming that *if* someone would inform him definitively about the nature of the Dowel-Dobet-Dobest mystery, he could then get on peacefully with his 'bedes' every moment of the day 'but when ich ete or slepe' (28). But the poem so far has shown that even the friars, who supposedly combined holiness and learning, had not been able to do this, so clearly there *cannot* be 'bokes ynowe / To telle men what Dowel is, Dobet and Dobest bothe' (17–18) or the friars would assuredly have found them![42]

The conclusion that seems to me to emerge from the foregoing analysis of Langland's deceptively simple self-defence is as follows. The making which he practises (only *som tyme*, he implies) is not 'spilling of speech'; it is not mere 'solace' after study or 'play' after and between prayers; it is not 'getting gold guiltless' (there is no suggestion, as I have argued above, that Langland's feeders accepted *passus* in place of psalms); it is, if a 'game', then a game 'of heaven' (blessed in origin and pleasing to God); it is, above all, as I hope the following chapters will substantiate, the product of *work*. And work in this context is not simply that 'labour' from which Chaucer's Eagle describes Geffrey as turning to 'another book' (*House of Fame* 652, 657); it is that which the *Winner and Waster*-poet claims 'witnesse will bere' to a serious tribunal 'at the laste, when ledys bene knawen' (*WW* 29–30). Langland, if my argument is well-founded, had no recognised position as a maker of mirths, no *locus standi* for his *apologia pro vita et arte sua*. In propounding the right of a clerk to 'make', he was re-defining the accepted role of both clerk and maker. This can have been no easy task, since the charge of idleness could have been urged as readily against the fourteenth-century chantry clerk as against the holders of tenured posts in twentieth-century university departments: unlike

42 This reading comes close to that of Burrow (op. cit. 118), though unlike him I do not 'suspect that Will would never be satisfied by *any* explanation' (my italics), while agreeing that no satisfactory explanation is offered in the text.

Chaucer, who was obliged to make his 'rekenynges', Langland had only his conscience to answer to. By the time he wrote the 'autobiographical' addition to Passus V of the C-text (which I discuss in the final section of this book) Langland had drastically reduced the scope of his apologia to his membership of the clerkly estate itself, and had accordingly excised from its place in the Ymaginatif section the passage on making which I have here examined. The causes and implications of those changes are matter for speculation, and will be speculated upon (but not too fancifully, I hope) in their proper place.

It may however be objected that I have already been engaging in speculation by speaking indifferently of Langland the author and of his character Will, to whom, after all, the speech of self-defence has been assigned. I do not deny that there are, at innumerable places in *Piers Plowman*, significant discriminations to be drawn between the two; but there is no serious risk of an autobiographical fallacy[43] here because what I am discussing is not the facts of the poet's life but the character and quality of his mind. The evidence for that, as with Wordsworth's *Prelude* (which exists in three versions and possibly more)[44] is the text of his work, in so far as we can establish its form, its sequence and its readings.[45] Langland could easily have written in the margins of his poem words like Gower's side-note to Book One of the *Confessio Amantis* (ll. 61ff): 'Hic quasi in persona aliorum . . . fingens se auctor esse *clericum*',[46] while in real life being nothing of the sort. That may well be the mode in which we should respond to his self-presentation in the opening of the poem as 'an heremite unholy of werkes' (Pr 3); but the condition of a lover is one thing, a subjective disposition of variable and uncertain duration, that of a clerk another, an objective estate marked by the *croune* and able, as Ymaginatif dryly observes, 'to take fro Tybourne twenty stronge theves, / Ther lewed theves ben lolled up' (XII 190–1). I think that the author of *Piers Plowman* was deeply concerned with the question of whether 'lyvynge after lettrure saved hym lif and soule' (XII 198) and especially, in the passage I have been considering, with the question of the place of making in a life of *lettrure*. That 'life' is known to us through the poem and its protagonist

---

43 See G. Kane, *The Autobiographical Fallacy in Chaucer and Langland Studies* (1965) and J. A. Burrow, *Autobiographical Poetry in the Middle Ages* (1983) esp. 390–5 (also n. 47 below).
44 See the Preface to *The Prelude: 1799, 1805, 1850*, ed. Wordsworth, Abrams and Gill (1979).
45 Universal agreement is still lacking about all three aspects, especially since the appearance of A. G. Rigg and C. Brewer's edition of the *Z Text* (Toronto, 1983). See further C. Brewer, 'The Textual Implications of the "Z"-text of *PP*' (unpublished D. Phil. thesis, Oxford 1986).
46 G. C. Macaulay, ed., *The English Works of John Gower*, I, 37. Gower, of course, has *amantem*.

Will, and 'the fact that Langland', as John Burrow has said in a relevant discussion of Passus XIII, 'portrays . . . Will's life in conventional fashion leaves untouched the question of whether Langland is talking about himself'. Like Professor Burrow, 'I believe he was'.[47]

---

47 'Langland *Nel Mezzo del Cammin*' in P. L. Heyworth, ed., *Medieval Studies for J. A. W. Bennett* (1981) p. 39.

Chapter Two

Versifying Fair

I. VERSIFYING AND ENDITING

'The next of our auncient Poets that I can tell of', wrote William Webbe in *A Discourse of English Poetrie* (1586), 'I suppose to be *Pierce Ploughman*, who in hys dooinges is somewhat harshe and obscure, but indeed a very pithy wryter, and (to hys commendation I speake it) was the first that I haue seene that obserued the quantity of our verse without the curiosity of Ryme'.[1] It is to Webbe's commendation, I feel, that he was able to appreciate Langland's versification, even though it will be the task of this chapter to argue that a very great deal of 'curiosity' went into the making of the verse of *Pierce Ploughman* (the poem) and that even rhyme was not entirely beyond the scope of the poet's interest as a maker in the alliterative tradition.[2] As with the account of the moral purpose of making in chapter one, I begin my description of Langland's versecraft with a negative critique of contemporary practice placed in the mouth of one of Will's interlocutors. Like Ymaginatif, and unlike Lewte, this character, Anima, is a 'noetic'[3] personification and his long, unbroken tirade against moral and spiritual and cultural decline in Christendom may be safely taken as expressive of Langland's own convictions (the role of Will in the opening dialogue (16–49) is largely to 'trigger' this tirade by embodying a stance of unchastened self-regard).

In the course of denouncing the radical failure in charity of 'Bothe lettred and lewed' (XV 353) Anima criticises the decline in knowledge of the crafts and then in education, the preserve of the clerical estate:

'Grammer, the ground of al, bigileth now children:
For is noon of thise newe clerkes – whoso nymeth hede –

---

1 Gregory Smith, *Elizabethan Critical Essays* I, 242.
2 See section viii of this chapter. Langland's rhyme is incidental, not systematic.
3 See ch. 1, n. 28 above.

That kan versifye faire ne formaliche enditen,
Ne naught oon among an hundred that an auctour kan construe,
Ne rede a lettre in any langage but in Latyn or in Englissh.'

(XV 370–4).

It is not my purpose here to discuss Langland's dislike of the new way of
teaching Latin without first learning French, which John Trevisa tells us in
a well-known addition to his translation of Higden, came in after the Black
Death and was firmly established by 1385.[4] I wish rather to isolate two
important points in this criticism for the purposes of my argument in this
chapter. One is the wide extent of meaning attached to 'Grammer, the
ground of al', which clearly covers not just the elements of Latin, but the
more advanced theoretical commentaries studied at the university in
close association with Logic and Rhetoric.[5] The other is the ascription to
clerkes not only of the means of acquiring knowledge ('rede', 'construwe')
but also the techniques of applying it, as we should say, creatively
('versifye', 'enditen').[6] It is on these that I shall concentrate to begin with,
by reference to what I take to have been the central tradition of grammati-
cal and rhetorical writing in the Middle Ages, and one that Langland
was probably acquainted with as a clerk brought up in *cloistre* and *scole*.[7]
The authors mentioned are not offered specifically as 'sources': though
Langland certainly knew works such as Isidore of Seville's *Etymologies*,
Alexander of Villedieu's *Doctrinale* and various works by Alanus de
Insulis (renowed as a teacher as well as poet)[8] he was not, as Chaucer was,
self-conscious about this knowledge; only mentions *retorik* once (XI 102);
and does not discuss, straightforwardly or ironically, the practice of

4 Sisam, *C14th Verse and Prose*, 149. See further A. F. Leach, *The Schools of
   Medieval England* (1915) 196–7; N. Orme, *English Schools in the Middle Ages*
   (1973) 73–4.
5 Grammar is 'origo et fundamentum liberalium litterarum' and Rhetoric 'con-
   iuncta . . . Grammaticae arti' according to Isidore of Seville (*Etymologiarum
   . . . Libri XX* ed. W. M. Lindsay (Oxford, 1911), I.v.4, II.i.5). See further R. J.
   Schoeck, 'On Rhetoric in C14th Oxford' (*Med. St.* 30 (1968) 214–25 and P. O.
   Lewry, 'Grammar, Logic and Rhetoric 1220–1320' in Catto, ed., *History of
   University of Oxford*, I, 401–33; and cf. E. R. Curtius, *European Literature and the
   Latin Middle Ages*, tr. W. R. Trask (1953) 45, 448.
6 This is the tradition of 'Preceptive Grammar, or the Rhetoric of Verse-
   Writing' as it is called by J. J. Murphy, *Rhetoric in the Middle Ages* (Los Angeles,
   1974), ch. 4.
7 The slender direct evidence (see my edn. xiii–xv) indicates that these would
   have been the school attached to Malvern Priory and Oxford University.
8 Isidore is quoted at XV 39*a*; Alexander at XI 267*a*; and Alanus at XVIII 410*a*.
   See Murphy, *Rhetoric*, 73–4 on Isidore, 138–9 and 148–51 on Alexander.
   Alanus and Alexander are listed as curriculum authors in Everard the
   German's *Laborintus*, in E. Faral, *Les Arts Poétiques du XIIe et du XIIIe Siècle*
   (Paris, 1924) 358ff.

applying terms, figures and colours.[9] Possibly, as a clerk, he took these things as read, and assumed that his audience knew the meaning of such phrases from the university milieu as *quodlibet*, used by Anima a few lines later (380).[10] I draw on these *auctours* here largely as a means of exploring what I regard as the most important issue relating to Langland as a clerkly maker: that he was as concerned about standards in the vernacular art of the maker as in the art of Latin versemaking to which Anima's comments of course *directly* pertain.

The gap in the evidence is, I believe, more apparent than real. While it is true that Langland's critique of the janglers, discussed above, is moral, and Anima's criticism of the *newe clerkes* is technical, I think it is not unreasonable to interpret the defence of his own *makyng* in the dialogue with Ymaginatif as both implying 'profitabille' matter and as aspiring to the ideals of 'fair' and 'formal' art held up by Anima in a speech from whose criticisms the author himself may be presumed exempt. I take it, then, that Langland, who could voice such ideals, was not so much 'a malcontent . . . bent . . . wholy to taxe the disorders of that age . . . a very true Prophet [whose] verse is but loose meetre, and his termes hard and obscure, so as in them is litle pleasure to be taken' (*The Arte of English Poesie* (1589) I.xxxi),[11] a view shared by many readers of *Piers Plowman* to the present day,[12] as (in the *Winner and Waster*-poet's words) 'the man that made it hymselven' and who, among the makers of his day, 'wirche kan beste' (*WW* 28, 30).

---

9 Langland draws on the terminology of grammar for the extended passage on *mede* and *mercede* in C III 332–405. The possible indebtedness of this to the *De Planctu Naturae* of Alanus is noted by Pearsall, ed. cit. ad loc.
10 Anima appears to be referring to *quodlibets* in both theology and arts; J. M. Fletcher (*Hist. of Univ. of Oxford* I 392–3) notes that *quodlibets* were held in the Faculty of Arts, though none have survived. Those in theology are discussed by Catto (ibid., 473–4, 504–5); to have attended them, Langland would have had at least to have begun study in theology – i.e. to have been destined for the priesthood; but his complaint may be at second-hand.
11 Smith, ed. cit., II.65.
12 Thomas Warton, *History of English Poetry* (1781 edn, section VIII) finds Langland's manner 'extremely perplexed' as a result of his 'perpetual alliteration'; G. M. Hopkins (*Letters of G.M.H. to Robert Bridges*, ed. C. C. Abbott (Oxford, 1935) 156) found *PP* 'not worth reading'; even C. S. Lewis, who wrote appreciatively of Langland's 'rare' excellence and sublimity, considers that he 'lacks . . . Chaucer's fine sense of language: he is confused and monotonous, and hardly makes his poetry into a poem' (*The Allegory of Love* (Oxford, 1936) 161). He shows 'as little regard for stylistic as for structural formalities' (Pearsall, *C-text*, Intro., 20) and 'Verse, for him, is to be used, not specially revered or respected for its own sake', E. Salter and D. Pearsall, eds., *Piers Plowman*, York Medieval Texts (1967) 54.

Of Langland's three terms *versifye, formaliche* and *enditen*, first recorded in this passage, the third (meaning 'compose, esp. poetry') is much the commonest.[13] *Versifye* 'write Latin verse, compose poetry in Latin' (from Latin *versificare* through French *versifier*; see *OED s.v.*) is used by Chaucer in a well-known passage of the *Monk's Prologue* stating how tragedies 'ben *versified* communely / Of six feet, which men clepen *exametron*' (B² 3168–9).[14] In context, this is to be understood as 'written in *meetre*' (cf. 3171),[15] which in the terminology of the grammarians was *metrum* 'quantitative metre' as opposed to *rhythmus* 'accentual-syllabic metre with or without rhyme' (Isidore, *Etym.* III.xviii; Bede, *De Arte Metrica*: 'De Rhythmo').[16] Langland quotes examples of both types of 'vers of Latyn' (Pr 143), *metrum* at XVIII 410a (from Alanus) and (unrhymed) *rhythmus* immediately before at XVIII 409. Elsewhere he often quotes metrical Latin from the *Distichs of Cato* and such rhyming forms as Leonine verse, e.g. at Pr 132–8 (the latter a popular 'Goliardic' form which Gervase of Melkley considered 'hardly worth discussing except by the way in an authoritative text-book' (*Ars Poetica*, under 'Leonitas').[17] There are no grounds for supposing that Langland thought *metrum* superior to *rhythmus* as a form of versifying; as a man of the Church he would be familiar with the great hymns of the Breviary (from one of which XVIII 409 is taken)[18] and could scarcely have shared Webbe's Renaissance prejudice against rhyme, let alone his erroneous belief that the alliterative long line is quantitative,[19] as reasons for choosing not to write in *rym*.

Our chief evidence that Langland esteemed the native form is the fact that *Piers Plowman* is written in it. But there may also be some basis for thinking that *versifye faire* is not exclusively restricted to learned verse-making if we read *formaliche enditen* not just as standing in (amplifying) apposition to it but as referring to verse-making in a vernacular, whether English or French. The early uses of *endite* which the *MED* cites from Chaucer and Gower support the sense 'compose orally, by dictation', and

13 See *MED* s.v. 1(a), which cites the Langland passage.
14 *The Works of Geoffrey Chaucer*, ed. F. N. Robinson, 2nd edn, 1957.
15 The *MED* quotations under *metre* show little or no awareness of a distinction in sense such as I suggest for *versifye*. Those from Gower (*CA* IV 2414) and Chaucer (*ML Pr* B 48) allow the sense 'rhyme' (not 'rhyming poetry') for the noun *rim(yng)* in the contrast drawn with *metre*, which may therefore mean simply 'metre', not *metrum*.
16 For Bede's treatise, see H. Keil, *Scriptores de Orthographia* (Leipzig, 1880) 258–9 (on *rhythmus*); for discussion, Murphy, *Rhetoric* 77–9, R. Palmer, 'Bede as a Textbook Writer: A Study of his *De arte metrica*' (*Spec.* 34 (1959) 573–84).
17 H. J. Gräbener, ed., *Gervais von Melkley: Ars Poetica* (Münster, 1965) p. 16.
18 See G. M. Dreves and C. Blume, eds., *Analecta Hymnica* (Leipzig, 1886–1922) II, 48.
19 See p. 21 above and n. 1.

Chaucer even contrasts enditing with written composition when he says that Philomena 'coude eek rede, and wel ynow endyte, / But with a penne coude she nat wryte' (*Legend of Good Women* 2356–7): she lacked active literacy and *a fortiori* was no clerk.[20] However, in context the natural way to take Langland's line is as referring to Latin primarily, even if the vernacular is not excluded; for although *faire* is a vague term of aesthetic praise, *formaliche* bespeaks conformity to rule, and the rules taught by 'Grammer' in its broad sense were of course those of Latin not of English poetry.[21]

The word *formaliche* also appears to be rare in early applications to *makyng* (*MED s.v.* cites only this example)[22] and its commonest use is in connexion with the third art of the Trivium, Dialectic, as in Troilus's 'That kanst so wel and formaly arguwe' (*Troilus* IV 497). *Forma* is assuredly a clerkly term, but one of largely philosophical function, and is not found much amongst those who discuss the *metricae disciplinae regulas* (Bede).[23] A term which is commonly used, and which covers the sense of 'ordered rule and principle' implied in Langland's *formaliche* is *ratio*, a key medieval term and one which did not undergo the specialisation in sense of *forma*. An example is from the discussion of the parts of 'Music' in Book III of the *Etymologies* (on mathematics):

Metrica est quae mensuram diversorum metrorum *probabili ratione* cognoscit, ut v.g. heroicon, iambicon, elegiacon, etc.

(*Etym.* III. xviii).

The italicised phrase means something like 'by systematic principles capable of being tested'[24] for Isidore regards music as a *disciplina* capable of being formally studied and metre, a part of it, as a teachable system. Writing in the early seventh century, he was certainly familiar with the (relatively new) art of *rhythmus*, too; but, doubtless because he knew it to be based on (variation-prone) speech-stress and not (rule-governed) quantity, Isidore finds it a more subjective affair, partaking less purely of the rational character of *ars musica* as a system of abstract number:

Rythmica est, quae requirit incursionem verborum, utrum bene sonus an male cohaereat (*ibid.*).

20 See further *MED* s.v. *enditen* 1(a).
21 See Murphy, *Rhetoric*, 115–16; a French verse 'grammar' of 1356 is known, but there is nothing similar in English from the period.
22 *MED* s.v. 1(a) 'in an orderly manner, correctly'.
23 *De Arte Metrica*, ed. cit., 251.
24 See C. T. Lewis and C. Short, *A Latin Dictionary* (Oxford, 1966), s.v. *ratio* II.2 (c), (d).

Here the 'aesthetic' terms *bene* and *male* may be contrasted with the 'formal' phrase *probabili ratione*.

Vernacular poetry is not mentioned by Isidore, and if Langland had consulted what Michael Haren calls 'the standard work of reference in monastic and cathedral libraries throughout Latin Christendom',[25] as he evidently did for the long definition of Anima at XV 39*a*, to find a formal basis for his practice as a maker, he would have been disappointed. Unlike 'Ysidorus' (XV 37) Bede, writing nearly a century later in a country with a native tradition not descended from Latin, reveals an awareness that vernacular verse is not a corruption of learned verse but something altogether different. Unfortunately his comments are tantalisingly brief, but nonetheless important (I translate, quoting the key phrases):

> *Rhythmus* seems to resemble metrical verse, being a measured and melodious putting-together of words (*verborum modulata compositio*), not according to the formal principles of metre (*metrica ratione*) but according to the number of syllables, and weighed according to the judgement of the ear, as is the case with the vernacular makers (*vulgarium poetarum*) . . . Metre is principle plus melody (*ratio cum modulatione*), while *rhythmus* is melody without rule or principle (*modulatio sine ratione*).[26]

Bede seems unwilling to recognise accent-count, which replaces quantity in vernacular scansion, as the *ratio* of native versifying, presumably because so much exception and variation (departure from rule) are possible where the ultimate appeal is to the judgement of the ear.

In this, Bede accords with Isidore's view of *rhythmus* as founded upon 'incursionem verborum' ('the flow and run of the words') and the quality of the sound-pattern (*sonus*). But he goes beyond him in conceding that

> often, by chance, you will even find an underlying principle (*rationem*) in *rhythmus* [in context evidently applied to Latin and English verse indifferently], one maintained not through a deliberate effort at regularity (*artifici moderatione*) but through the effect of the sound and the melody itself. This the vernacular poets do, necessarily, without benefit of learning (*rustice*), while learned poets do so as a result of it (*docti faciant docte*).[27]

The exact sense of *rustice* probably lies somewhere between 'instinctively' and 'clumsily', but the play on *docti, docte* clearly suggests that

25 M. Haren, *Medieval Thought: the Western Intellectual Tradition from Antiquity to the 13th Century* (1985) 69.
26 Ed. cit. p. 258. In his *De Orthographia* (ed. cit. 288, 7) Bede glosses *rhythmus* by *modulatio* and *rhythmizo* by *modulor*.
27 Ibid.

Bede, himself one of the vernacular makers,[28] believed the intermittent 'regularities' of their work to be the happy result of latent poetic feel, not the product of clerkly training. Disappointingly the only example he gives is a Latin *rhythmus*, the hymn-verse *Rex aeterne domine*, which he finds 'does this very beautifully after the manner of the iambic metre';[29] it would have been worth much to have his judgement on a piece of English making. Bede, then, we conclude, believes that *metrum* has all the qualities of *rhythmus* while *rhythmus* only occasionally strays into the perfection belonging to metre. This throws light on his story of Caedmon as the account of a *rusticus* who is awakened to awareness of what is possible in poetry without the advantages of a clerkly education: for the first named English poet is clearly to be seen as an exponent of *rhythmus*,[30] one who endites formally to the extent that *ratio* can be grasped intuitively but who does not and cannot practice the *disciplina* that pertains to clerks.[31]

II. THE STRUCTURE OF LANGLAND'S VERSE

The traditional alliterative long line as used in the fourteenth century is constructed on the basis of what the *Winner*-poet calls 'three wordes togedire', which are 'wroghte thurgh witt' (*WW* 25) and, this time in the *Gawain*-poet's celebrated phrase, 'With lel letteres loken, / In londe so hatz ben longe' (*Sir Gawain* 35–6).[32] The key principle of this, the traditional verse-form of the Germanic peoples, is not, as in the *rhythmus* of Romance

28 C. L. Wrenn (*A Study of OE Literature* (1967) 63) speaks of *Bede's Death-Song*, his one extant vernacular poem, as having 'the same rather stiff competence as does his Latin verse'. For text and discussion see E. V. K. Dobbie, *The Anglo-Saxon Poetic Records VI* (New York, 1942) 107, c–cvii, 199.
29 Ed. cit. p. 259; for the text, see *Analecta Hymnica* LI, 5.
30 Bede states how Caedmon set about 'quendam sacrae historiae siue doctrinae sermonem . . . *in modulationem carminis transferre*' (*Historia Ecclesiastica* IV.24, in C. Plummer, ed. *Venerabilis Baedae Opera Historica* (Oxford, 1896) 260). On *modulatio* as a synonym for *rhythmus* see n. 26 above.
31 Bede nonetheless recognises the inspired songs of the cow-herd as *uerba Deo digni carminis*, acknowledged as such by *multis doctioribus uiris* (ibid.).
32 Ed. J. R. R. Tolkien and E. V. Gordon, 2nd edn. rev. Norman Davis (Oxford, 1967). This recalls the *Beowulf*-poet's *word oper fand / sope gebunden* (ed. F. Klaeber, 3rd edn. Boston 1950) 870–1 (cf. also Cynewulf's *Elene* 1250, *leoðucræft onleac*, with its somewhat different metaphor (G. P. Krapp, ed., *The Vercelli Book* (New York, 1932) 100)). Davis notes (ed. cit. ad loc) that both *lel* and *sope* may be taken to refer to the *story*, not the verse-technique, but like him I think the metrical sense to be the more likely.

languages, the binding together of two *lines* by rhyme (whether immediate or alternate) but the binding together of two *half*-lines by alliteration. The point of division between the 'a' and the 'b' half-line is almost as marked as that between the 'a' and 'b' line of a rhyming couplet, as can be seen by comparing a line from the 'Z' text of *Piers Plowman* (a typical alliterative poem, whether or not we believe it is by Langland) with a couplet from Chaucer:

> For word ys but wynd / ant so my wyt telleth   (Z, V 34)[33]

> Soun ys noght / but eyr ybroken,
> And every speche / that ys spoken, . . .   (*House of Fame* 765–6).

The Chaucerian couplet has an internal caesura, of course, like the alliterative line, but it is not as marked as the latter's, which more nearly approximates in weight to the couplet's line-end pause. In both types of verse, this pause may be reduced to varying degrees by enjambement, which is essentially a metrical result of a syntactical choice. Langland differs from most alliterative makers in his partiality towards enjambement, the product, perhaps, of his clerkly training in Latin, with its preference for hypotactic syntax.[34] However, he never lets us forget for long the basically end-stopped character of his line, which encloses a single sense-unit, as in this typical sequence of five lines from about the middle of the poem:

>   1)   2)
> And yet me mervelled moore: many othere briddes ∫
> Hidden and hileden hir egges ful derne ∫
>   2a)
> In mareys and moores   for men sholde hem noght fynde,
>   3)   3a)
> And hidden hir egges whan [hii] therfro wente,
> For fere of othere foweles and for wilde beestes   (XI 350–4).

Here it will be seen that two of the five lines have enjambement (marked by the symbol ∫), that in 351 being noticeably weaker than in 350 and permitting an initial closure of the sense-unit which is then 'undone', so to speak, as we read 352 and discover its syntactic relation to the preceding line. Disregarding sentence 1, which is merely introductory, we find that the other two sentences each contain one main clause (2, 3) and one subordinate clause (2a, 3a) (I take 'Hidden and hileden' as in effect one verb). Despite the enjambements, the lines show considerable respect for the traditional end-stopped pattern, as can be seen from the

---

33 Rigg-Brewer, ed. cit.
34 Enjambement is discussed in section iv of this chapter.

symmetrical parallel between 2a and 3a, each of which ends with a finite verb followed by a strong pause. The end-position of the verb in 3a causes the only case of inversion in these lines (*therfro*), which otherwise follow prose order; in Langland, who is unrestricted by the 'curiosity of Ryme' (in Webbe's phrase), inversion is more often the product of rhetorical and syntactical purpose than metrical need.

Langland thus has at his disposal a verse-form with a freedom comparable to that of blank verse, having an internal *ratio* (structural alliteration) which resists the tendency of unrhymed metre to dissolve into prose, with syntax predominating over rhythm, and the line becoming subordinate to the verse paragraph, as in Milton (this never happens in Langland). Nonetheless, the verse of *Piers Plowman* seems to me no less ordered than it is flexible. I believe that its freedom is productive of richness and variety of pattern of a kind that has not been adequately appreciated; it does not betoken a malcontent's (or even a Prophet's) concern with his 'message' above all else. It is not possible here to give a comprehensive account of Langland's metre in all the versions of his poem (including the 'Z' text, which I regard as authentic). The description that follows is, however, based upon a study of all the lines of all four versions, both during and after the process of editing one of them, the B-text, to which I shall confine myself here. I hope to publish all the relevant evidence in a separate book on the metre of *Piers Plowman*,[35] so I shall spare the reader mainly interested in the art of the poem any lengthy lists of percentages and line-references. But it is necessary to set out briefly what I take to be the fundamental principles of Langland's metre, the *ratio* of his versifying, before examining the variety of ways in which he contrives to make it 'fair'. The state of Langland's text does not permit of absolute certainty about the scansion of every line; but the apparently irregular lines which might serve to challenge the validity of my account are relatively few, as it happens, and do not justify the amount of space that detailed textual analysis entails.[36] What I hope my schema will do is to enable the reader to 'test' the text of *Piers Plowman* as I have done in using it as a heuristic tool, and, at the same time, to evaluate the utility of the schema as a tool for critical (and textual) analysis.[37]

Langland's line consists of not fewer than four and (with rare exceptions such as XVI 20 and XVIII 59) not more than five stressed syllables,

---

35 *The Metre of Piers Plowman* (in preparation).
36 Where such comment is necessary, I have tried to keep it brief in the main text or else to confine it to the footnotes.
37 See further my 'The Authenticity of the Z Text of *PP*' (*MÆ* 53 (1984) 295–300).

separated from each other by a varying number of unstressed syllables, and with optional unstressed syllables at the end and beginning of the line:

In ă sómĕr sésŏn, // whăn sóftĕ wăs thĕ sónnĕ   (Pr 1).

The line is divided into two halves, with a medial break or caesura (//), but the 'halves' are not always of equal metrical weight, since there are sometimes three stressed syllables in the first or a-half (possibly four in B XVI 20, depending on the textual reading),[38] though never more than two in the second or b-half (except for XVIII 59). The stressed syllables are 'lifts' (a term denoting their heightened volume and pitch) and the unstressed syllables 'dips' (in which volume is reduced and pitch falls). The smooth-flowing effect generated by the alternation of lifts and dips is sometimes deliberately interrupted by the omission of the dip between lifts, usually at the caesura, so that two points of high intensity are immediately juxtaposed. This may occur in lines of average length, like Pr 20:

Somme pútten hem to the plóugh, // pleíden ful sélde

or in short, terse, stabbing lines like X 128:

Or Júdas the Jéw // Jésu bitráye

or V 461, where the juxtaposed lifts occur not at the caesura but together in the b-half:

'Ĭ shăl sékĕn trúthe ĕrst // ĕr Ĭ sé Rómĕ!'[39]

Langland displays great resourcefulness in exploiting the rhetorical and emotional potential of varying line-length, a matter of some importance in so long a poem; irregular he has been (wrongly, but understandably) thought, but not monotonous.[40]

Of the four lines quoted above, and the five quoted earlier (XI 350–4), eight have no alliteration on the last lift, which is *blank*. Where a lift has both alliteration and stress we have what I call a 'full stave', the most essential feature of native English verse in this period, as rhyme is of the accentual-syllabic Romance-derived verse written by Chaucer and Gower. So common is it, not just in Langland but in other alliterative

---

38 See my textual note ad loc., and 'Inner Dreams' (*MÆ* 55 (1986) p. 30 and n. 19).

39 Possibly *erst* should fall in the dip of the b-half; but I regard the scansion of the a-half with *shál, séken* stressed and *truthe* unstressed (given in the first printing of my edition, p. 359) as unnatural and wrong.

40 That the alliterative long line is as prone to monotony as blank verse can be seen from the unvarying *aa/ax* pattern of *The Destruction of Troy*.

poets, for the fourth lift to be blank, that the scansion pattern *aa/ax* (where *a* denotes a full and *x* a blank stave) has been called by Kane and Donaldson 'normative'.[41] However, it is possible for the blank stave to become 'enriched' with alliteration, producing the pattern *aa/aa*, as in the very first line of the poem. This enrichment creates a *variant* upon the normative line, but not a distinct type, since it satisfies (while also adding to) the norm's requirement. From one standpoint, 'enrichment' may be reasonably seen as not creating a structural but only an ornamental variant, or, if it is to be judged 'functional', its function is rhetorical not metrical. In Pr 1 the extra *s* stave helps to create the desired atmosphere of balmy languor, just as an extra *b* stave serves the *Gawain*-poet in his effort to convey the stark harshness of the winter landscape:

> Þay boȝen bi bonkkez þer boȝes ar bare   (*Gawain*, 2077).

The matter is not so straightforward in the case of the five-lift or extended line with three lifts in the a-half (scanning *aaa/ax*), which is used by both Langland and the *Gawain*-poet among others, or its enriched variety (*aaa/aa*), both of which occur in succession at Pr 125–6:

> 'Críst képe thee, sire Kýng, and thi kýngrýche,
> And léne thee léde thi lónd so léaute thee lóvye'

(with which we may compare *Gawain* 2018 and 2080 respectively). The rhetorical function of the enrichment in lifts 3, 3 and 5 cannot be denied; at the same time, the increase in *metrical* weight of the three-lift a-half is surely due in part to the enrichment by alliteration of lift 3. This becomes even clearer if we compare with these two variants the lines in which the extended a-half contains a *blank* stave, usually in position 3, but sometimes in position 2, as in these two successive lines respectively:

> 'Into a déep derk hélle to dwélle there for évere.
> And mó thoúsandes mýd hym than mán kouthe nómbre
> (I 115–16).

Although these last lines must be regarded as variants upon the normative line, and not a distinct type, their character seems to me so different from that of the other pair that I would regard enrichment as having metrical significance, therefore as being virtually a structural feature.

The blank extended line (scanning *aax/ax* or, less commonly, *axa/ax*) is also found in the *Gawain*-poet (e.g. *SGGK* 2313, 2319) and this, together

---

41 George Kane and E. Talbot Donaldson, *Piers Plowman: the B Version* (1975) ('K-D' hereafter) 137; they acknowledge however (p. 136) 'that the normative *number* of staves . . . is three' (my italics), thereby including in 'normative' what I call Type II (the 'clustered' type). This usage is confusing, so I confine *normative* to the *aa/ax* type alone (see below).

with the frequency of occurrence of all five variants so far discussed constitutes a reason for calling the entire category the 'Standard' line in Langland or 'Type I':

a)	Normative	*aa/ax*
b)	Enriched	*aa/aa*
c)	Extended	*aaa/ax*
d)	Enriched extended	*aaa/aa*
e)	Blank extended	*aax/ax* or *axa/ax*

The overwhelming majority of Langland's lines belong to one or other variant category of the Standard Type, in which it may be said that there are *at least* three full staves, of which one is in the b-half. The 'variety' he achieves is therefore *largely* a matter of working within these limits and drawing on a number of devices of ornament (*ornatus*) which will be described below. But in a small number of lines (about eighty) he uses a line in which the three full staves are grouped or clustered in the a-half (*aaa/xx*) sometimes with the two lifts of the b-half alliterating on a second sound (*aaa/bb*):

(a)   That Méde móste be máynpernour, Réson thei bisóughte

(IV 112)

(b)   And álle that hólpen hym to érye, to sétte or to sówe (VII 6).

This type may be regarded as an adaptation, in its (a) form, of Type Ic, with blanking of the first stave in the b-half (the 'key-stave'),[42] and in its (b) form as related to Type Id, with substitution of a new stave-sound in the b-half. This type is not found in the *Gawain*-poet but occurs occasionally in *The Parliament of the Three Ages*, a poem of uncertain date which could be later than (and therefore influenced by) *Piers Plowman* (see e.g. T 371, 382).[43] Its melody is very different from that of Type I, since its alliterative sound is not 'given' by the key-stave, and the *lettres* are not *loken* according to traditional practice. This line may be called 'Type II':

a)	Single clustered	*aaa/xx*
b)	Double clustered	*aaa/bb*

As the examples given show, this is a line of slow, heavy movement, with an unusual freshness and beauty in its (b) form (cf. also VII 30 and X 78). Its rarity ensures that it remains a felicity rather than becoming a fault.

---

42 Also called 'head stave' or 'chief stave' (*Hauptstab*, after ON *Hǫfuðstafr*). In a 'Standard' line we may rely on the first lift of the b-half to furnish the 'key' that unlocks the letter-pattern of the whole line.

43 M. Y. Offord in her edition of *PTA* (EETS 246 (1959) xxxvi) prefers a date before 1370, Turville-Petre (*Allit. Revival* 5) the late fourteenth century. I favour a post-B text date (see my edn., Introduction, xvii).

In a third type, the 'lettres' *are* 'loken', but with only two, not three words:

(a) 1 Yeldynge for this thyng at one *y*eres ende (II 105)

   2 For thei *l*eveden upon hym that *l*yed in this manere (I 118).

This 'minimally'-staved line (found also in *Sir Gawain*, 650, and the *Parliament*, TW 325) is considered unoriginal by K-D,[44] partly because the C-text often revises such lines to the standard type.[45] But the fact of revision, though proof of a wish for change, is not proof (or, I think, even evidence) of unoriginality in B, especially in face of lines such as V 14 ('And the south-westrene wynd on Saterday at even'), which are uniformly attested in all versions (A V 14 / C V 116 / Z V 32).[46] This type (*ax/ax*) must have a 'full' key-stave. It can also have an enriched fourth lift (*ax/aa*):

(b) 1 And with that *h*é séide, that *H*óly Chirche it hérde (VI 243)

   2 And the *é*llevene stérres *h*aílsed hym *á*lle (VII 161).[47]

In a third variant (found also in *Gawain*, 906) alliteration is 'crossed' (*ab/ab*):

(c) And whoso *b*ummed ther*of b*oughte it ther*a*fter (V 219).[48]

The three variants make up what I call the 'Reduced' Type III:

a)	Minimal	*ax/ax*
b)	Enriched	*ax/aa*
c)	Crossed	*ab/ab*

The 'chiastic' pattern (*ab/ba*), found, e.g. in *Sir Gawain* 335, 544, does not appear.

III. LANGLAND'S 'LEL LETTRES'

My account of Langland's line-structure, with its ten variants grouped in three main types, shows him working in the same broad tradition as the

44 K-D, 137; the exceptions they recognise are lines containing Latin.
45 Neither I 118 (emended by K-D to scan normatively) nor II 105 (retained by K-D without comment) is in C; but an example of such revision is I 42 (= A I 40 (ed. Kane, 1960)) but omitted from Z (Pr 129/30) and revised to scan normatively on *w* in C I 40). K-D retain, but scansion normatively on /v/ seems to require a wholly unnatural stress-pattern and is surely mistaken.
46 The objection that Langland left the line unrevised in C because it was so well known logically tells *for* rather than *against* the authenticity of *ax/ax*.
47 K-D emend VI 243 to read with A VII 227 but (inconsistently) retain VII 161, which is so attested in all three versions (A VII 144, C IX 311).
48 K-D again retain V 219 inconsistently (so attested in A VII 137, C VI 229).

Gawain-poet, the 'maker' *par excellence* in this period.[49] But whereas the latter employs a diction rich in words derived from the Old English poetic lexicon, and augmented by items of dialectally restricted provenance, Langland, though originating from the South-West Midlands,[50] uses a much simpler language that probably reflects both his residence in London and his interest, as a clerk, in wide, even nationwide dissemination of his urgent 'national' matter.[51] The 'clerkly' character of his making can be investigated above all in his choice and handling of stave-words, the *lel lettres* of the alliterative poet. If I differ somewhat from the interpretations offered by Kane and Donaldson in their edition of the B-text and, more recently, by Kane in a separate treatment of Langland's metre, it is while acknowledging my indebtedness to both studies as fundamental to our understanding of the subject.[52]

Kane and Donaldson defend Langland's use as *staves* (metrically significant alliterating syllables) in what they describe as 'several hundred lines' of 'grammatical' or 'little' words (prepositions, adverbs, conjunctions) against the charge that 'his attitude to alliteration was careless or perfunctory'.[53] Such a view is to be found, for example, in Skeat, who observes that Langland 'frequently neglects to observe the strict rules',[54] and also in J. Lawrence, who finds Langland 'the least scrupulous of the fourteenth century poets in admitting words of slight sentence stress to alliterative rank'.[55] Skeat's illustrative scansion of I 58 ('Thanne I fráyned hire fáire, for Hým that hire máde') seems to me correct, and to recognise implicitly the nature of the 'rules' that I believe Langland *did* observe (though he won in their service an all-but perfect freedom). Lawrence's remark may well be patient of the same interpretation, in which case I find their analysis acceptable but not the evaluative judgement they make. By contrast, Kane and Donaldson seem anxious to 'defend' Langland's practice without recognising a clear-cut distinction between the presence or absence in an individual stave of the two separate components of alliteration and stress. They even speculate that 'linguistic change will have obscured many effects of his otherwise well instanced technical

---

49 This judgement is based on the range and variety of alliterative style represented in the four poems of BL MS Cotton Nero A. x.
50 See M. L. Samuels, 'Langland's Dialect' (*MÆ* 54 (1985) 232–47, esp. 244.
51 See ch. 3; for a recent re-statement of the question see Anne Middleton, 'The Audience and Public of *PP*' in D. Lawton, ed.: *ME Alliterative Poetry* (Cambridge, 1982) 101–123, esp. 103–4. The sharpness of her distinction between regional and social 'location' is not entirely convincing to me.
52 See K-D 132–40 and Kane, 'Music "Neither Unpleasant nor Monotonous"', in P. L. Heyworth, ed., *Medieval Studies for J. A. W. Bennett* (Oxford, 1981) 43–63.
53 K-D, 134–5.
54 W. W. Skeat, ed., *PP: in three parallel texts* (Oxford, 1886), II, lxi.
55 *Chapters on Alliterative Verse* (1893) 106.

virtuosity'.[56] This is doubtless plausible; but a much better 'defence' of that virtuosity is provided in Kane's more recent theory of 'modulation', the aim of which is to show the existence in his verse of two separate and indeed separable (because independent) patterns – one of alliteration and one of metrical accent. This 'modulation' can be found to occur

> in lines where at some point metrical accent and alliteration must be differently located because the alliterating syllable is (less commonly occurs in) a 'grammatical' as opposed to a 'lexical' word, one which would not normally bear stress in connected speech and upon which the context does not confer relative importance.[57]

One of the examples Kane quotes is Pr 80:

> Ac it is noght *by* the bisshop that the boy precheth.

Now I think that both Kane-Donaldson and Kane are making important and valuable points about a real and fundamental feature of Langland's alliterative practice which I shall discuss below. But I cannot agree with Kane that in Pr 80 'accent and alliteration must be differently located' (ibid.) or with Kane-Donaldson that 'the alliteration appears to throw a stress' on the 'little words' (an earlier account with which Kane presumably no longer agrees) in such lines as VI 47 ('That he worth worthier set and *with* moore blisse'),[58] where the grammatical word in question is *with*. In the first case, Pr 80, the sense of *by* 'in accordance with the intentions of' necessitates that it be stressed, and so metrical accent and alliteration are located in the *same* not in a different position. In the second case, the demands of the sense require the stress to fall on *moore* (not, as here used, clearly a 'grammatical' word) rather than on *with*, which carries the line's stave-sound.

It is undoubtedly true that there are several hundred small-word staves in the poem. *With*, to take only one example, occurs forty-five times;[59] but in only one of these instances can it be plausibly maintained that 'the alliteration appears to throw a stress on *with*':

> [Thei] ne wédde no wómman that [thei] *wíth* deéle (VII 89).

56 K-D, 135.
57 Kane, '"Music . . ."', 53. Cf. also K-D 132, on Langland's 'sense of disciplined, subtly *modulated* progression' (my italics). This anticipates Kane's later expression; but though he refers us to Priscian ('"Music . . ."' 55, n. 24) he does not seem to have Bede's notion of *modulatio/rhythmus* in mind.
58 K-D 135. Their comments on *to* at XVI 147, XIX 218 (K-D 217) seem to me equally unconvincing; cf. Kane, 'Music . . .' 54–5. Like Skeat, Turville-Petre (op. cit. 137, n. 24) recognises the existence of modulation (cf. his reference to *Gawain* 987) but he does not correctly scan *for, fro* in A VII 11, 13.
59 Examples are Pr 22; I 150; II 91; III 74, 227, 239, 282; IV 34; all key-staves.

Langland's stress-pattern is generally that of ordinary speech, and the inversion of the order of preposition and verb (which was permissible in Middle English) serves to bring out even more forcefully a sense which is clearly present in an equivalent modern English sentence, where such inversion is *not* possible:

They wéd no wóman that they have íntercourse wíth.

But the Kane-Donaldson account is, I believe, *generally* mistaken with regard to the several hundred other cases of small-word staves. Stressed small words occur in only twenty-two lines (in addition to VII 89). All but one involve the five words *bi, for, so, to* and *with*[60] (in the form *myd* at XVII 170, a slighty doubtful case); the exception is XV 171:

Córseth he no créature, ne he *kán* bere no wráthe

where the model auxiliary *kan* acquires full-word (or 'lexical') status through here having the sense 'know how to'.

The value of the Kane-Donaldson theory was to draw attention to Langland's demonstrable skill in the use of small-word staves. That of Kane's later theory is, in my view, that it is essentially correct, though I do not always agree with his application of it and would prefer to give a simpler description of the facts that will fit into our existing understanding of the stave. To do this I wish to introduce the notion of the 'mute' stave.[61]

By a 'full stave', it will be recalled, I mean a syllable carrying both stress and alliteration, and by a 'blank stave' one with stress but no alliteration. A 'mute stave' is a syllable that carries alliteration but no stress. It may be understood as 'correlative' to the blank stave, fulfilling half the notional requirement for 'full-stave' status, the other half being fulfilled by an adjacent (always *following*, never preceding) syllable. So important is the mute stave in Langland's versification, that it seems worthwhile to discuss several examples. I have chosen the four which occur in the Prologue:

1 And *w*ónnen that thise *w*ástours *w*ith glótonye destrúyeth (22)
2 Mánye of thise *m*aístres *m*owe clóthen hem at líkyng (62)
3 Bísshopes and *b*áchelers, *b*othe maístres and dóctours (87)
4 I *s*éigh in this ass*é*mblee, as ye *s*hul hére áfter (218).

60 E.g. *bi*: III 10; XV 284, 568; *for*: XI 64 (= 'because'), XV 324 (= 'on behalf of'); *so*: XV 495 (=adv.), XVI 130 (= conj.); *to*: XVI 148; *with*: XV 245 is a doubtful second case. (These all occur in various stave-positions).
61 I have already used the term in the revised Appendix of my B-text edition (359) and, with fúller explanation, in my 'Authenticity of "Z"' (n. 37 above).

The first point to notice here is that each of the mute staves is a 'small'-word stave (a 'grammatical' or 'form' word) – a modal and a tense auxiliary (2, 4), a preposition (1) and a determiner (3). By no means all of the 750 or so mute staves in the B-text *are* small-word staves, but the overwhelming majority are,[62] because, quite understandably, it is after words such as auxiliaries, prepositions and determiners that potential *blank* staves (which are usually 'full' or 'lexical' words, as with the two nouns and verbs here) will appear. Secondly, in all four examples the muted stave is the *key* stave (the first stave of the b-half, from which the line's stave-sound is established). This is also to be expected, since a Langland line often divides into two phrase-groups on either side of the caesura of which one contains a verb (1,2,4) preceded by auxiliaries, prepositions or determiners and similar words. As it happens, some five in every seven muted staves occur at the key position, though in at least one example in the Prologue it occurs in the *a*-half:

> 5 The *máze* among us álle, theigh we *mýsse* a shérewe (192).

It is theoretically possible, of course, that 192 is a blank extended line of Type 1e, with *among* a full and not a mute stave, and that is why 5 is listed separately from nos 1–4; but a reading of the line with natural speech-stress will, I believe, favour *among* as a mute stave (the *line*-type to which 192 is assigned, should, however, remain Ia).

We encounter in 5 what may be called 'stave-type ambiguity' but no real 'line-type ambiguity'. In 4, however, we have a genuine line-type ambiguity that arises out of uncertainty (or lack of complete certainty) about which stave *is* the key-stave, and therefore, whether it is muted or not. For if we take *shul* as the key-stave (and Langland regularly alliterates *s* with *sh*) it becomes mute and the blank stave *here* forms the third lift. But there is evidence that Langland (on at least 25 occasions in B) created staves by the ingenious expedient of *liaising* the final consonant of a word with the vowel of the word following, as in the following two examples:

> 1 Fáls or Fável or any of híse féeris (II 194)
> 2 That Móyses or Méssie be come ínto this érthe (III 303).

The b-half of 2 was emended (differently) by both Kane-Donaldson and by myself in the first edition of my B-text, where I read (quite plausibly):

> That Moyses or Messie be come in [myddes] this erthe

---

62 See e.g. Pr 47 (*Seint*); V 366 (*wroght*), 443 (*fette*); VI 174 (*hente*); ?XI 176 (*lyveth*); ?XIII 60 (*drank*); ?XVII 108 (*suwen*); ?XVIII 28 (*fals*), ?400; XX 143 (*leet*). This list is almost complete (*Seint* occurs several times).

(Kane-Donaldson: into [myddel] erþe) to produce a line of normative scansion (*aa/ax*). Both Kane-Donaldson and I were agreed in requiring that the third lift should bear alliteration, our editorial experience leading us to believe that absence of it here indicated scribal corruption in a line. What we failed to see was that 2 scans in its archetypal form because the third *m* stave is generated by the *liaison* of *come* and *into*. The generation of a stave through 'a word alliterating by help of the end-consonant of the word preceding it' had been recognised by Lawrence and named by Schumacher (the 'liaisonal stave' = *Stab der Liaison*).[63] There is no difficulty in explaining, therefore, how in both 1 and 2, the compound stave-phrase created by the liaison requires to be stressed on a 'form' word (*ofhíse, comeínto*). As this is true of most of the liaisonals, if they are accepted, the effect is almost to double the number of non-muted (i.e. 'full') small-word staves.

Even more significant than this (possibly controversial) consequence is the creation in 2 of a new species of *line*. For whereas 1, with liaisonal stave, gives a Type 1b or 'enriched' line that scans *aa/aa* (a 'Standard' variant), example 2 displays the lineaments of a plausible alternative scansion, in which the *m* of *come* is not liaised fully with the vowel beginning *into*, but allows articulation of the latter word's initial glottal stop so that *into* alliterates with *erthe* producing a pattern *aa/[a]bb* (the caesural break *must* come after *Messie*). There is, therefore, a real possibility of '*line*-type ambiguity' (uncertainty as to which of two line-types III 303 should be placed in). And the same line-type ambiguity may be said to exist in 4 (Pr 218). If we find a liaisonal stave in *as yé* we have a line scanning normatively (*aa/ax*) with a small-word key-stave (and yet another addition to the repertory of small-word staves). But if, as I prefer, we analyse *shul* as the *muted* key-stave, then the following two (blank) staves, which are vowels, alliterate together giving the pattern *aa/[a]bb* once again. This pattern, which occurs in what I regard as undisputable examples such as Pr 163:

Bothe in wáreyne and in wáast where hem léve líketh

(with which compare III 18) is arguably present in about 100 cases in B (about half that number in C). I call it the 'transitional' or 'T'-type line, as it is transitional between Type 1a (with muted post-caesural stave, as in Pr 22) and Type IIb (as in V 370, 407).[64]

63 Lawrence, op. cit. 86; K. Schumacher, *Stüdien über den Stabreim in der mittelenglischen Alliterationsdichtung* (Bonn, 1914) 57–62. The possibility that B originally read *or of hise feeris any*, and was scribally inverted to prose order, is weakened by the identical form of the line in A II 155.
64 For a discussion of the 'T'-type line with special reference to Z, see 'Authenticity . . .' 296ff.

The major characteristics of the 'T'-type line are two. The first is that the b-half now assumes a weight more nearly equivalent to that of the a-half because the (new) stave-sound heightens the prominence of its lifts. The second is a direct consequence of the muting of the key-stave, and differs only in degree from what happens in *any* line with muted key-stave: a greater flexibility in retaining conversational word-order and rhythm without resort to inversion, wrenching of stress or *recherché* synonym-choice.[65] The 'T'-type lines are distributed randomly over the poem, every passus having at least one, but the reader can gauge their quality easily by reading through in succession the fifteen examples occurring (for no particular reason I can ascertain) in Passus XI.[66] Here it must suffice to quote a couple which appear in a sequence of three lines (372–4):

1   And thanne I rébukede Réson, and right til hymsélven I séyde,
       'I have wónder of thée, that wítty art hólden,
2   Why thow ne sewest mán and his máke, that no mysféet hem fólwe'

The mere existence of the T-type line becomes more credible when two examples are placed in such proximity (a feature obscured in Kane-Donaldson's text, which deletes *-selven* following the C-text revision).[67] However the type is interesting not simply as a variant for variety's sake but because it illustrates how the b-half can be strengthened in such lines and also, in 2, how the T-type's second- stave-sound enhances the witty pun on *feet . . . folwe* with which Will challenges his 'witty' interlocutor (*mysfeet*, a Fench loan first recorded here, presumably had terminal or at least variable stress).[68]

If the argument outlined above is sound, then it emerges that emendation of the text can often be avoided by appeal to one or other of the metrical criteria set out in my typology. The latter may be understood as constructed on an inductive basis, without resort to models or theories. I shall end this account of Langland's stave-practice by considering four cases in which I believe that major textual emendation proves unnecessary if the problematic lines are read in the light of one particular writer on grammar whose work Langland knew, Isidore of Seville.

---

65 This is not to deny 'inversions of word order in many second half-lines' (K-D 138), as in XI 373, quoted below, or XVIII 159 (where such inversion furnishes the rationale of emendation); or 'wrenched stress' (see p. 42 below); or words such as *gome* at XI 379 or (conjectured) *mid* at XI 343, forms that Langland normally avoids as not current in London English.
66 See XI 74, 77, 92, 116, 134, 148, ?176, 258, 274, ?276, 323, 349, 372, ?374, 436.
67 See C XIII 182, a revision perhaps in response to corruption by scribal mislineation in Langland's working-copy of B (corrected by K-D and followed in my edition).
68 See *MED* s.v. *misfait* (< OF *mesfait*). As *no* other examples are given, it may be an original borrowing of Langland.

Generally speaking I am in agreement with the masterly exposition of Langland's alliterative technique in the Introduction to Kane and Donaldson's edition (pp 132–3) and, apart from two small points,[69] there is only one issue on which I would wish to challenge them. This is their contention that Langland does not 'rhyme' (I prefer 'alliterate') *b* with *p*, *d* with *t* or *g* with *k*, that is to say, the voiced and unvoiced modes of the bilabial, alveolar and velar stops respectively. They therefore judge the instances where they occur as indicating unoriginality and requiring textual emendation. I prefer to regard them as metrical licences akin to the alliterating of *s* and *sh* (very frequent in Langland), which they consider 'approximate rhymes' (with no suggestion that they were undistinguished in the poet's idiolect). The alliteration of *p* with *b* occurs once, in V 208:

> To *b*roche hem with a *p*ak-nedle, and *p*layte hem togideres

where the textual evidence in both the A and the B traditions massively attests both *p* as the key-stave and *b* as stave 1 (A V 126; K–D V 210). Kane-Donaldson emend *broche* to *prochede*.[70] Alliteration of *d* with *t* occurs once also, in XVIII 294, which is identical in C (C XX 325):

> 'Certes, I *d*rede me', quod the *D*evel, 'lest *T*ruthe wol hem fecche'.

Here the key-stave, which should determine the line's stave-sounds, is *t* as the text stands, and Kane-Donaldson accordingly emend *wol* to *do* in order to obtain the required *d* sound, thereby producing a reading objectionable on grounds of sense.[71] Finally, *g* and *k* alliterate twice. In XIX 213 (identical in C):

> And *c*ride with Conscience, 'Help us, *G*od of *g*race!'

where the key-stave is *g*, Kane-Donaldson emend *God* to *Crist* (this is plausible but no reason for the substitution appears)[72]. Finally, in XIX 323 (also unchanged in C):

> And *G*race *g*af hym the *c*ros, with the *c*roune of thornes,

69 These are (i) regarding alliteration of *f* with *th* (voiced or unvoiced) as an 'approximate' rhyme (I see the dental and labio-dental fricatives as all levelled to /v/); (ii) understanding the word *who* as rhymed with both /w/ and with aspirated or unaspirated vowels (I think Langland's vowels were *all* unaspirated and *who* is always pronounced /ɔː/; in the three examples K-D quote (fn. 15) of apparent *w* alliteration, *who(m)* is not a stave-word in my analysis.
70 See my discussion, *B-text*, 269–70. Schumacher (op. cit. 123, 126–7) discusses these and other (more doubtful) cases of voiced and unvoiced stops alliterating.
71 Ibid., 297.
72 The account below disposes of my earlier speculation that the scansion *aa/bb* 'was acceptable to Langland' (*B-text*, 300).

the key-stave is *k*, and there may be two *g* staves in the a-half if we scan the line as Type Ic ('extended'). Kane-Donaldson emend *croune* to *garland*, citing XVIII 48 in support.[73]

There are, I believe, good grounds for not emending to be found in both the MS evidence and the sense of the attested archetypal readings in all four cases. But there is also reason for thinking that the alliteration of these three pairs of stops has a 'clerkly' origin. Isidore of Seville notes a 'kind of relationship' (*quaedam cognatio*) between the letters B and P and between C and G ('De Orthographia', *Etym.* I. xxvii, 4), giving as examples words like 'trecentos' / 'quadringentos'. He does not speak explicitly of the *cognatio* between D and T but finds them closely linked nonetheless, in that the same word (spelt *haud*) may be an adverb of negation or a conjunction depending on whether the final stop is voiced or unvoiced (he speaks of the presence or absence of 'aspiratio'). The spirit of Isidore's chapter as much as the letters themselves is useful to bear in mind when reading Langland, who may well be deliberately choosing an alternative form of the preterite (*gaf* for *yaf* in XIX 323 above)[74] because he is not merely a maker in search of staves but a clerk determined to practise *rhythmus* in accordance with a *ratio* learned in *cloistre* or *scole*.

IV. THE DIMENSIONS OF MAKING: ENJAMBEMENT

The foregoing discussion of Langland's versification has followed the assumption (intuitive, not theoretical) that he adheres to the normal stress-patterns of speech in the case of both individual words and whole sentences. The notion of 'mute staves' or of 'modulation' also helps obviate unnatural ways of reading lines that are supposedly enjoined by the requirements of the metre. Alliterative lines, however, though in some ways freer than the accentual-syllabic lines of Chaucerian rhymed verse (alliteration probably exerts less influence on word-choice than does couplet-rhyme), are not as free as, say, blank verse. Accordingly, the pressures of his form occasionally compel Langland to stress words in a way that probably differs from that common in speech or prose. It is hard to tell how these 'wrenched stresses' would have struck the ear of a contemporary alert to the 'incursionem verborum, utrum bene sonus an male cohaereat'. But we need to recall that many words in the fourteenth century, if of French or Latin origin, would possess variable pronunciation, and as the influx of Romance loan-words increased, that tendency

---

73 See K-D 118, and my comment, ed. cit. 323.
74 His usual form is *yaf*: see, in stave-position, VIII 53 (and cf. X 47).

might also have spread in part to words of native origin. I have counted about 75 lines with wrenched stresses, a small number in a poem of 100 times that length. If we leave aside cases of probable variable stress, such as *Délited* in I 29:

> *Délited* hym in drynke as the devel wolde

where we have a loan-word bearing stress on the first or the second syllable in speech,[75] or those where the native stress is *shifted* to satisfy the metre,[76] such as *welcómed* in XIII 27:

> Conscience knew hym wel and *welcómed* hym faire

(cf. also XV 21, XX 60), lines in which the demands of alliteration and speech-stress conflict are very few indeed.[77]. I have not space here to discuss or even to enumerate all the cases in which this conflict appears, but a close look at one may suffice to show the degree of skill Langland could bring to the solution of the problems posed by his form.

The example occurs in the second of the two lines I 17–18:

> And therfore he highte the erthe to helpe yow echone
> Of wollene, of lynnen, of liflode at nede.

Since (as appears to be the case) it is Langland's practice never to have a blank stave in the *first* lift of a line, it would follow that *wollene* will have to be stressed on the second syllable, contrary to speech-norms, given that the line seems to scan on *l*, producing a very clumsy *sonus*.[78] I suspect that most readers would prefer to assume that Langland has simply been defeated by the form here or that 'his verse is but loose metre', as Puttenham thought, not versified fair according to the precepts of Ars

75 See also *dévyne* (Pr 210), *dévýsede* (XIX 331), *dísputyng* (VIII 116); *éxcepte* (IX 141), *éxperience* (XVIII 151); *Ýmaginatif* (X 117, and throughout XII).
76 See V 108 (*Áwey*, a graphically mimetic instance); V 292 (*Bísette*: cf. also *Bífore* XIII 47, *bíleven* XV 73, with wordplay on *bileve* in XV 72). For wrenching of stress to *final* position, see XVI 71 (*Maidenhóde*), XIX 334 (*Preesthód*).
77 In native words, see *nevéremoore* (XI 103); *estwárd* (XVI 169), *afterwárd* (XVI 228), *hellewárd* (XVIII 114); and (with possible rhetorical justification) *pecókkes* (XI 358), *Mýself* (XVI 236), *hýmself* (XVI 239). In loan words, see *pharisées* (XV 603), *norrisséth* (XVI 33: unless the line scans on *n* and *nyce* has been lost archetypally before *wordes*), *maynpríse* (XVI 264: reverting to original stress). J. P. Oakden (*Alliterative Poetry in ME* (1930), I, 178) wrongly calls wrenched stress 'very common' in *PP*.
78 There is a small number of lines with awkward a-halves, e.g. XIV 270 and XVII 226 (discussed in my edn. ad loc) where satisfactory emendations do not suggest themselves. But most such lines contain Latin (e.g. III 339, 343; VI 236) and may be governed by special licensed rules. These and other (apparently anomalous) lines will be discussed in my forthcoming study of *The Metre of PP*.

Grammatica. I would agree that the pronunciation *wolléne* is impossible; but does that mean that Langland, in following speech-stress, has broken metrical rule? I think the opposite is in fact true, for the line seems to me to contain a pattern of triple liaisonal staves that actually enhance the natural-sounding quality of the verse while fully satisfying the strict metrical requirement:

> Of wóllene, of lýnnen, of líflode at néde.

The liaisonal stave in all probability is the *product* of fidelity to speech-norms, rather than a device constructed to overcome the problems of composing alliterative verse. Here, the scansion on voiced *f* is given delicate support from the 'buried' medial *f* of the compound *liflode* while the 'notional' stave-pattern (on *l*) remains prominent (thanks to the key-stave) even while the line's first *l* stave is effectively muted in reverse. What makes this rich and complex structural patterning seem plausible, the product of a keen artistic awareness, is the fact that line 18 runs on without interruption from line 17.

Enjambement[79] is one of the most important means by which Langland creates an impression of conversational naturalness rather than rhetorical formality: we speak, after all, in sentences, not in lines of verse. It is also one of his favourite devices, developed with great resourcefulness and variety as a technique for sustaining the rhythmic pulse of his poetry. It occupies an important place on the 'axis' of rhythm, the other being that of Langland's formal metric as already described (for further clarification see the simple diagram at the end of this chapter).

At its most basic, enjambement arises because of the primacy of syntax over metre at a particular point in the flow of the verse. Simple examples, in which no special rhetorical emphasis or other expressive value is being sought, are those like the following two. In the first, the *enjambing* line introduces a subordinate clause, in this case a noun clause:

> And mette ful merveillously *that* in mannes forme
> *Antecrist cam thanne* . . .   (XX 52).

In the second, the subordinating conjunction appears as the line-headword in the *enjambed* line:

> 'And if ye coveite cure, Kynde wol yow tellé
> *That* in mesure God made alle manere thynges .. .' (XX 253–4).

---

79 G. N. Leech describes enjambement as 'the placing of a line boundary where a deliberate pause, according to grammatical and phonological consider-ations, would be abnormal' (*A Linguistic Guide to English Poetry* (repr. 1979) 125). Oakden (op. cit., I, 158) notes the relative frequency of enjambement in *PP*, but without discussing its implications.

Commonly, too, the subordinate clause is one of comparison, as at XX 62–3:

> Whiche fooles were wel *gladdere* to deye
> *Than* to lyve lenger sith Leute was so rebuked.

Very often, however, the enjambing line introduces a main verb that has been *suspended* until the enjambed line, or a suspended subject, direct or indirect object, or complement. In many of these instances syntax and rhythm come together in such a way that the *incursio verborum* is laid at the service of subtle expressive effects, sometimes with and sometimes without the aid of textural ornaments. Space forbids discussion of all of even the most interesting examples, but most of them are referred to in the notes and enough will be said, I hope, to indicate how important enjambement is in Langland's verse, even though it recurs in fewer than fifteen lines per passus on average.

Three examples of suspended main verbs occur in the Prologue (55/6, 128/9, 147/8), in each of which the enjambement serves to generate a rhythmic pulse at the line-end, a point of relatively low tension in the normal line,[80] and to impart an extra emphasis to the first stave-word (in each case also the first *syllable*) of the enjambed line:

1 Grete lobies and longe that lothe were to swynke
   Clothed hem in copes   (55/6)
2 . And sithen in the eyr on heigh an aungel of hevene
   Lowed to speke in Latyn   (128/9)
3 And smale mees myd hem: mo than a thousand
   Comen to a counseil   (147/8).

In all three, the syntax is that of prose, except for the two inversions in 1 (*and longe, were*), the second of which helps to sharpen the profile of the key-stave *lothe* and thereby clarify its links with the assonating *lobies* and the rhyming *clothed*; but the line is noteworthy mainly for the way in which the terminal *swynke* is cunningly juxtaposed with the initial *clothed* to generate the ironic sense 'though they hate work, they nonetheless manage to clothe themselves' (the stated sense is '*because* they clothe themselves [sc. as hermits] they manage to *avoid* work – which they hate'). In 2, there is a vivid impression of dramatic 'enactment', the 'angel' hovering at the line-end, and then 'lowing'; but again irony is prominent, as there must be a slight pause after either *lowed* or *speke*: 'the angel descended (physically) but did not *con*descend to speak in the *lewed*

---

80 Leech (op. cit.) 124 calls the line-end pause 'a silent stress'. I would argue (paradoxical as it may seem, put this way) that this feature becomes more not less prominent in an enjambed line because there is no lowering of pitch (as is normally the case with the line's last lift).

tongue'. In 3, the enjambing fourth lift 'retroactively', as it were, sharpens the key-stave (*mó*); yet again, there is irony as the grand word *counseil* is applied assonatingly to a *thousand mees*.

It is surely not fanciful to hear behind these deftly-manipulated enjambements the subtle voice of Langland the clerk reading to an informed and appreciative circle not of *lordes* but of *clerkes*, in the first instance, like himself. Such could best have understood St Augustine's admonition to *argueres* (X 118) in a brilliant line-pair which Langland (very unusually) repeats almost *in toto* and which exemplifies a suspended *infinitive* after an auxiliary very common in this position:

> 'Wilneth nevere to wite why that God *wolde*
> *Suffre* Sathan his seed to bigile' (X 119–20; cf. 126–7).

The witty contrast here between a human wilfulness equated with human curiosity (*Wilne . . . wite*) as against the absolute and inscrutable divine Will (*wolde*) is pointed up by the enjambement, which causes us both to linger over terminal *wolde* (thereby almost transmuting it from a modal to a lexical verb)[81] and to come down with a heavy stress on *Suffre*, a key word in the poem and one rich in varied theological and scriptural meanings which are only hinted at here but are more fully explored in XI (esp. 379) and XVIII (esp. 335–40).[82] (A similar instance of 'de-modalising' an auxiliary is XI 312/13: 'That crouneth swiche Goddes knyghtes that konneth noght *sapienter* / Synge . . .', where the enjambement both forces attention onto the contrast between knowledge and wisdom or *sapientia* in 312 and points forward to the specific inadequacy of scandalous liturgical incompetence in the clergy).[83]

Enjambement is usually unmistakable, but sometimes its ambiguity at the syntactic-rhythmical plane can mirror a semantic ambiguity, as in the 'Janus-faced' lines XVIII 211/12:

> 'So God that bigan al *of his goode wille*
> Bicam man of a mayde mankynde to save'.

Here the italicised 211b need not enjamb, until we realise that it is from the same 'goode wille' that the Redemption springs as did the original Creation, a realisation that enables us to link more closely *bigan* and *bicam*. In this example the outer surface or texture of the verse is plain rather than rich, the chime of *bigan* and *bicam* sounding as a soft under-music, not an emphatically crescendo outburst, as in the following two 'main-verb'

81 On this distinction see, e.g. B. M. H. Strang, *Modern English Structure* (2nd edn, 1968) 144, 155.
82 I discuss this in 'The Inner Dreams in PP' (*MÆ* 55 (1986) 35–7).
83 Here the fact that the adverb is *Latin* helps to restore the 'silent stress' since it inhibits or counteracts the normal run-on. 'De-modalising' is also assisted by the *position* of the adverb (between auxiliary and infinitive).

examples. In XX 218–20, a combination of running and translinear alliteration[84] helps to build up the climax reached on the first lift of 220:

> Próude préestes coóme with hym – *p*ássynge an húndred
> In *p*áltokis and *p*ýked shóes and *p*ísseris longe *kń*yves
> Cóomen ayein Cónscience . . .[85]

These are lines of extraordinary skill and power, in which the unobtrusive *coome* of 218 (where it is a blank stave in a Type Ie line) becomes transformed into the huge and menacing 'suspended' verb of 220, its deadliness sharpened by the *knyves* of 219 that initiates the *k* alliteration of 220, even before we encounter the pivotal and all-explaining key-stave:

> with Cóveitise they helden.

In XIII 328/9 a translinear pattern of assonance (on short *e*) conveys the unrelenting quality of Haukyn's malice with the insistence of a drum:

> 'Or with myght of mouth or thorugh mannes stréngthe
> Avénged me féle tymes, other fréte myselve withinne'

– and the drum continues echoing in the following line 'As a shépsteres shere . . .'

In some instances of enjambement it is not the verb but the *subject* that is 'suspended', as in the 'lewed vicory's' cynically assured statement at XIX 413/14:

> 'I am a curatour of Holy Kirke, and cam nevere in mý tyme
> *Mán* to mé that mé kouthe telle of Cardinale Vertues . . .'

where the headword of 414 introduces a stabbing Type IIa line that sets the impossibility of 'virtuous cardinals' (for that is how the *vicory* sees them) against the certainty of what 'I' know (*my* 413 translinearly linking with *me . . . me*). Another splendid example is XIX 132/3, with its 'clerkly' macaronic[86] *b*-half stave:

> 'And tho was he called in contre of the comune peple,
> For the dedes that he dide, *Fili David, Ihesus*'

where the simple faith of the 'comune' expresses itself in a 'vers of Latyn' which, in strong contrast with that of Pr 143, expresses a profound

---

84 *Translinear* alliteration occurs when 'the last unalliterated stressed syllable . . . set(s) the alliteration for the next line', *running* alliteration when consecutive lines are grouped together 'by identical alliteration in two or more lines' (Oakden, op. cit., 154, 155).

85 I follow K-D in removing Skeat's comma after 218 (ed. cit., I, XVIII 217) but not in placing one after *knyves* 219 (though there is no enjambement; cf. Leech 125 on identifying enjambement 'by the absence of end-punctuation'.)

86 On macaronics as a feature of clerkly style, see ch. 3 below, pp. 93–102.

intuitive wisdom (the vicory is bound to recall the earlier priest de-
nounced by Piers in the memorably ironic words '*Lewed* lorel', VII 137).
Another fine example of 'suspended subject' (more strictly, complement)
is also from Passus XIX, where Conscience's act of kneeling (XIX 12)
anticipates his awed utterance of the title won by 'Jesus the justere' (10)
through the blood that now furnishes his armorial tinctures:

> 'ac he that cometh so blody
> Is Críst with his cros, conquerour of Cristene'   (13/4)

– with its heavily emphatic enriched fourth lift growing, as it were, out of
the root *Crist* planted as the (anticipated) first *k* lift of line 14.

The largest and most variously developed category of enjambements
involves suspended *objects*, which receive added emphasis because of the
build-up of syntactic energy in the enjambing line, containing the verb:

> 'Yeldynge for this thynge at one yeres ende
> Hire soules to Sathan, to suffre with hym peynes'   (II 105/6).[87]

This is a typical pattern, with the verb separated from its object by an
adverbial phrase or phrases. Here the pitch rises dramatically at the end of
105, where the word *ende* hovers ominously like a sentence of judgement.
Enjambement here involves both pause and advance, the two forces
being locked in suspension like the opposed streams of a tidal river. Also
common is the *juxtaposition* of verb and direct object, as in this vivid
mimicking of incredulous voices:

> 'How?' quod al the comune. 'Thow conseillest us to yelde
> Ál that we ówen ány wight ér we go to hóusel?' (XIX 394/5).

Here the sharpness of the five vowel lifts in the Type Id line 395 is
heightened by the 'background' music of secondary *w* alliteration on *we*,
wight.[88]

Enjambement is a means of attaining fidelity to the contours of living
speech. This is true even when the speaker is one of Will's wise instruc-
tors, not a fully realised dramatic character. An example is Ymaginatif
warning him against his *wilde wantownesse*:

> 'To amende it in thi myddel age, lest myght the faille
> In thyn old elde, that yvele kan suffre
> Poverte or penaunce, or preyeres bidde'   (XII 7/8/9).

---

87 Skeat (ed. cit.) destroys the enjambement with an unnecessary comma after
   ende.
88 There may also be 'echoic counterpoint' in XIX 394 (see section vi, p. 65
   below) which scans on either vowels or *k*.

Here the second of the two enjambements is much stronger than the first, which introduces only an adverbial phrase. Its potency lies in the way that both modal and prolative in line 8 are made to relate to grammatically discrete components in 9, *suffre* to the two nouns in the *a*-half and *kan* to a second prolative, *bidde*, in the *b*-half. The writing is extremely economical, and it has the weight and authority of Wordsworth's

> But there may come another day to me –
> Solitude, pain of heart, distress, and poverty
> > *(Resolution and Independence, l. 35).*

in which the alexandrine solemnly proffers four additional subjects for the verb *come*, 'borrowed' from the preceding line, where it already has an immediate subject, *day*.[89]

In some more complex instances, Langland builds up the pressure behind the 'suspended' object by *delaying* it, as here, where the syntax gets somewhat out of hand:

> 'To alle trewe tidy men that travaille desiren,
> Oure Lord loveth hem and lent, loude outher stille,
> Grace to go to hem and ofgon hir liflode'   (IX 105/6/7).

The initial *To* of 105, like the second *to* of 107, slightly blurs the clarity of the two linked statements 'Our Lord loves honest workers', 'He shows this love by giving them "grace" [every kind of means][90] to earn a living'. Langland seems to need the greater freedom afforded by repetition-with-variation, as in this case, where Will himself is reflecting on what will become of a 'renegade' Christian

> 'But if Contricion wol come and crye by his lyve
> Mercy for hise mysdedes with mouth or with herte'.
> > 'That is sooth', seide Scripture; 'may no synne lette
> Mercy al to amende, and mekenesse hir folwe'
> > > (XI 135/6, 137/8).

In this double instance of enjambement on the same word, we see the 'mercy' which is only a word to be 'cried' (vocally or inwardly) become a force, even a person ('hir') as the lines skilfully move from separating verb and noun by an adverbial phrase (135/6) to juxtaposing them, with only the line-end pause between (137/8). This reduction of verbal space between key components is mirrored in the rhythmic contraction of the

---

89 Possibly, as Prof. Burrow has suggested to me, *preyeres bidde* is also dependent on *suffre*: 'when you will barely have strength to endure poverty or penance, or even the exertion of prayer'.
90 See *MED* s.v. 1(d) and 2, the apparent sense(s) at XIX 228 (XIX 218 echoes IX 107).

two-syllable dip (*by his*) to near-zero (*sýnně létte*). The effect of syntax and rhythm co-active in the lines is almost to mimic a physical struggle between 'sin' and 'mercy', with mercy proving victorious when aided by humility.

A similar urgency of response to the concept and experience of the divine mercy is illustrated in another example, where Abraham, model of faith, is expressing his trust in God's promise of both earthly prosperity and spiritual grace:

> 'Myn affiaunce and my feith is ferme in this bileve,
> For hymself bihighte to me and to myn issue bothe
> Lond and lordshipe and lif withouten ende.
> To me and to myn issue moore yet he me grauntede –
> *Mercy* for oure mysdedes as many tyme as we asken'
> (XVI 238–42).

The great climactic force of *Mercy* in 242 is due to its surprising our expectation, and this in turn is the result of *bothe* 239 seeming to exhaust the possibilities of divine bounty:[91] what could be more than 'lond and lordshipe' *and* 'lif withouten ende' (called elsewhere 'hevene in . . . here-beyng and hevene thereafter' XIV 140)? Langland's answer to this question is *Mercy*, God's supreme gift (with *moore yet* XVII 241 compare *above Goddes werkes* XI 139), the unique expression of generosity *per se* inasmuch as it is 'grauntede' in the face of hostile opposition ('synne'). Langland has dramatically put into his figural personage's mouth all the jubilant emotion of the humblest sinner experiencing the certainty of being 'saved'. This jubilation is reflected in the enriched structure of 241, which unexpectedly inverts the lift-pattern of the *b*-half so as to generate a translinear alliterative pattern carried over from the line-end to 242 and attaining its crest in that line's first lift:

> 'To mé and to mýn issue moóre yet he mé gràuntede –
> Mércy for oure mýsdedes as mány tyme as we ásken'.

These lines display the 'roll, the rise, the carol, the creation'[92] of the clerkly maker's style at its barest – relying on small-word staves and upon the full resources of rhythm and syntax and wrenched stress.[93]

The same urge to exploit 'articulate energy'[94] to the full can be seen

---

91 As in the 'Janus-faced' XVIII 211b (see p. 45 above) *bothe* goes either with *issue* as adj. (*MED* s.v. 2a) or with *Lond*, etc. as correlative conj. (*MED* 4a).
92 'To R.B.', *The Poems of Gerard Manley Hopkins*, ed. W. H. Gardner and N. H. MacKenzie, 4th edn. (Oxford, 1970) 108.
93 On 'wrenched stress' see note 77 above.
94 The phrase is Donald Davie's describing the syntax of verse, *Articulate Energy* (1955); see esp. pp. 29–30.

in some lines expressing a view that evidently went against the grain
for Langland, as the rigorous ideal of Christian Charity (expressed
supremely in charity to the unworthy) runs hard against natural instinct
and was felt to do so by this poet:

> Ac Gregory was a good man, and bad us gyven *alle*
> That asketh for His love that us *al* leneth (VII 74/5).

Two points need noting here. One is the semantic ambiguity that 'sur-
vives', so to speak, the *dis*ambiguity of disyllabic *alle*.[95] This word, which
could qualify *us* in 74, in fact refers to 'them' (those who ask for alms); but
the near-repetition in *us al* ('everything to us') at 75 momentarily destabil-
ises the fixed meaning, so that we wonder if Gregory's injunction was not
'to give all' as well as 'to give to all'. I believe that *this* sense – which
ultimately is in accord with Langland's deepest apprehension of God's
love as unconditioned – is made both possible and perceptible through
the skilful control of syntax and, to some degree, the recourse to trans-
linear alliteration, which initiates the *incursionem verborum* running
through *ásketh*, *Hís* and *ús* to meet *ál* again and be, as it were, 'resurrected'
in the initial-*le* of *léneth*.

The amount of oral effort required to articulate vowel lifts tends to
endow the staves in question with a heightened prominence, as is
beautifully clear from this simile comparing the action of the Trinity to the
sun upon ice:

> – as men may se in wyntre
> Ysekeles in evesynges thorugh hete of the sonne
> Melte in a mynut while to myst and to watre
> (XVII 229/30/31).

Here there is a perceptible pause at the end of 230 as we contemplate the
slow but irresistible operation of the sun upon the stiff icicles. Once again,
the 'idea' that has fired Langland's imagination is that of the rigidity of
power relaxing into the liquid suppleness of mercy. Glottal-stopped
vowels[96] 'enact' stiffness and nasals and liquids fluidity. Of the consonant

95 The *alle/al* distinction is lost in Skeat's text (based on Laud Misc. 851), which
has *alle* twice, giving a plausible but more commonplace meaning.
96 I disagree with Oakden's view that there is no glottal stop in vocalic lifts and
that frequent alliteration of 'an unstressed verbal prefix' may be due in part to
a wish to appeal to the eye as much as the ear (op. cit. 159–60). The strongest
evidence for my view (that of J. Lawrence, *Chapters on Alliterative Verse*, 111,
who believed that the glottal stop had greatly weakened by the C14th) is the
de-aspiration of native words in, e.g. XVI 239. This surely suggests com-
pensatory emphasis at the vowel-onset, and thus in effect a glottal stop,
which I see as extending to the key-stave's vowel lift (cf. the converse
situation in XVII 230). (See also XX 185–90, quoted below, with fifteen vowel
staves in six lines).

stops it is velar *g*, further hardened through being 'loken' with rolled *r*, that best betokens violent action, especially of the forces of evil against weak or vulnerable good. Two examples must suffice; both reveal how Langland turns from the sheer power of syntax to the various devices of what I have inadequately called 'decoration' to achieve a maximum of poetic *expressiveness*.

In the first it is necessary to quote the lines preceding and following the enjambing pair to bring out sufficiently the cumulative force behind the 'hostility' key-stave:

> 'Now is Piers to the plow. *Pride* it aspide
> And gadered hym a greet oost: *greven* he thynketh
> Conscience and alle *Cristene* and Cardinale Vertues –
> Blowe hem doun and *breke* hem and bite atwo the mores
> (XIX 337–40).

Here *greven* takes to itself something of the meaning of *greet*, with which it has close alliterative links. The drop in pitch and loudness at *he thynketh* is quickly seen as a *reculer pour mieux sauter*: *gr-* links translinearly with *Cristene* (stave 2 in 339) by virtue of that *cognatio* between the voiced and unvoiced palatal plosives of which Isidore speaks (discussed above in relation to XIX 213 and 323). But the 'force' of *Cristene* is insufficient against that of *Pride*, and the *P* of that word is transformed into the harder, heavier *b* of *breke* (the other pair between which Isidore observed 'a certain close relationship'). The syntax relies to an unusual extent on parallelism and repetition: the caesuras of 337 and 338 are both exceptionally strong, and the metrical pattern of 337b and 338b is very similar. But there seems little doubt that the expressive energy largely resides in the stave-patterning across the lines (*Pride, greven, Cristene, breke*), which determines as much as it is determined by the syntax.

The grieving or afflicting of Conscience is seen by Langland as such a grave matter because Conscience is the soul's power to say 'no' (to temptation) or 'yes' (to grace) (cf. XV 39*a*). To oppose the grace of God, therefore, is 'to prick God in the palm' (XVII 200):

> So whoso synneth ayeins the Seint Spirit, it semeth that he *greveth*
> God that he grypeth with, and wolde his grace quenche
> (XVII 203/4).

In this final instance, the crucial word *greveth* is translinearly linked with *God*, the headword of the enjambed line. The power of *sin* here is such that it can extinguish the divine 'sonne', stop up the access and passage to God's pity, effectively *lette* that Mercy which is above all God's works.[97]

---

97 Langland renders Ps 144:9 ('Miserationes eius *super* omnia opera eius') as 'Mercy . . . and mekenesse . . . / . . . beth . . . *above* Goddes werkes' (XI 138–9). (The sense of *super* is probably 'upon, towards').

These words of the Samaritan – before the Crucifixion and Harrowing scene – have to be set in counterpoise with those of Scripture at XI 137–8, quoted and discussed above. And if Mercy, now wholly personified, is given the last word –

> So shal grace that al bigan make a good ende   (XVIII 160)

it is not until Langland has first graphically demonstrated the *cost* of salvation to 'God that bigan al of his goode wille' and 'Bicam man of a mayde mankynde to save' (XVIII 211–12).

A close examination of the device of enjambement, here attempted only in a few selected instances, has taken us deep into the thematic heart of *Piers Plowman*. The same will, I think, be found to be true of those other varieties of *ornatus* that I have grouped together somewhat arbitrarily under 'Texture', and it is to these that I now turn.

V.   TRANSLINEAR AND RUNNING ALLITERATION

The patterns of complex alliteration used by Langland may be divided into two classes – those which occur within *individual* lines and those which span *two or more* lines. I begin with the latter, both because they are more easy to establish as unambiguously present and because I have already illustrated both in the course of discussing enjambement, the device which 'strides' across individual lines 'locked' together through 'letters'. It is especially appropriate to begin with *translinear alliteration*[98] because, as my first example will show, it serves a particular function of *counteracting* the tendency of enjambement (a product of syntactic pre-dominance) to dissolve the structural autonomy of the individual line. This instance is one of *double* translineation,[99] a feature which occurs in 20 out of the total of some 455 (there are also four examples of *treble* translineation):

> 'But thoo that feynen hem foolis and with faityng *l*ibbeth
> Ayein the *l*awe of Oure Lord, and *l*yen on hem*s*elve,
> *S*pitten and *s*puen and *s*peke foule wordes . . .'   (X 38–40).

---

98 This is found both in OE and in transitional works such as Laȝamon's *Brut*, where it occurs on average once in every 30 lines (see Oakden, op. cit., I. 148–9). Langland has almost twice the frequency of Laȝamon (455 examples in 7275 lines; Oakden's *PP* figures (ibid., I. 154) of 371 examples in 7089 lines are incorrect).

99 This may be *plain* (on different letters in successive lines) – e.g. II 64/5, 65/6 (*th* (= *v*), *b*); or *enriched* (on the same letter in successive lines) – e.g. II 32/3, 33/4 (*l*, *l*; these lines also carry *running* alliteration on *m*).

Here we see created a fluid pattern (larger than, but arising from, the individual line), which helps to strengthen the stave-pattern of the subsequent line (38/9 enjamb, 39 and 40 do not). The overall effect of this device is to increase the notional density of the full staves in the poem by a sort of attraction. Although in most cases (the exceptions being line-types Ib, Id and the rare IIb and IIIb) the 'trigger' stave is actually a blank stave *within its own line*, it becomes attracted into the alliterative 'orbit' of the following line and so acquires a quasi-stave status in that line. This can be seen by comparing the impact of the (notionally blank) fourth stave in the following pair of enjambed lines:

> 'By my feith, frere!' quod I, 'ye faren lik thise *wow*eris
> That *w*edde none widewes but for to welden hir goodes'
>
> > (XI 71–2).

Here *woweris*, which belongs metrically with line 71 but semantically with line 72 (through the collocation with *wedde* and *widewes*) may be heard as triggering a sequence which culminates in *welden*. Thus 'wedding' and 'wielding (wealth, power)' become intimately associated, and the exposure of the friars' duplicity attains maximum rhetorical force.

The cases of translinear 'trebles' show Langland building up a tone of peculiar intensity, though they vary from the mnemonic-didactic (VI 242/3/4 (followed by a change of stave in 244/5)) to the hypnotic-soporific (XV 9/10, 10/11, 11/12: three separate trigger-staves) and the logico-deictic (XI 262/3, 264/5, 266/7: 'quasi-doubles' with intervals between each trans-lineating alliteration). There is space here to quote only one example (XX 187/8, 188/9, 189/90: with changed central trigger-stave), especially in-teresting as a sequence because its *first* initiating stave (*heddes* 187) is *anticipated* by the stave-pattern of the preceding line 186, which in turn has been triggered by the final (vowel) stave of 185:[100]

> So harde he yede over myn heed it wol be sene *e*vere.
>   'Sire *y*vele ytaught Elde!' quod I, 'unhende go with the!
> Sith whanne was the wey over menne *h*eddes?
> Haddestow be hende', quod I, 'thow woldest have asked *l*eeve!'
>   'Ye – *l*eve, lurdeyn?' quod he, and leyde on me with *a*ge,
> And *h*itte me under the ere – unnethe may I here.   (XX 185–90).

The passage is one of the two (there is a third in the A-text, A VII 166) in which one character 'hits' another an allegorical 'blow', with serious consequences (cf. Piers at XVI 87) for the person hit. Both scenes are

---

100 If the fourth lift of line 186 is in fact *with* and not *the* (as it may well be) the sequence will constitute a unique translinear 'quintuple' (vowel/vowel; *w/w*; vowel/vowel; *l/l*; vowel/vowel).

moments of grotesque fantasy, with comedy and tragedy in tense prox-
imity. What is remarkable here is the way in which Langland sustains the
action by vivid dialogue and constantly varying metrical and rhythmic
artistry. The words are of the very simplest, all monosyllabic or disyllabic:
here is Biblical *sermo humilis*[101] indeed – Jerome's 'simplicitas et quaedam
vilitas verborum'.[102] Now the formal control displays an alert and
resourceful maker: consider, for instance, the placing of the caesura in 187
as opposed to 190, with its wordplay and internal rhyme. Yet what
Langland is doing here is clerkly more than makerly – exacting the full
value out of the flattest and most colourless of stave-sounds, the vowels,
which seem to mimic the emptiness and impotence of toothless age
itself.

The lines that immediately follow, with their violent explosion of *b* and
g staves ('buffeted . . . bette . . . gyved . . . goutes'), take us with an
almost parodistic abruptness from the subdued 'clerkly' world of sugges-
tive monochrome into the knockabout arena of *rum, ram, ruf* of which
Langland is in his own way as critical as Chaucer. For it is, of course, with
heavily stressed stop-consonants that the form was associated right up to
the time of Holofernes' 'pretty pleasing pricket' (*Love's Labour's Lost*
IV.ii.53). Langland does not 'affect the letter, for it argues facility' (ibid.),
though he exhibits that quality at full in the following passage, which will
serve to effect a transition to the feature of running alliteration. 'I marvel',
Will tells the friar at XI 75,

> 'Whi youre *c*ovent *c*oveiteth to *c*onfesse and to *b*urye
> Rather than to *b*aptize *b*arnes that *b*en *c*atecumelynges.'
>
> (XI 76–7).

Here we have a remarkable specimen of what might be called 'crossed
translineation', as a metrical analysis discloses. If, as seems likely, *con* – 76
is a muted key-stave,[103] then an additionally heavy stress falls on the
translinear trigger-stave *b*, which is quickly attracted across the anacrusis
of 77 to 'collide' with *b*aptize (earthly profit from physical death being
counterposed against heavenly profit from spiritual life). As I read it, 77 is
also a 'T'-type line scanning *aa[a]bb*, with muted key-stave *ben* and two

101 See E. Auerbach on 'a new sermo humilis . . . which . . . encroaches upon the
deepest and the highest, the sublime and the eternal' (*Mimesis* (1968) p. 72;
see also his article on '*Sermo humilis*' in *Romanische Forschungen* 64 (1952)
304–64).
102 Letter LIII (to Paulinus), in I. Hilberg, ed., *Sancti Eusebii Hieronymi Epistulae* I,
463.
103 Langland's *con*- words are generally stressed on the first syllable (e.g. XX 229,
372), but they presumably bore a shifting stress which could prove useful to
an alliterative poet; the more usual pattern is likely to have been with stress
on the second syllable, as today (cf. *contrárieth* V 54).

even stresses on *cáte–cúmelynges*.[104] The resulting structure of this trans-linearly linked pair of lines becomes 'crossed': *c,c,b*, // *b,b,c*, with a flowing syntactic unit (from 'to burye . . .' to 'barnes') separated off from 'covent coveiteth . . . catecumelynges'. The impression we are left with is that if the friars *did* 'covet' baptismal fees (to which no legacies were annexed) they would not be really guilty of *coveitise* at all: but by failing to baptize they are effectively 'burying' the infants alive (*catecumelynges* is first attested here and *catacumb* not before the C15th (see *MED s.vv.*) but one is tempted to find a sardonic clerkly pun on this strange, waif-like polysyll-able with its dying fall).

Running alliteration – the repetition of the same stave-sound over two or more successive *lines* – achieves for groups of lines what the enriched lift does for the individual line (e.g. in Types Ib and Id): it increases the density of the texture and makes for greater weight and memorability, in a manner similar to patterns of rhyme in normal verse. The distinctively clerkly character of Langland's use of running alliteration can be seen if we compare his one example of a six-line run with one by a typical maker such as the *Morte Arthure*-poet.[105] Trajan has been arguing for the superiority of simple faith over book-learning or *clergye*, especially those forms of it which offered contemporary English clerks the best prospects of worldly advancement:[106]

> 'Thanne is bileve a lele help, above logyk or lawe.
> Of logyk ne of lawe in *Legenda Sanctorum*
> Is litel alowaunce maad, but if bileve hem helpe;
> For it is overlonge er logyk any lesson assoille,
> And lawe is looth to lovye but if he lacche silver.
> Bothe logyk and lawe, that loveth noght to lye,
> I conseille alle Cristene, clyve noght theron to soore . . .'
> (XI 218–23, with 224 added).

The passage from the *Morte* describes Arthur's ravaging of Tuscany:

> Thus they springene and sprede, and sparis bot lyttille,
> Spoylles dispetouslye, and spillis theire vynes;
> Spendis vn-sparely, that sparede was lange,

---

104 For Langland's 'occasional location of two staves in a single word' (*sc.* in standard lines) cf. K-D 133 (referring to V 122, VII 154, XI 206 etc).
105 Oakden (*op. cit.* 156) rightly notes the high frequency of this device in the alliterative *Morte* but is mistaken that '*PP* has the device very rarely'. The B-text has 402 cases of single runs and another 61 of runs of three or more lines. 'Fours' in *PP* are admittedly rare (8) and 'fives' rarer (3). Brock is nearer the mark (*Morte Arthure*, ed. cit., xiii).
106 See Dunbabin, 'Careers', in Catto, *op. cit.*, esp. 573.

Spedis theme to Spolett with speris inewe!
ffro Spayne in-to Spruyslande the worde of hyme sprynges,
And spekynngs of his spencis, disspite es fulle hugge!

(*AMA* 3158–63).

I have chosen a relatively subdued passage from the *Morte* rather than one of the more blatantly clangorous pieces of battle-description such as 1368–73 (alliterating on hard *g*) because it actually resembles Langland in some respects. One is the wordplay (*paronomasia* with *annominatio*) on *springene* and *sprynges* (3158, 3162), used of troops and reputation respectively, on *sparis* 'spares' (3158) and *sparede was* 'had been saved, accumulated' (3160) and *vn-sparely* 'unsparingly / unstintingly' in the same line, and on *dispetously* 'pitilessly' and *disspite* 'spite, hatred' (3159, 3163), with its ironic vacillation between laudatory and condemnatory points of view. Yet the passage is as a whole directed to the ear, aiming to overwhelm us with a sense of epic scope and scale, so that the immediate relevance of 'Spain' and 'Spruyslande' in the context of the Italian campaign becomes unimportant.

The Langland passage, by contrast, makes little sensuous appeal, and the fourfold repetition of *logyk* and *lawe* occurs as part of a demonstration, carried out in gradual stages ('Thanne . . . For . . . And . . . Bothe') in the clerkly mode of those two arts, of their inferiority to a *bileve* 'faith' that is demonstrated in love. Yet it cannot be denied that the running alliteration imparts a real intensity to the *argument* as such, the appeal to the 'ear' becoming in effect an appeal to the intellect *through* the ear. In this most dense of all the poem's passages of sustained alliteration, the resources of the maker's art seem decidedly subordinated to the requirements of *clergye*; but those resources are abundantly displayed, nonetheless. Whereas the *Morte*-lines are all of the same metrical type (in 3162 the blank key-stave is perhaps due to a textual corruption and the b-half should read *sprynges of hyme the worde*), Langland's lines contain only two of the same type, 220–1, and even these differ in the placing of the slack syllables in the a-half. 222 is Type Ie, 223 is Ib, while 219, formally Ia, subtly differs from the normative by having a mute key-stave and a Latin b-half. 218 is a cross between Id and Ie, with blank third and enriched fifth stave. In 219 and 223 the phrase *logyk and lawe* occurs in the same position, because these lines are parallel; its other appearance is in the b-half of 218, while *logyk* and *lawe* by themselves appear in positions 2 and 1 respectively. The antithetical pair, *bileve* and *lovye*, likewise appear in corresponding a-half and b-half positions in 218, 220 and 222, 223 respectively. The upshot of the unrelenting *l*-alliteration (21 staves) is to fix our minds firmly on the key oppositions almost as if we were reciting a mantra rather than a reasoned argument. Despite the bevy of abstractions, too, Langland keeps our attention by resorting to occasional 'emotive' words (*lele, litel, longe, looth*) and by one deft piece of concreteness, *silver*.

This is not the place to explore at any length Langland's possible 'reasons' for writing this singular piece of running alliteration. What matters is that the one who is 'broken out of helle' (XI 140) is articulating a set of crucial antinomies (logic, law: belief, love) which will not be finally resolved until the one who has broken *into* hell claims that 'by lawe . . . lede I wole fro hennes / Tho [leodes] that I lov[e] and levede in my comynge' (XVIII 401–2), 'leodes' who include Trajan, exemplar of 'leel love and lyvyng in truthe' (XI 161). And this theme, that of the relationship between justice and love, reason and faith, is as fundamental to *Piers Plowman* as it was central to the poet's age and to his presumed audience.[107] The sustained intensity of the alliteration underlines its importance; and the abrupt termination of the *l*-pattern at 224, with its peculiarly heavy key-stave *clyve*, almost enacts a physical gesture from the speaker before he resumes the tone of argument, turns to 'wordes . . . of Feithes techyng' (225) and concludes: 'Forthi lerne we the lawe of love as Oure Lord taughte' (227).

There is not space here to look in any detail at the three instances of five-line runs and the eight instances of four-line runs; but it is worth drawing attention to a distinction which applies also in the much larger range of three-line runs (about 50) and simple runs of two lines (about 402). This is the distinction between runs which *repeat* a stave-word, in whatever position, and those which do not. The six-line example discussed above displayed functional repetition in a high degree, and I attempted to defend it as both art and argument. But it has to be admitted that Langland is not always so successful, and it is useful to find out how often he fails and why, since I suspect that it is the dry, flat, didactic lines that have led readers to share Hopkins's judgement that Langland's poetry was 'not worth reading'. Such lines are often passages of exposition, of which one is inclined to feel that prose would have done as well, and if as well, then probably better. An instance like XIX 26–30, where Conscience distinguishes the titles of Christ as knight, king and conqueror, is a case in point. Here, in spite of the genuine effort to avoid monotony by, e.g., shifting the third use of *called* from first to second stave-position and by muting the key-stave in 30, there is real relief when the *k* alliteration ceases at 31 and the rhythmic flow is restored as the demands of expository logic are relaxed:

> 'Ac to be conquerour called, that cometh of special grace,
> And of hardynesse of herte and of hendenesse' (XIX 30–1).

107 See M. Stokes, *Justice and Mercy in PP* (1984) 27ff, 83–5; J. Coleman, *PP and the 'Moderni'* (Rome, 1981), esp. ch. 2.

This passage repeats *knyght* three times and *kyng* and *conquerour* twice each, and while their shared *k* stave helps to convey the notion of an ascending order of 'degrees', the repetitions are not functionally dynamic as in XI 218–23, where *lawe* and *logyk* are in constant semantic movement under the pull of their antithetical pair *love* and *bileve*.

Clearly, running alliteration achieves greatest expressiveness and also, I believe, gives most pleasure to the ear, when the successive staves are all, or nearly all, different words. This can be seen in the course of Patience's magnificent exposition to Haukyn of the power of divine mercy to 'amenden us as manye sithes as man wolde desire' (XIV 187). Here the threat of despair coming from the devil is countered by the comfort to be derived from the Passion of Christ, a 'document' of release from the bonds of sin. The full effect of Langland's contrast between 'punishment' and '(saving) passion' requires quotation of the preliminary and concluding *p*-lines, not themselves part of the running sequence, which 'bracket' the run and are separated from it by a line alliterating on another stave:

'Ac if the *pouke* wolde plede herayein, and punysshe us in conscience,
We sholde take the acquitaunce as quyk and to the queed shewen it –
Pateat &c: Per passionem Domini –
And putten of so the *pouke* and preven us under borwe.
Ac the *parchemyn* of this patente of poverte be moste,
And of pure pacience and parfit bileve.
Of pompe and of pride the *parchemyn* decourreth,
And principalliche of alle peple, but thei be poore of herte.
Ellis is al on ydel, al that evere we wr[ogh]ten –
Paternostres and penaunce and pilgrimage to Rome . . .
(XIV 188–96).

Here the only stave-word to be repeated is *parchemyn*, the most important word in the whole passage, the symbol of the Passion in which all the power of *pacience* and *poverte* (suffering and humility) is centred and concentrated, along with the 'complete faith' (*parfit bileve*) that makes such virtues possible: the *parchemyn*, of double strength through its twofold utterance, puts off the *pouke* and his worldly trappings of pomp and pride. The 'T'-type line 195 (as I read it), with its heavy stresses on *wé* and *wróghten*, affirms the impotence of mere human effort without grace (an effort that can be understood as a form of pride) and the outer 'bracketing' *p*-stave line 196 enumerates various empty acts of piety that count for nothing against the 'pleading' of the Devil (cf. 188, the introductory 'bracketing' line), being *al* that is *ydel* (195) in comparison with the *acquitaunce* (189) won by Christ. In this run, even the Latin quotation contributes to the pattern of the verse, since it contains in its juxtaposition of *Pateat* and *Passio* (with its 'clerkly' pun on *pateo* and *patior*) a hint at the liberating and quickening potential of suffering taken in patience, which is basic to Langland's religious understanding.

Repetition of a stave-*word* once or more occurs in all but twelve[108] of the 62 instances where the same stave-*sound* runs over three or more lines. In 24 of these, the stave-*position* is the key one, sometimes for both occurrences, as here:

> Clerkes that were confessours coupled hem togideres
> Al to construe this clause, and for the *Kynges* profit,
> Ac noght for confort of the commune, ne for the *Kynges* soule
> > (IV 149–51).

'Rhetorical *repetitio*'[109] like this can doubtless be defended because it serves to heighten the contrast between 'profit' and 'soule', but carried to excess it would soon induce fatigue. This would be *a fortiori* true where the run is a 'simple' one, i.e. only two lines long.[110] But to do Langland justice, he seems aware of this danger, and generally makes an effort to vary the stave's *form* (a sort of *annominatio*)[111] or, failing that, the half-line's rhythmic structure. This can be seen in the following pair of *l*-alliterating runs, the first showing rhythmic and the second formal variation within the repetition:

> 'Ĭ léve wĕl, *lády*', quod Conscience, 'that thi Latyn be trewe.
> Ăc thŏw ărt lík ă *lády* that radde a lesson ones,
> Was *omnia probate*, and that plesed hire herte –
> For that lyne was no lenger at *the leves ende*.
> Hadde she loked that other half and *the leef torned*,
> She sholde have founden fele wordes folwynge therafter'
> > (III 337–42).

Repetitions understandably bulk large in speeches of an admonitory, exhortatory or even, virtually, 'catechetic' type, e.g. in those of authoritative personages like Holi Chirche or Theologie. Here it is very important to avoid boredom through monotonous insistence; and more often than not, Langland achieves this by varying the stave-word's *position*, as in II 135–6:

---

108 These include I 92–4, V 386–8, X 90–2, 424–6, and XI 129–31.
109 A. C. Spearing's 'Verbal Repetition in *PP* B and C' (*JEGP* 62 (1963) 722–37) claims that Langland owes more to *ars praedicandi* than to *ars poetica*; but too sharp a distinction should not be drawn, since an Alanus, for instance, was both a poet and a theorist of the art of preaching.
110 Compare the inert Pr 124–5, I 28–9, 37–8, with the more expressive Pr 15–16 or the subtly-nunaced Pr 108–9.
111 E.g. Pr 104–5 (*closynge/close*); II 31–2 (*Mercy/merciful*), 56–7 (*men/man*).

'And ledeth hire to Londoun, there *lawe* is yshewed,
If any *lawe* wol loke thei ligge togideres'

(where there is also a subtle difference in the senses of *lawe* in each case)[112]
or by filling the *stave-word* itself with a range of associations that are
'squeezed out', so to speak, by the pressure of the repetitions, as in
II 120–1 (Theologie again speaking):

'And God graunted to *gyve* Mede to truthe,
And thow hast *gyven* hire to a gilour – now God *gyve* thee sorwe!'

This last example effects variation through *annominatio* (the verb-forms
are the infinitive, the past participle and the subjunctive respectively) and
also through a *second* stave-word *repetitio*, with *God* performing two
strikingly different roles in the declarative of 120a and the imprecation of
121b.[113] Patterns of even greater complexity become visible to the reader
who is willing to conclude, against Hopkins, that Langland is worth
reading and worth reading attentively. One final example must suffice,
which varies the *double* stave-word repetition with enjambement, *annominatio*, *paronomasia* and change of both metrical sub-type (Ie to Ia, or Ic, if
that 68 is stressed) and rhythmic contour:

'Fóoles that *faúten* Ínwit, I *fýnde* that Hóly Chirche
Sholde *fýnden* hem thát hem *faúteth*, and faderlese children'
(IX 67–8).

Here the inversion of the order of the two repeated stave-words occurs
not merely *cross*-wise (*fynde/fynden*) but also *mirror*-wise (*fauten–fynde*:
fynden–fauteth).[114] There are many such instances where Langland the
maker strives to match the demands of Langland the clerk and, to a
remarkable extent, succeeds.

It would be appropriate to end this section with some account, however
brief and inadequate, of the relationship between the two textural *ornatus*
I have been discussing and between them and the rhythmic resort of
enjambement. If enjambement, a product of the desire to follow the
natural sequence of English syntax, tends to undermine the metrical
autonomy of the line, translinear alliteration, a metrical device, serves to
reinforce the authority of the stave: the one loosens, the other binds.
Running alliteration, finally, groups together sequences of lines, whether
enjambed or end-stopped, and does this with special effectiveness when

112 Cf. also *love/loven* at III 53–4, and contrast *peple/peple* at III 81–2.
113 See also *love* in III 158–9; at III 220 (itself translinearly linked to 219) the
speaker's *repetitio* subtly blurs related but distinct conceptions.
114 Another, even more complex example of cross- and mirror-wise *repetitio* is IV
92–3 (*Bettre . . ./ bettre; boote: bale, bale; boote*), with ironic *paronomasia* on
bettre ybet.

conjoined with translinear alliteration. Langland uses these techniques so freely and unobtrusively that he can deceive a casual reader, concerned only with following his meaning, into thinking him indifferent to his art. This art, as I have been arguing, is as natural as speaking (if only because it is based upon speech); but we should never forget that speech itself, which is the most natural of skills, can become an art. This passage from Passus XX will serve to draw together several of the points that have been discussed in sections iv and v of this chapter:

Ia   Conscience of this counseil tho comsede for to laughe, ⎫
Ia   And curteisliche conforted hem and called in alle freres, ⎬
IIa   And seide, 'Sires, soothly welcome be ye *alle* ∫
Ia   To Unitee and Holy Chirche – ac ó thyng I yow preye:
Ib   Holdeth yow in *unitee*, and haveth noon envye ∫
Ia   To lered ne to lewed, but lyveth after youre reule.
Ia   And I wol be youre borugh, ye shal have breed and clothes
Ia   And othere necessaries ynowe – yow shal no thyng *l*akke,
Ib   With that ye *l*eve logik and lerneth for to *lovye*.
Ic   For *love* lafte thei lordshipe, bothe lond and scole –
Ie   Frere Fraunceys and Domynyk – főr *love* to be holye.' (242–52)

 I have indicated by marginal marks some of the ways in which these eleven lines abound in devices of rhythmical and textural variation while preserving with the minimum of deviation the sound of a speaking voice engaged in natural conversation. All the features discussed are present, but none is over-present, and this helps to preserve the naturalness: the art is so consummate it makes itself almost invisible. The six instances of Ia-type lines support the view of this pattern as the norm. The enriched Ib type at 246 is half concealed by, but also serves to counter-act, that line's enjambement, while in 250 the extra stave in lift four imparts enormous weight and authority to Conscience's sweeping injunction. The trans-linear *l*-stave that ends 249 helps to bind the notion of 'lacking nothing' with that of the all-sufficiency of love, to which it is attracted as the climactic lift of the following line. In 244, the enjambing *alle* is also a translinear 'trigger', and this word seems to lean across the line towards its opposite and complement, the word 'One' *hidden* in initial syllables of the Latin-derived *Unitee* and the native Ho – *ly* and plainly *disclosed* in the small-word key-stave *ó* (preluding the one thing necessary) which con-tinues to echo faintly in the first lift of 246 *Holdeth* (for stability is both needed for unity and is the product of unity, without which things fall apart). The lower-case *unitee* of 246 thus reveals itself transparently as the condition and guarantee of the upper-case *Unitee* in 245 (editorial devices, but dictated by the sense). Finally, the third translinear stave in this passage, *lovye* 250 both initiates the dual phrase *For love* (251a/252b:

repeated 'cross-wise' with subtle modification of sense and stress) and stretches across the length of 251 to make visual and aural contact with *holye*, which sinks to an awed whisper under the burden of the preceding *love*, the crucial 'key' word to which all the energy of the muted key-stave is transmitted.[115]

VI.   CONTRAPUNTAL ALLITERATION

In addition to types of alliteration which serve to link individual lines and groups of lines, there is a type or group of types the purpose of which is to produce greater density of texture *within* individual lines. These patterns are recognised by Oakden in the three versions of *Piers Plowman* as 'complex groups'.[116] I prefer to see in them four varieties of what may be called for convenience alliterative *counterpoint*.

In any 'Standard' line, the pattern created by reference to the key-stave is the *thematic* pattern, and the staves are 'theme-staves'. These may be 'full', 'blank' or 'mute', and the presence of blank staves can generate a *type-variant* (Ie: *aax/ax*) and that of a mute stave in key-position can generate a type *transitional* between Ia and IIb ('T'-type: *aa/[a]bb*). Now in the 'T'-type and in the related IIb, the second set of thematic staves (*bb*) are set off against the first (*aaa* or *aa[a]*) by the presence of the caesural gap: *two* melodies, one primary and one secondary, are stated, of unequal prominence but equal independence (except that in the 'T'-type the *bb* theme pattern is further subordinated by the presence in the b-half of the line of a muted *a* stave. The relationship between the two opposed stave-groups (*aaa* and *bb*) may be described as 'antiphonal', but it is not 'contrapuntal', because the two patterns do not interweave. Accordingly types IIb and to a lesser degree 'T' do not fully exemplify the essential character of the alliterative long line as a distinct form of verse: the *lettres* are not *loken*. In counterpoint, on the other hand, they are locked with a double mechanism, as in IX 24:

1   1   2   1   2

Til Kynde come or sende to kepen hire hymselve

115 This reading takes *love to be holy* as a single phrase and so allows no *variation* in the rhythmical structure of the twice repeated *for love*. An almost equally acceptable reading would make *for* 252 not a mute but a full small-word stave: 'they left their lordship, etc. to be holy *for the sake of* love', and this *will* allow variation in the cross-wise repeated phrases.

116 Op. cit. I, 179. Oakden rightly calls such patterns 'ornamental' rather than 'structural', but his view of their alliteration as 'excessive' (ibid) implies a lower valuation and a different understanding of ornament than mine.

This 'standard' or basic form of contrapuntal alliteration scans *aab/ab*.

The 'standard' form of counterpoint shows obvious similarities to the 'crossed' pattern of Type IIIc (*ab/ab*); but that pattern cannot be classed as contrapuntal because it assigns an equal prominence as well as independence to the stave-sounds represented in *a* and *b*. Although the key-stave is formally identifiable, and so gives us the thematic pattern, it lacks the prominence lent to it by the extra staved lift in the true contrapuntal line, which is always, in its standard form, a line of Type Ie. In counterpoint the thematic pattern is distinct and dominant, the contrapuntal pattern distinct and subordinate; their interweaving creates a melodic conjunction which counteracts the rhythmic disjunction caused by the caesura. Counterpoint is, in a sense, alliterative making raised to its highest power.[117] In effect, the two blank staves of a Type Ie line become enriched with a second pair of mutually alliterating stave-sounds.

Contrapuntal alliteration is as common in other poets as translinear, and commoner than running alliteration,[118] and it must be regarded as one of the standard textural ornaments of the traditional maker. But in Langland it acquires new qualities, for in addition to the standard type he uses variants that I call *inverse*, *echoic* and *running* counterpoint. Even *within* the standard type, he varies the pattern by his favourite device of muting. This can occur in the thematic key-stave, as in IV 76:

> Méde overmáistreth Láwe and *m*uche trúthe létteth

or in thematic stave-position 2:

> Bótrased with Biléef-só-or-thow-béest-noght-sáved   (V 589).

In both examples, the stressing of lifts whose sound does not form part of the thematic *or* the contrapuntal pattern seems to result from the desire to avoid stressing a 'small' word (*muche*) or wrenching stress onto an unstressed prefix (a morpheme, which is of even lower semantic rank than a form-word). Langland evidently is unwilling to sacrifice natural speech-rhythms to the requirements of ornament.

The urge to pattern is nonetheless strong, as appears from the four or five examples of *inverse* counterpoint, in which the positions of the thematic and contrapuntal staves are reversed in the a-half, giving the scansion *aba/ab*, as in V 28:

> Tomme Stowue he *t*aughte to *t*ake two staves.[119]

117 Unlike Oakden, I do not find the second stave-set 'excessive' because it seems to me to arise from the basic principle of the form, 'lel lettres *loken*'.
118 Cf. Oakden, op. cit. I, 154–5. Other examples are VII 70, VIII 51, XI 317. For instances in other writers see, e.g. *Alexander A* 998; *Winner and Waster* 30; *Morte Arthure* 2704; *SGGK* 1331, 370; *Purity* 11, 1776; *St Erkenwald* 34, 77.
119 See also XVII 160, also X 437, XIII 423; and cf. *SGGK* 123, *Purity* 493.

Another example seems to hover between being a contrapuntal Ie with inversion and an echoic type (see below). It is worth quoting the preceding line, an enriched reduced line of the rare Type IIIb, because the final lift is a word in close semantic association with the contrapuntal stave of the line under discussion:

> And whoso éte of that séed hárdy was évere
> To súffren ál that God sénte, síknesse and ángres   (XIX 292–3).

Here the struggle and tension between the metrical patterns mirrors that of the meaning. Helped by the enjambement, *evere* 292 seems on the point of becoming a translinear 'trigger' stave of a line 293 which would then have the unique 'chiastic' pattern (*abba*) hitherto not found in *Piers Plowman*. But so important is the word *suffren* (to 'suffer' what *God* sends is to become 'like' God, who suffers *al* man does: cf. XI 379–81) that it resists the facile optimism that might be engendered by too close a conjunction of *hardy*, *evere* and *al*. The seed of *this* virtue can only grow in and through suffering and sickness: that, for Langland, is the *differentia* of true fortitude as opposed to its corrupt simulacrum invoked by the 'lord' in XIX 467 – the spirit of 'fecche it – wole [he, nel he]'.[120] 'The line too *labours* and the Words move *slow*'[121] because for Langland the understanding of virtue, and the articulation of that understanding in speech, is as laborious a task, almost, as the practice of the thing itself.[122]

A very similar sense of extremity, of being 'laced with fire of stress',[123] can be felt in another example of inverse counterpoint that seems to hover between two alternative possible inverse types. Once again, quotation of the preceding lines helps place the account of sense and sound in proper focus:

> Thus relyede Lif for a litel fortune,
> And prikked forthe with Pride – preiseth he no vertue,
> Ne careth noght how Kynde slow, and shal come at the laste
> And kille alle erthely creature save Conscience oone
>   (XX 148–51).

Here the line in question is the last, which may scan as inverse contrapuntal with either the *k* as thematic stave (*aba/ab*) or with the vowel as

---

120 Cf. XIX 294–8*a*, echoing Patience's teaching in XIV 56–8 and contrasting with Haukyn's attitude at XIII 394–8*a*.

121 Pope, *Essay on Criticism*, l. 371 (*Poems*, ed. J. Butt (1963)).

122 Cf. Geoffrey Hill on that 'heaviness' in poetry 'which is simultaneously the "density" of language and the "specific gravity of human nature"' (*The Lords of Limit* (1984) p. 15).

123 G. M. Hopkins, *The Wreck of the Deutschland*, st. 2 (*Poems*, ed. W. H. Gardner and N. H. Mackenzie, 4th edn. (Oxford, 1970) 52).

thematic stave (*aab/ba*), with an extra 'half-stressed' *k*-stave (*kille*) as in *running* counterpoint (on which, again see below). The difficulty in deciding between the alternatives is due to the fact that the line contains six important words, three vowel-staved and three *k*-staved. However, the formal key-stave is *k* (*Conscience*), the running alliteration lends it prominence (150 scans on *k*) and the formidable power of the 'Deeth of Kynde' is only adequately communicated if *kille* carries full and heightened emphasis. Nevertheless, the opposition between *alle* and *oone* is of very great significance, even if they rank lower than the lexical words carrying the *k*-stave, and they function in what might be called a semantic as well as a melodic counterpoint to *kille, creature* and *Conscience*. Once again, the line *labours*, under its great burden of grave and portentous meaning.

In *echoic* counterpoint, the two contrapuntal staves occur at either end of the line. The first is *mute* (though strictly it is half-stressed rather than unstressed) and is echoed by the second:

> Allàs, that mén so lónge on Mákometh sholde biléve!
>
> (XV 490).[124]

Here, if *allas* is *un*stressed, the line is scannable as Type IIIc. Similarly, in

> Sèlden fálle thei so fóule and so fér in sýnne   (X 470)

to *un*stress *selden* will produce a line of Type Ia. But in this example, there appears to be a secondary alliteration of a stronger kind than in XV 90, the double *so* recurring in what could be key-stave position if the line were judged as scanning on 'small-word' staves (*sholde* in XV 490 is not so readily interpretable as a key-stave). The result is to make X 470 type-ambiguous with the fourth type, which I shall discuss somewhat more fully.

In a few striking lines Langland opposes the expectation that the thematic staves will be lexical words, as in XIII 349, indignantly 'arating' the paganism of Haukyn's lechery:

> And as léf ín Lénte as óut of Lénte, álle tỳmes ylíche.

Here the key-stave is unmistakably *alle*, but the half-stressed *l*-pattern is substantially re-inforced by the *l* of *yliche* (which has full stress). An exactly similar structure is found in Holi Chirche's denunciation of clerics who lack not just supernatural charity but natural family affection:

> Únkỳnde to hìre kýn and to álle Crístene   (I 192).

---

124 The scansion of this variant may be expressed as [*b*]*ab/ab*. See also X 430, XX 325, X 437 (possibly inverse) and many C-text examples – e.g. II 102, 105, 234; III 276; X 160, 245; XII 127.

Again *alle* is the key-stave, but in this line it seems impossible to avoid stressing *kyn* rather than *hire*. The result is to wrench the stress on the first word of the line with a violence which dramatically mimics the speaker's revulsion. The play of stresses upon form-words as against lexical words[125] may be felt as establishing a pattern of *running* counterpoint, although the first example bears a close resemblance to the *echoic* type. In two other cases the guidance of the key-stave (which *appears* to be a consonantal lexical word) is insufficient for determining the scansion. In III 254:

> Taken híre mède hére as Màthew ús técheth

the final decision not to scan as a simple Type IIIa ('minimal') line with stresses on the words of highest semantic rank is influenced by two factors. One is the rhetorical play on the form-words *hire* and *here*, which pararhyme and also pun on *hire* 'reward, payment', a synonym of 'mede'. The other is the context provided by the preceding line

> That taken mede and moneie for masses that thei syngeth
> (III 253)

which scans on *m* but which creates a *syntactic* impetus that suffices to direct the pattern of emphasis in 254 away from the repeated *mede* and onto the possessive and the adverb. In V 544:

> Withínne and withoúten waìted hís pròfit

once again the choice of *his* rather than the lexical word *waited* as key-stave is influenced by two considerations: the impossibility of 'wrenching' the stress of the two *w-* words in the a-half,[126] and the context of the preceding and following line(s). Piers is strongly affirming that he has been the servant of *Truth*, and no one else:

> IIIa I have ben hís fólwere ál this fourty wýnter –
> Ia   Bothe ysówen his séed and súed hise beéstes,
> Ia   Withínne and withoúten waìted hís prófit,
> 'T'   Idýke[d] and id[ó]lve, idò that hé hóteth   (V 542–5).

The fourth of these metrical categorisations is doubtless open to

---

125 Found also in lines without counterpoint, e.g. XIII 260 (unless *moot I* is an archetypal error for *burde I*, a form not otherwise found in *PP*).

126 Contrast *unkynde* (I 292, above) where the prefix is quasi-separable. The spelling *WiÞInne* (retained from MS W by K-D) *may* indicate that the word was sensed as a compound with separable elements (they are separate in MS L and hyphenated by Skeat but printed without hyphen by Bennett), thus allowing an optional shifted stress; but unlike *un-*, *with-* is semantically 'opaque'.

question,[127] as is often the case with transitional-type lines;[128] but it seems to me to yield, in context, the most 'dramatically' satisfactory available scansion.

If *standard* counterpoint is clearly a species of textural *ornatus*, capable of great rhetorical heightening:

Súffraunce is a sóverayn *vér*tue, and a *swíft vén*geaunce (XI 378)
And *l*ove shal *l*epe out *a*fter into this *l*owe *er*the (XII 141)

running counterpoint is primarily an expressive device, with little obvious ornamental appeal. It stands on the axis of 'expression and decoration' somewhere between rhythm and texture. This is borne out by the fact that both III 254 and V 544 are Type Ia lines, with muted key-stave in the former; standard counterpoint occurs only in Type Ie lines, where there are two blank staves capable of bearing contrapuntal enrichment.

VII. PARARHYME

Pararhyme, or 'vowelling-off',[129] as Hopkins called it, occurs over a hundred times in *Piers Plowman*, and it is one of the devices of *ornatus* in which the native and learned sources of his versecraft are put equally under service. English is a language naturally rich in monosyllabic pararhymes, because of the system of vowel-gradation in strong verbs (*break/broke*) and the general abundance of monosyllabic words (para-rhymes on more than one syllable are much less common in English than in Latin, with its wealth of inflexional endings). Langland never uses final pararhyme, the form most familiar to modern readers from the haunting effect it produces in the work of Wilfred Owen:

> Think how it wakes the seeds, –
> Woke, once, the clays of a cold star
> Are limbs, so dear-achieved, are sides,
> Full-nerved – still warm – too hard to stir? ('Futility').[130]

127 So too is that of V 542 in the light of C VII 189 *foloware*, which is trisyllabic, yielding a Type IIIc line. If Samuels's case for the high authenticity of C-MS X's language is accepted (*MÆ* 54 (1985) 244) *foloware* may be the original form (so also many A-MSS – see A VI 30 – but not 'Z').
128 See e.g. I 43, 108; II 37; IV 120; V 166, 419; VIII 14; IX 141; XI 176.
129 Or 'changing of vowel down some scale or strain or keeping', *Notebooks and Papers of G. M. Hopkins*, ed. H. House (Oxford, 1937) p. 243.
130 *Collected Poems of Wilfred Owen*, ed. C. Day Lewis (1963), p. 58. Also notable here is the 'vowelling-off' in *nerved, warm, hard* and *stir* and the translinear pararhyme of *wakes . . ./ Woke*; see p. 73 below.

As far as I know, it was never employed in Latin *rhythmi*, and is not found in vernacular English verse before the present day. Langland uses pararhyme only *within* the line – whether across the two halves of the line, within the half-line, or, in a few cases, from one line to another.

It is not surprising that pararhyme should bear some similarities to counterpoint, since it is in essence a form of *compound alliteration*. In the pair *laike* and *loke*, for example (Pr 172), we have a triple alliterative sequence – initial consonant, vowel, and final consonant. Although not a structural necessity in alliterative verse, pararhyme has a structural value. What it does is to bind even more closely the staves of the a-half and the b-half by adding a *second* alliterating consonant to each of two words that are already joined by *initial* alliteration, the enclosed vowels being caught up, as it were, through the mutually attractive power of the enclosing consonants:

> And if hym list for to *laike*, thanne *loke* we mowen (Pr 172).

This type of *cross-caesural pararhyme*, with a dip[131] between the associated words, is common in Langland but rare in other alliterative verse.[132] It is found, however, in rhetorical Latin poets of the eleventh and twelfth centuries such as Marbod of Rennes, who wrote a treatise on 'versifying fair', the *De Ornamentis Verborum*. Here it appears in a line that is also stuffed (almost to bursting) with internal and cross-caesural rhyme:

> Tu mihi rex, mihi *lex*, / mihi *lux*, mihi dux, mihi vindex.[133]

Langland pararhymes not only lexemes but a lexeme and a segment (*lunatik/leene* Pr 123)[134] or two segments (*Paradis/persone* XVIII 336),[135] a device he could also have found in Marbod:

> Crimina si repe*tat*, repe*tit* quod crimina perdit.[136]

But he is no mere imitator of learned masters, and assimilates the device to a verse-form with totally different metrical principles.[137] Thus he can *mute* the pararhymed key-stave:

131 Or a dip and a lift, as in Pr 26, I 91, 143; or two lifts, as in III 22 (Type Ie).
132 This is my impression; the subject needs a more systematic study.
133 J. P. Migne, ed., *Patrologia Latina* CLXXI 1687. On Marbod (1035–c.1123) see F. J. E. Raby, *A History of Christian-Latin Poetry* (Oxford, 1927) 273–77.
134 See also VII 122, IX 184, XI 162, XII 180, X 89, 105 (both with long + short syllable), V 58 (macaronic).
135 Other examples are XIII 343, XIV 6, XV 204 (long + short), XI 321, XIV 263, XIX 155 (each with *two* segments and a lexeme).
136 *Carmina Varia* xxxvi, *PL* CLXXI 1671.
137 Gervase's discussion of alliteration (ed. cit. 11) quotes only Latin examples, as we might expect, but it seems reasonable to assume that he, like Bede, was aware of the importance of this feature in vernacular verse.

And er thow *lákke* my líf, *loke* if thów be to préise   (XI 386)

here placing the first member of the pair in position one (not two), with a full lift (*lif*) and not just a dip between it and the second member. Or – an excellent instance of his clerkly mastery of both languages – he can pararhyme two segments of which one occurs in a macaronic half-line:

For the dedes that he *dide, Fili David, Ihesus* (XIX 133).

While most of these examples illustrate a thoroughly 'makerly' delight in thickening the texture *ut bene sonus cohaereat*, one line from the Prologue reveals a complexity rare in either vernacular makers or learned *poetes*. It needs to be quoted with the line preceding so that the function of the translinear 'trigger'-stave in winding up the spring of the following line emerges:

For a cat of a court cam whan hym *l*iked
And over*leep* hem *light*liche and *laughte* hem at his wille
(Pr 149–50).

Here the enormous superiority of Langland can be clearly seen both in the staccato stopped palatal staves of 149 (entirely composed of mono-syllables) and in the sudden expansion of word- and line-length, mim-icking the action of the creature. The thin front vowel of *lightliche* (enact-ing the leap) widens ominously into the broad back diphthong of *laughte* (imaging the spread of claw and jaw) with its accompanying change in the quality of the terminal spirant (from hiss to growl). The pun on 'cheer-fulness' and 'laughter' is also visible if we look hard enough at *lightliche* and *laughte* (cf. XVIII 327: 'And tho that Oure Lord lovede, into his light he laughte', where the play is on 'light' (*lumen*) and 'light' (easy)).[138]

A less common variety of cross-caesural pararhyme occurs between the first and third stave, with intervening lift and dip. A good example, with a *gradational* pararhyme (where the second item is a form of the first – here present and infinitive of a verb) is XVIII 224:

To *wite* what alle wo is, that *woot* of alle joye

where the 'knowing' (= experience) of human *wo* seems to be retained or encapsulated in the vowel-structure of *woot*.[139] Gradational forms, this time working in an opposite direction, also function to powerful effect in a

---

138 The type of wordplay characteristic of the Latin poet-clerks is that we find in, e.g. Alanus's '[Clerici . . . nostri temporis] . . . potius col*ligunt* li*bras* quam le*gant* li*bros*' (*Summa de Arte Praedicatoria* xxxvi (*PL* CCX 180)) or Walter Map's 'Roma mun*di* ca*put* est; sed nil ca*pit* mun*dum*' ('Golias in Romanam Curiam' l. 13, in T. Wright, ed., *The Latin Poems commonly attributed to Walter Mapes* (1841) 37).
139 So also VII 76; further V 543, VII 96, VIII 66 (double 'vowelling-off'), X 435 (muted), XII 286, XIX 119, 418.

third variety, which resembles the first except that there is no dip, and the pararhymes are starkly juxtaposed, as in Hopkins's 'ghost guessed', whose clashing stresses illustrate 'markedness of rhythm – that is rhythm's self – and naturalness of expression':[140]

> For blood may suffre blood bothe hungry and acale,
> Ac blood may noght se *bloód bléde*, but hym rewe
> (XVIII 395–6).[141]

Here there is a disconcerting momentary hesitation as to the primary sense of *blood* 396: the shock of recognition comes with the realisation of the *literal* meaning of the phrase 'one's own flesh and blood'. The speaker is the victorious Christ who himself 'tholed deeth' (XVIII 71) because, as the Samaritan 'so ful of pite' (XVII 86), he had been moved to help humanity – 'wounded', 'semyvif' and 'naked' (XVII 55, 57, 58). Here *blood* 396 carries the accumulated force of its two earlier, less dramatic occurrences, and the violently clashing stresses enact the full horror of physical penetration, the rounded vowel of the noun narrowing to the long slit of the verb. The *Morte Arthure*-poet's 'That the groundene stele glydes to his herte' (1371), brilliant as it is, seems shallow by comparison: one cannot read the Langland 'but hym rewe'.

With the exception of a single case (XVIII 327, already quoted above (p. 69)) pararhyme *within* the half-line always occurs in the a-half. As with some of the true gradational examples, these display Hopkins's 'native and natural rhythm of speech, the least forced, the most rhetorical and emphatic of all possible rhythms' –[142]

> And *gad*rede hem alle to*gid*eres, bothe grete and smale (XVI 80)

or

> Was never *wrighte* saved that *wroghte* theron, ne oother werk-man ellis
> (X 397–8).[143]

140 *Letters of G. M. Hopkins to Robert Bridges*, ed. C. C. Abbott (2nd edn, Oxford, 1955), p. 47 (commenting on the phrase *lashed rod*, from *Deutschland*, st. 2; *ghost guessed* is from 'Spring and Fall', *Poems*, ed. cit., 88).
141 Clashing-stressed cross-caesural pararhymes are very rare: see III 131, X 326 (the same at IX 123 but *muted*), and XVII 95. The perceptible loss of tension occurring when even a monosyllabic form-word dip intervenes can be seen in XVI 59 (same pararhymes as XVII 95); cf. also V 527, XIV 230, XV 454, XVII 245 and XVIII 31 for other examples.
142 Letter to Bridges; see note 140 above.
143 Other *quasi-gradational* examples are XIV 66, XV 180 and XIX 280. *Segments* pararhyme in XII 110, XVI 40 and XIX 256. The *same* words recur at XII 229, 230; V 117, VII 88 (cf. also XV 364, 475 and XVII 294); X 390, XIII 356 (with which cf. XVI 9, XVII 131, 269); XVII 124, XVIII 232, 234. Others are I 149 (cf. V

The first acquires a frightening immediacy as we reflect that the 'apples' Satan is collecting are human beings 'both great and small' (with all that implies). The second, in the effort at articulation that it exacts, mirrors the idea of the difficulty of salvation through outward works (in this case the mere going through the motions of one's duty as a clerk). In more complex examples, the lift may pararhyme both *internally* (with either a whole lexeme or a segment) and cross-caesurally. The effect may range from the simple 'rhetorical and emphatic rhythm' of XIV 263:

> And for Goddes *love lev*eth al and *lyv*eth as a beggere

(which links self-abandonment for love with 'life') through the punning syllable-dance of XIV 185:

> And if us *fille* thorugh *folie* to *falle* in synne after

(which takes the most indulgent view of moral failure compatible with a belief in free will)[144] to the extraordinary mimetic inventiveness of XVIII 10, where the advantages of the 'T'-type line are turned to good use:

> Oon *sém*blable to the *Sam*áritan, and *som*deel to Píers the Plówman

a line whose rotating pararhymes (*sem-*, *Sam-*, *som-*) appear to enact the experience of likeness-in-difference in Will's dream of the three-personed *figura* Christ-Samaritan-Piers. As so often, some of Langland's greatest and most characteristic lines, those in which 'the rehearsal / Of own, of abrúpt sélf there so thrusts on, so throngs the ear'[145] (and, one must add, the mind and memory), are macaronics like line XVI 151:

> '*Ave*, raby!' quod that *rib*aud, and right to hym he yede.[146]

This is not one of Judas' children (Pr 35) but Judas himself who 'With *turpiloquio*, a lay of sorwe' (XIII 456) leads himself to Lucifer's feast even as he hands his '*raby*' over to those who will 'warante hym a wicche' (XVIII 46).

In addition to cross-caesural and half-line pararhyme, there is a more complex type still, which spans two lines. This is often found in pairs of lines with running alliteration, as here in symmetrical positions (lifts 2 and 1 respectively):

---

485); III 185, 87 (with ironic effect); V 452, 469; VI 261; IX 123, 132; X 427; XI 39, 104; XII 8; XIV 86, 263; XV 56, 299, 360, 534, 554 (muted and macaronic); XVI 4, 30, 166; XVIII 195.

144 Also similar is the 'echoic' pararhyme with paronomasia in XII 229 (*Kynde, kynde*).

145 G. M. Hopkins, 'Henry Purcell', *Works* (ed. cit.) p. 80.

146 Repeated, doubtless with deliberate ironic echo-effect, at XVIII 50.

Though ye be myghty to *mote*, beeth meke in youre werkes,
For the same mesure that ye *mete*, amys outher ellis,
Ye shulle ben weyen therwith whan ye wenden hennes

(I 176–8).

Here the caesural pause is so strong that the *sonus* of half-lines 176a and
177a comes very close to that of Owen's

not flowers
For poets' tearful fooling:
Men, gaps for filling   ('Insensibility').[147]

But the main function of the device is to help create the lines' solemn,
almost ritual enactment of the process of *redde quod debes* so central to the
poet's thought: after each pararhyme there is a warning pause to enable
the hearer to reflect and take stock, and to become aware that whatever
happens here, in the next life the scales will inevitably balance.[148] In the
second example, from the description of Haukyn which is one of the
poem's high points:

Lakkynge lettrede men and lewed men bothe;
In *likynge* of lele lif and a liere in soule   (XIII 286–7)

the negative and positive sides of the 'Actif Man' are seen to add up to a
neutrality which is a nothingness: his 'lakkyng' and his 'likynge' are both
essentially hollow ('a liere in soule').[149]

Double-line pararhyme also enriches the texture of line-pairs linked by
translinear alliteration, as in these three cases. When Mede gives

Rynges with rubies and richesses *manye*,
The leeste man of hire *meynee* a moton of golde   (III 23–4)

we seem to see the 'least man' grow under our eyes through the power of
her wealth, the quantity of which ('richesses manye') is the reason for her
having so large a company of followers ('meynee') in the first place.[150] In

147 Owen, *Complete Poems* (ed. cit.) p. 37.
148 The lines' source, Lk 6:38, implies a measuring scoop rather than scales, but
    Langland's *mote* was perhaps suggested by the preceding verse ('Nolite
    iudicare'), the Matthean parallel/source of which links judgement and mea-
    sure in the same verse (Mt 7:2). However, it is Lk not Mt that he quotes at XII
    89a commenting on Jn 8:6 (XI 90 may be either).
149 Langland perhaps puns here on *MED* sense 1 'lack' and the stated sense 2
    'disparage': Haukyn *lacks* the 'lele lif' he lyingly professes to *like*. Formally,
    this type is 'symmetrical', with both words in position 1 (so I 176–7: both in
    lift-position 2).
150 Here *man* is caught up trans-linearly just as *Sam-* is *intra*-linearly in XVIII 10.
    This line is formally asymmetrical (pararhyme in positions 4 and 2; cf. VI
    91–2).

XV 391–2, translinear alliteration has been itself enriched further into translinear pararhyme:[151]

> For Sarsens han somwhat semynge to oure bi*leve*,
> For thei *love* and bi*leve* in o [Lede] almyghty.

Here we have a sense that since what the Moslems share with Christians is *love* of God and since that, for Langland, is the kind of 'belief' that alone counts, it is hard to see why their belief 'in' (= *leel lyvyng*) should not also turn into belief 'that' (= *'oure* bileve').[152] In this example, there is a dip between the pararhymes (the anacrusis of 392). In the next, they are juxtaposed in a way that almost turns the line-break into a half-line caesura:

> I have yseyen charite also syngen and *reden*,
> *Riden*, and rennen in raggede wedes;
> Ac biddynge as beggeris biheld I hym nevere   (XV 225–7).

Anima's broad-minded but nonetheless unequivocal statement may be paraphrased thus: charity is possible amongst the learned, the rich and the (genuine, honest) poor, but *not* among mendicants – and you know who *that* means! (He in fact goes on to make this point explicitly in 230–2). The effect of the translinear conjunction of *two* of these categories (clerks and knights) in such an intimate way is to draw in the third ('raggede wedes') so that the whole sequence of *r*-alliterating terms holds together as a single entity. A block, *linked to* 'charite' by 'syngen' (which is syntactically bound to the translinear 'trigger' word *reden*) is *locked off* from the 'biddynge as beggeris' sequence both by the line-end pause (aided by the blank stave) at *wedes* and by the abrupt *Ac* that opens 227 and functions like a finger-post pointing towards the excluded group (Langland subtly balances the two contrasted groups by the syntactical mirror-inversion of *I have yseyen* (225a) in *biheld I hym nevere* (227b)).

The more intricate of the double-line pararhymes may owe something to the example of Marbod and others like him:

> Jure moritur homo; sed homo qui jure *moritur*,
> Flendo *meretur* opem; sed opem quam flendo *meretur*
> Crimina si repetat, repetit quod crimina perdit.

The device used here is described by the early thirteenth-century rhetorician Gervais of Melkley as *'gradatio* (per inflexionem)'.[153] Another

---

151 The weightiness of these lines owes something to their combination of translinear and intralinear pararhyme (*love*: bi*leve* 392) with cross-caesural pararhyme (*som*: *sem*- 391; cf. XVIII 10 again).
152 As with the pagan Trajan (see XI 161). There may also be a punning allusion to *bi-live* 'sustenance, that by which one lives' in *bileve*.
153 *Ars Poetica*, ed. Gräbener, 20.

example is this from Hildebert of Lavardin, a writer whom Langland might have read:

> Surgit, et exorto *sol sole* videtur in horto,
> Magdalenae *soli* dicens: Me tangere noli
> (*Carmina Miscellanea* XCVIII).[154]

Marbod himself uses intralinear pararhyme to illustrate *adnominatio*:

> Inju*stis* ju*stos*, inhone*stis* aequat hone*stos*   (*De Orn. Verb.* XV).

and Gervase remarks that the device is 'iuxta annominationem'.[155] But none of these illustrations sound 'native and natural' even if they are 'rhetorical and emphatic' (in Hopkins's words).[156] This can be seen by examining one final example, where the Langlandian pararhyme communicates a maximum of meaning with a minimum of formal display.

Abraham, speaking to Will of how the mystery of the Trinity can be approached by the analogy of human relationships, compares the Second Person's Incarnation (which meant separation from the Father) to the loss of her husband by a widow:

> That is, creatour weex creature to knowe what was bothe
> (XVI 215).

The source of this *idea* may be a passage such as Hildebert's

> Ergo *factorem factura* Deum sciat esse,
> Cui mirabiliter mirabile competit esse
> ('Versus de fide sanctae Trinitatis') [157]

or perhaps these (in *rhythmus* not *metrum*) by a later twelfth-century master, Walter of Châtillon, contemporary and countryman of Alanus de Insulis:

> Factor factus est factura
> iuxta nostram sortem
> et refregit armatura
> fortiore fortem
> ('Obtinente monarchiam', st. 4) [158]

---

154 *PL* CLXXI, 1127. On Hildebert (1056–1133) see Raby, op. cit., 265–73.
155 *PL* CLXXI, 1689; Gervase, *Ars Poetica*, ed. cit., 18.
156 See p. 70 and n. 142 above.
157 *Carm. Misc.* LXXIV, *PL* CLXXI, 1417. The piece is not certainly Hildebert's.
158 K. Strecker, ed., *Die Lieder Walters von Chatillon* (Berlin, 1925) p. 7. On Walter (1135–84) see Raby, *A History of Secular Latin Poetry in the Middle Ages* (Oxford, 1934) II, 190–204.

– lines which Langland's almost seems to translate. The difference lies in the skill with which the English maker has avoided the flat obviousness that would have gone with using 'maker' and 'maad' (for *factor . . . factus*) and has chosen instead a word with variable stress in which, by muting, the speech-accent can be made to fall on the terminal syllable whose function it is to carry the whole load of semantic difference:

> créatour wéex creatúre to knówe what was bóthe.

Such variation is beyond either the rhythmical or the metrical Latin poet (as is, though not for linguistic reasons, the audacious wit of *weex*, which is appropriate to Christ as a human infant in the womb but paradoxically at odds with his nature *in deitate Patris*, as the divine son of the Father).[159]

VIII.   RHYME

The low opinion of *leonitas* expressed by Gervase of Melkley[160] is not likely to have been shared by Langland, who not only quotes leonine verses several times[161] but clearly imitates the form in half a dozen lines (one already quoted above in another connection, p. 60 above). In this type, the last word in the line rhymes with the word before the caesura:

> And of his baptisme and blood that he bledde on roode
>
> (XIX 325)

which perhaps echoes Paul's phrase 'the blood of his cross' (Col 1:20). A more expressive example is XVIII 249, which describes how at the Harrowing

> Lo! helle myghte nat holde, but opnede tho God tholede

which rumbles like a stone being rolled away, suggests the future impotence of the devils when it comes to 'holding' the patriarchs, and

159 See XVI 101 ('Til he weex a faunt thorugh hir flessh') and cf. XVIII 26.
160 See p. 24 and n. 17 above. As Raby notes (*Secular Latin Poetry* II, 1) Leonines escape monotony if the poem is brief (or, one may add, if they occur only rarely). Curtius (*European Lit.*, 151–2) is more positive about the form.
161 See Pr 132–8, 141–2, 145 (verses found in Lambeth MS 61, f. 147 v; see J. A. W. Bennett, *PP: Prol. and Passus I–VII* (Oxford, 1972) 99); I 141*a*, repeated at V 441*a* (proverbial; see Bennett, ed. cit., 112); IX 183 (? John of Bridlington, in T. Wright, *Political Poems* I (1859) 159); X 258*a* (source unknown); XIV 59*a* (proverbial; see H. Walther, *Lateinische Sprichwörter und Sentenzen des Mittelalters* (Göttingen, 1963–9) no. 28959: noted by Pearsall, *C-text* XV 261 *ad loc*; cf. also C III 189, XVII 286–7).

relates the 'opening' of hell with the opening of the saviour's body by the spear of Longinus.[162]

Langland's cross-caesural rhymes, however, are by no means always of the Leonine kind. Sometimes they chime out in adjacent lifts that resemble his commonest pararhyme usage (see above), as in III 226:

> Marchaundise and *mede* mote *nede* go togideres

where the emphasis given by the rhyme (visually and aurally conjoining the ideas, making them *go togideres*) compensates the loss of stress from *mote* through its muting. Mede is a skilled rhetorician, and her aim is to persuade; but her enemy Holi Chirche is no less adroit, as here, when she warns against becoming the *fendes liknesse* through pride, since 'mo . . . than man kouthe nombre' (I 114, 116) fell from a state of grace

> Into a deep derk *helle* to *dwelle* there for evere   (I 115).

Here once again the rhyme restores force to a stave (*helle* is blank, not mute), links the idea of perpetual imprisonment with depth and dark, and through the assonance of *evere* with the two rhymed words, leaves the admonition echoing eerily in our ears as if down a long vaulted cavern. In another example, an unusual one in which the rhymes are only half-rhymes and stand at opposite ends of the line, Langland wittily plays on the connection (*per oppositionem*) between mistreating one's serfs and prospering in the next life:

> And mys*bede* noght thi bondemen – the bettre may thow *spede*
> (VI 45).

This is a case where the *cognatio* of *p* and *b* discussed by Isidore of Seville is cunningly and unobtrusively laid under service: the proper way for a maker to 'bede' those hard-working bondmen, his *lel lettres*.[163]

The rhymes in alliterative long lines please partly at least because they surprise, like silence in a city. Internal half-line rhyme, which Langland permits only in the b-half, produces a plangent tune like a striking clock:

> And there gat in glotonie *gerles* that were *cherles*   (I 33)
> But right as the lawe loketh, lat *falle* on hem *alle* (II 198)

(where *falle* gains extra impetus from the energy given up by the muted *lat*)

> To be buxom at his biddynge, his *wil* to ful*fille* (III 265)

162 Other Leonines, not all of them perfect, are XVI 275, XVIII 170, 216, VI 307. Another is V 199, if B is emended to read with A V 117; see also C XII 217.
163 Two other cross-caesural rhymes with one- or two-syllable dip are VI 269, XVI 116. See also C VI 193 (after mute auxiliary) and C XII 185 (a mute rhyme).

(where the heavy rhyme – satisfyingly enacting the sense through the harmony of 'buxom' sounds – more than compensates for the light-weight, almost notional first stave (*be*)). Langland never formally mutes the first lift, but this line reads better as [*a*]*áá*/*x̂x̂* than as a clustered Type IIa.) The most memorable example, already quoted in an earlier discussion (p. 51 above) is so like Hopkins's

My heart in hiding
Stirred for a bird
('The Windhover')

that it might (if Hopkins had admired Langland) have challenged recognition as its source:

Now is Piers to the plow. *Pride it aspide*   (XIX 337).[164]

Langland uses *identical* rhyme, a device rare in English poetry (but favoured by a modern poet born not far from Malvern, Geoffrey Hill),[165] in four instances. Two of them are worth giving here since they seem genuine specimens of rich rhyme, with a real differentiation of meaning between the two occurrences of the identical lexeme:[166]

Loke thow suffre hym to seye, and sithen lere it after;
For thus witnesseth his word; worche thow therafter
(I 146–7)

Here there is arguably a shift of stress in 147 from *after* to *ther*, since Holi Chirche is drawing a contrast Truthe's 'word' and that of some (non-existent) teacher who might improve on it. In the second example, where Truthe himself is promising the merchants protection if they deal honestly, there is no shift of stress but a subtle association and distinction of senses:

'And sende youre soules in saufte to my Seintes in joye.'
Thanne were marchaunts murie – manye wepten for joye
(VII 36–7).

Whereas the overt contrast is simply between the joy of heaven and the joy of relief, the rhyme draws attention to the way in which the one

---

164 Other internal b-half rhymes are VI 254, XI 129 and XX 55 (imperfect); cf. also A VII 2 and C XII 75.
165 See *Collected Poems* (Harmondsworth, 1985) 52, 62, 64, 138, 143. Ricks (*The Force of Poetry*, p. 307) comments on Hill's 'rhyming a word with its bracketed self, so that the rhyme is not truly a *rhyme*, . . . and yet is on a different plane or in a different dimension'.
166 Chaucer normally rich-rhymes *distinct* lexemes (e.g. *seke: seeke, GP* 17–18) but Langland's are more like Hill's 'bracketed' rhymes (though without the brackets).

should be properly the ground of the other and *both* different from worldly *suffisaunce*, that 'bely joye' Piers resolves not to be so 'bisy' about (VII 119). The 'merriness' of the merchants is reflected in their tears, which may be understood on closer consideration to be not just physical symptoms but symbols of a new concern for the 'saufte' of their 'soules'.[167]

The 'surprise' that is part of the pleasure these rhymes give becomes all the greater when they are not internal or identical but recognisable *full rhymes in end-position*, as in 'normal' English verse. Langland uses these sparingly, for he is borrowing from another convention (as is Chaucer when he writes 'alliteratively'),[168] but he always does it for a reason, and with remarkable success. A simple example comes from the description of Sloth in the infamous catalogue of wedding gifts Fals has drawn up for Mede:

> And thanne wanhope to awaken hym so with no wil to *amende*,
> For he leveth be lost – this is his laste *ende* (II 100–101).

Here the rhyme, rendered doubly emphatic by the preceding pararhyming *laste* (with no intervening lift), simply rams home the idea of the finality of the sin of despair, which loses the *amen* from *amende* and retains only its last, lost termination.[169] A more complex pattern of repeated internal rhyme precedes the end-rhyme in the flurried conclusion of the prophecy to England's slothful or greedy labourers at the end of the Half-Acre passus:

> For Hunger hiderward *hast*eth hym *faste*!
> He shal awake [thorugh] water, *wast*ours to *chaste* . . .
> (VI 321–2).

The four-fold repetition here is like a drumbeat warning of an approaching army.

One of the most beautiful and moving of Langland's rhymes occurs in the Harrowing Passus, that anthology of all that is best in his total repertory of alliterative technique:

> I faúght so, me thúrsteth yet, for mannes sóule *sáke*;
> Máy no drynke me moíste, ne mý thurst *sláke*
> (XVIII 368–9).

---

167 For other examples, see Pr 127–8 (*hevene: hevene*), XX 48–9 (*nedy: nedy*).
168 Most notably in *LGW* 635–48 and *KtT*, A 2602–2616, but cf. also *TC* II 906–9, and compare *CYT*, G 658 with *PP* B II 217.
169 Other 'simple' examples are C IX 92–3, A III 245–6, V 115–6 (both rhyme-words changed in B V 197–8). For 'imperfect rhymes' see XI 344–5, XV 277–8; 'penultimate rhymes' IV 113–4–5, XVIII 341–2; assonance XVIII 61–2.

Almost more striking here than the rhyme is the deft alteration of stresses from lexical words in the 'T'-type 368 to form-words in 369, which points up the difference between Christ's 'thirst', its nature and scope, and all other thirsts before and since;[170] but the rhyme serves exquisitely to lengthen the pause at the line-end before Christ moves on into the terrifying vision of what *will* be necessary to 'slake' divine thirst:

> ne my thurst slake
> Til the vendage falle in the vale of Josaphat   (369–70)

with its tremulous *falle* lengthening out in the flat, level desolation of *vale*.

A final example, of what might be called *deferred* rhyme, may be found in another passage prophesying destruction to Christ's enemies, the speech of Anima in which he speaks of the defeat of the Jews:

> Ac thei seiden and sworen, with sorcerie he *wroughte,*
> And studieden to struyen hym – and struyden hemselve,
> And thorugh his pacience hir power to pure noght he *broughte*
> (XV 594–6).

Here, whether we stress *pure* or *noght* in 596, the line conveys an overwhelming sense of the divine 'power' (founded in *pacience*), which exhibits its paradoxical creativity in death and in de-creating (bringing to nought) that which has no metaphysical substance when seen from the ultimate perspective of eternity – the 'power' of those who 'study' to 'destroy'.[171]

'I mean by it' [wrote Hopkins of the word *sake*] 'the being a thing has . . . and that is something distinctive, marked, specifically or individually speaking . . .'[172] I have written this chapter, it might be said, for Langland's 'sake' – a 'virtue' that I believe Hopkins would have discovered had he persisted in reading *Piers Plowman*. For despite their many and obvious differences, both poets have a great deal in common; their work is 'distinctive, marked, specifically *and* individually speaking': *well* worth listening to – or reading.

---

170 For a detailed study of this pattern of images, see my 'Treatment of the Crucifixion in *PP* and in Rolle's *Meditations* . . .' (*Analecta Cartusiana* 35 (1983) 174–96, esp. 181–4), and P. Dronke, 'Two 13th-century Lyrics', in *Medieval Poet and his World* (Rome, 1984), esp. 341–7.

171 Also interesting is the third-lift symmetrical deferred rhyme of *songen* and *throngen* at V 509–10. XIII 230–1 and VIII 63–5 contain 'trailing' rhymes (part final and part internal), and V 199–201 combines with pararhyme.

172 *Letters to Bridges*, ed. cit., p. 83.

The Dimensions of Langland's Making

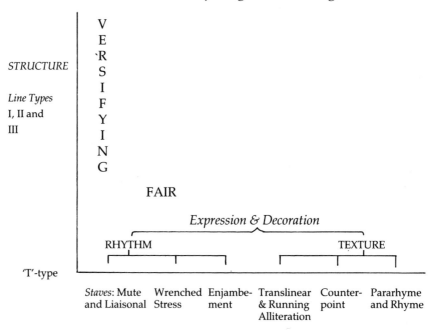

Chapter Three

Formally Enditing

I. CONSTRUING AND KENNING

In the opening chapter of his *De Vulgari Eloquio* Dante distinguishes between two kinds of language, the vernacular (*vulgarem locutionem*) which we learn at the outset of our lives from our immediate family without recourse to any rules (*sine omni regula*), and *grammatica*, which we learn only by regular instruction over a period of time. Of the two, he regards the vernacular as *nobilior* 'the more excellent' because it is primary, universal (i.e. common to all, despite dialectal variations) and natural, whereas *grammatica* is secondary, restricted to a few, and *artificialis* 'an acquired skill'.[1] It is of course ironic that Dante's bold claim for the dignity of the common speech has to be itself couched in the language of the learned: for only Latin is universal to the learned of all lands and hence to all speakers of (otherwise mutually-incomprehensible) vernaculars; and only a language which has regularity and precision will avail for the purposes of scholarly exposition.

A major part of such exposition is *definition*, saying what a word is, in Haukyn's phrase, 'proprely to mene' (XIV 274). This is not a question only of grammatical correctness, but of truth to the genuine, the intrinsic, the *propre* nature of the concept signified by the word. As early as the Prologue, the close bond between name and thing has been emphasised by the *goliardeis* when he declares that a king who fails to observe the laws has the name of king only, not the substance (*Nomen habet sine re*) since his very title of *rex* comes from *regere* 'to rule' (Pr 141–2).[2] However the *goliardeis*, it goes without saying, is engaged in a dialogue with the Latin-speaking angel to which the *lewed commune* (Pr 129, 143) are not privy. The irony of their own utterance of a 'vers of Latyn' affirming their

1 *Opere di Dante*, ed. Moore, 379; all subsequent refs. to *De Vulg. El.* are to this edition and page.
2 For discussion of this phrase, see J. Mann, 'Satiric Subject and Satiric Object in Goliardic Literature', *Mittellateinisches Jahrbuch* 15 (1980), 66–9.

implicit obedience to royal edict (Pr 143, 145) is thus pointed up by the parenthesis 'construe whoso wolde' (Pr 144) with its dual implication that the *lewed* cannot interpret the maxims they mouth and therefore become vulnerable to the 'will' of those who can: ignorance is weakness *because* knowledge is power.

Piers Plowman, as is well-known, records a protracted effort to discover whether the weakness of the ignorant may not, in some ways, be preferable to the power of the wise and the would-be wise.[3] Thus Dame Studie blames indifferently both the 'crabbede wordes' that 'heighe men . . . carpen ayein clerkes' when they 'Carpen as thei clerkes were' and the 'motyves' (with perhaps a pun) that are 'moved by' (and move) 'thise maistres in hir glorie': for both end in *mysbileve*, whether that be 'heresy' or 'unbelief' (X 103–116).[4] But it is interesting that the Pauline text she adduces as 'Austyn's' riposte 'to swiche argueres' (the learned and the would-be learned alike) is *Non plus sapere quam oportet* (Rom 12:3) (X 118–118*a*). The content of this allows that there is something which *is* necessary to know, while its form implies that part of that something at least is knowledge of *locutio secundaria* (as Dante calls it) *quam Romani 'grammaticam' vocaverunt*. Thus, although speculative learning and un-learned speculation may both be vain in the face of the divine mysteries, and may prove spiritually dangerous by leading to *glorie*, there remains a need for *some* to be able to 'construwe', if only to 'kenne' those who cannot.

Ymaginatif's subsequent defence of 'clergie for Cristes love, that of clergie is roote' (XII 71), adumbrated by Dame Studie at X 117, contains no more striking statement than the lines glossing Christ's action of writing on the ground in Jn 8:3–9:

> Holy Kirke knoweth this – that Cristes writyng saved;
> So clergie is confort to creatures that repenten,
> And to mansede men meschief at hire ende   (XII 82–4).

These lines both defend learning against the charge of vanity by affirming its essential neutrality (it only becomes 'positive' when the *right* dispo-sition is at hand) and defend it *simpliciter* by asserting what Holy Church 'knows' (i.e. what could not *be* known without the *clergie* that enables the Church to 'construwe' the Gospel of Christ, 'that of clergie is roote').

Ymaginatif's fundamental solidarity with the teaching of the authority he quotes from is shown in the way that his first words to Will, associating the virtue of patience with growth in religious understanding –

---

3 See, e.g., Frank, *PP and the Scheme of Salvation*, 48, and B. Raw, 'Piers and the Image of God in Man' in Hussey, ed., *Critical Approaches*, 172–5.
4 See *MED* s.v. *misbileve*, n., 1a and 2a.

Formally Enditing

'Haddestow suffred', he seide, 'slepynge tho thow were,
Thow sholdest have knowen that Clergie kan and conceyved moore
thorugh Reson –'
(XI 411–12)

echo and accord with the admonition of Holy Church, Will's first instructor:

'To litel Latyn thow lernedest, leode, in thy youthe:
Heu michi quia sterilem duxi vitam iuvenilem!
It is a kynde knowynge that kenneth in thyn herte
For to loven thi Lord . . .
who kan teche thee bettre,
Loke thow suffre hym to seye . . .'   (I 141–3, 145–6).

The fault does not lie in the Dreamer's *clergie* (if anything, he has too little, not too much) but in his will, his refusal to listen with and to his heart:

'For Reson wolde have reherced thee right as Clergie seide.
Ac for thyn entremetynge here artow forsake:
Philosophus esses, si tacuisses'   (XI 413–14a).

It therefore falls to Patience, in the Fourth Vision, to show Will how a philosopher can be silent (i.e. 'suffer others to have their say') and so become qualified to teach by example (as he teaches Will at Clergie's dinner) and by precept (as he instructs Will's *alter ego* Haukyn in the second half of the Vision).

It is in this encounter, when Patience is attempting to explain the objective or outward and symbolic or inward meaning of *poverte*, that the necessity of Latin learning for some, and the inevitability of incomprehension for most, finds fullest expression. But we have come a long way from the Prologue-exchange between Angel and Goliardeys, with the *commune's* uncomprehended 'vers of Latyn' which 'construe whoso wolde' (Pr 143–4). Haukyn, though as *lewed* as the Folk of the Field (whom he figurally recapitulates), is further advanced in moral understanding than the latter, who confessed through fear of punishment and then 'blustreden forth as beestes' (V 514), as blind in their quest for the 'corsaint . . . that men calle Truthe' (V 532) as in their cry '*Precepta Regis sunt nobis vincula legis!*' (Pr 145). Haukyn, though unlearned, is neither as brutishly servile as the Folk nor, it must be added, as crabbedly contentious as Will up to and including the first half of Vision Four. Thus when Patience embarks on explaining to him 'What is poverte . . . proprely to mene' with a Latin definition drawn from Vincent of Beauvais and Augustine, he neither re-iterates the phrases parrot-like ('as beestes') nor 'rebukes' his instructor with 'rude speche' (XI 372, 418, where the irony of

83

rude 'unlearned' as well as 'uncivil' should not go unremarked).[5] Instead, he both admits his own ignorance and affirms the obligation of his learned interlocutor to teach him:

'I kan noght construe al this . . . ye moste kenne me this on Englissh'

to which Patience replies:

'In Englissh . . . it is wel hard, wel to expounen,
Ac somdeel I shal seyen it, by so thow understonde'
(XIV 276–8).

Haukyn's incapacity is not only literal, through having learnt 'too little Latin in his youth' like Will earlier: Will's failure had been in the *use* of his learning, where Haukyn never had any at all. Rather, he cannot make any personal 'sense', cannot derive any spiritual benefit, from the substance of Patience's exposition of *Paupertas*, because of the *locutio artificialis* in which it is couched. For the *kynde knowynge* of truth (including the truth of his own sinfulness, 'that deere God displesed' XIV 325) described by Holy Church *is* able to 'kenne' in Haukyn's 'herte'. This is revealed by his genuinely heartfelt repentance at the end of the Vision, an act in which, as it were, he figurally enfolds into himself not only the Folk but Will also. The scene brings out with skill and economy that, however hard it may be 'In Englissh . . . *wel* to expounen' (*vulgaris locutio* lacks the richness and philosophical precision of *grammatica*) it is nonetheless imperative to *try*, for there is no other way to 'kenne' the 'lewed' save through the common speech which is 'humano generi usitata' and which 'naturalis est nobis', as Dante puts it. What Patience is well-equipped to recognise in Haukyn (as Conscience had earlier recognised in Patience himself) is 'the wil of the wye', the 'goode' and 'trewe wille' of Haukyn which is also the 'trewe wille' of Will himself, since it is demonstrated in his capacity to 'moorne for [his] synnes' (XIII 190–3).[6]

The scene also demonstrates the mutual inter-dependence of *lettred* and *lewed*, cleric and layman, Latin (finally) and English. For Patience to 'construe' there must be someone to construe *for*, and someone to 'understonde' (278) once the construing has been done. That is the tacit logic that underlies the movement in this brief and pregnant dialogue from 'I *kan* noght' to 'ye *moste*' to 'I *shal*'. These three modal verbs encapsulate the whole rationale of Langland's enterprise as a clerkly maker, which involves a reciprocal interchange between the voices of *vulgaris elocutio* and *grammatica*, admitting incapacity, affirming obligation, accepting responsibility. Where Langland differs from Dante is in

---

5 See *OED* s.v. *rude*, 1 and 4.
6 See F. Vernet, *Medieval Spirituality* (1930), 120–25 (on compunction and tears).

not asserting explicitly that the *vulgaris* is *nobilior*. Such claims as he makes *for* it are wholly implicit in the demands he makes *upon* it. Like Chaucer, troubled 'for ther is so gret diversite / In Englissh' (*Troilus*, V 1793–4), and Dante, who qualifies his praise of the vernacular thus: '*licet* in diversas prolationes et vocabula sit divisa' (*De Vulg. El.* I.i), Langland concedes a peculiar limitation of 'oure tonge': that 'In Englissh . . . it is *wel* hard, *wel* to expounen' (XIV 276). Yet even in the making of the concession his skilful play on the adverb's two senses points to aspects in which the common speech may well be as noble as, or nobler than, the learned.

If the discussion so far has tended to suggest that the relationship between 'construing' and 'kenning' is simple and unproblematic, that suggestion needs to be severely qualified now. In an ideal state of affairs, learning may be both sought and applied out of love of God and one's neighbour, since the prime aim of study, affirmed by Holy Church and echoed by Kynde (I 142–3, XX 208), is nothing other than to learn to love.[7] Such an ideal may even approach realisation in a particular *cloistre* or *scole* (cf. X 297–302). But the poem shows insistently, through such representative figures as the priest (VII), the minorites (VIII), the Doctor of Divinity (XIII), the 'lewed vicory' (XIX) and the friar-confessors of III and XX, that the clergy as a collective entity have forgotten their true 'root', Christ, and, though themselves 'the roote of the right feith', have become 'roten' with hypocrisy and greed (XV 100–1). The result may be described as a fissure between 'signifier' and 'signified', between the Church's learning and its love, between *veritas* and *caritas*, which prevents the Clergy from becoming the 'sign' or sacrament of Christ and from bearing leaves of 'lele wordes' and 'the fruyt Charite' (XVI 6, 9). The failure of churchmen to match 'loore' with 'ensaumples' and their coupling of 'prechen' with 'preven it *noght*' (XV 108–10) creates a yet further fissure, between clergy and laity, which threatens to widen into an unbridgeable chasm at one point, the quarrel between the priest and Piers at the end of Passus VII.

When the Pardon arrives, a priest (on a 'naturalistic' interpretation the parish priest of Piers' village) declares

'thi pardon *moste I* rede;
For *I shal* construe ech clause and kenne it thee on Englissh'
(VII 105–6).

---

7 Cf., e.g., J. S. Wittig, '*PP* B, IX–XII: Elements in the Design of the Inward Journey', *Traditio* 28 (1972) 274 and *idem*, 'The Dramatic and Rhetorical Development of Long Will's Pilgrimage', *NM* 76 (1975) 64; J. Simpson, 'From Reason to Affective Knowledge: Modes of Thought and Poetic Form in *PP*', *MÆ* 55 (1986) 7, 15 and my 'The Inner Dreams in *PP*', ibid, 34–5.

There is a very different atmosphere here from that of the scene between Patience and Haukyn in Passus XIV discussed above: it is now the cleric not the layman who employs both the modals of necessity/obligation *and* that of intention, uttered not in the hesitant and tentative tones of Patience but with the arrogant insistence of a 'maister in glorie' (X 115). It is not my concern here to explore the structural parallels between the earlier and the later scene; rather I wish to concentrate on the way in which the action of construing and 'kenning' is used to emblematise not the gap between educated cleric and ignorant layman but that between a 'carnal' and a 'spiritual' understanding of religious truth. For the power of this strange episode derives in no small measure from Langland's bold re-interpretation of what it really means to 'construe' the language of liturgy, scripture and creed. At one level, the literal, the priest *does* 'construe' the Latin lines correctly; but he 'kan no pardon fynde' (VII 111) because his criterion for recognising a 'pardon' is purely literalistic, that is, 'carnal'. Piers, as I understand it, 'recognises' the 'two lynes' (in both senses) as a 'witnesse of truthe' (110) – as a true pardon, graphically demonstrating his 'spiritual' understanding of the *meaning* of the Latin in his tearing of the paper on which it is written, followed by his dramatic resolve to make prayer and penance the centre of his life (118–30).

There is, I believe, no strict necessity to take Piers' Latin quotations from Psalms and Gospel (116–17, 124*a*; 127), any more than his earlier ones at VI 47*a* and 75–76*a*, as betokening a *literal* capacity to 'construe', which would be out of keeping with his character as one of those '*lewed* juttes' who are later contrasted with 'thise konnynge clerkes that konne manye bokes' (X 455–8). I say this in spite of the fact that Piers' evident comprehension of the priest's sarcastic gibe about preaching with '*Dixit insipiens* to thi teme' (VII 136) would seem to presuppose such a capacity. For not only would Langland fail to establish a valid *spiritual* contrast between the two antagonists if he made Piers anything so odd as an 'educated' ploughman, he would undermine his case for the efficacy of a simple, sincere faith for those 'That inparfitly here knewe and ek lyvede' (X 462). For Piers, though spiritually exceptional, must surely be regarded as socially representative: otherwise his role as a *model* for the transformation of society would lack real conviction. And it is of interest that when the priest 'apposes' him with the condescending words 'Thow art lettred a litel – who lerned thee on boke?' (VII 132) his reply is not a claim that he *is* 'lettred' but that he has learned from a long experience of what the 'paynym' Trajan is later to call 'leel love and lyvyng in truthe' (XI 161):

'Abstynence the Abbesse', quod Piers, 'myn a.b.c. me taughte,
And Conscience cam afterward and kenned me muche moore'
(VII 133–4).

Piers' point is precisely that it was not a literal nun who instructed him in a literal alphabet but a virtuous mode of *life* – based, of course, on the *literally* exiguous regimen of the poor[8] – that grounded him in the elements of religion and a progressively developed moral *habitus* that widened his grasp of its *grammatica.*

Piers' outburst in lines 137–8*a*, therefore, should not be read as an attempt to confute the priest by exclaiming *'Contra!* . . . as a clerc' as Will is to do some 80 lines later in the poem, when he is still unable to absorb what Piers' words and example have to teach (VIII 20):

> 'Lewed lorel!' quod Piers, 'litel lokestow on the Bible;
> On Salomons sawes selden thow biholdest –
> *Eice derisores et iurgia cum eis ne crescant &c'.*

Difficult and ambiguous, perhaps dangerously ambiguous, these lines may be, with their potential suggestion that a spiritual (and educated) layman might be more truly 'priestly' than a carnally 'derisive' ordained minister, especially in the post-Pestilence years when actual priests might be all too often of low mental and moral calibre;[9] and there could be several good reasons why Langland deleted them from the C-text. However, I think they make better sense if read in a symbolic way. The priest is *not* literally 'lewed', nor need we see Piers as charging him, *more Wycliffitae,* with actual ignorance of scripture.[10] The point is rather that his formal acquaintance with the Bible is as unfruitful as his merely formal criteria for 'recognising' a pardon: he is *spiritually* 'lewed' where Piers is only *literally* so; and it is a brilliant poetic stroke of Langland's to figure the latter's capacity to 'construe' the pardon with his conscience by allowing him to quote the Latin text of the Bible *literatim.* There was, after all, no authorised 'version' of scripture; quotation, as opposed to paraphrase, was thus properly of the Vulgate itself (whether directly or indirectly), which would then have a peculiar point, and pointedness, for the clerics among his audience (men such as the Rector of St Alphage, Cripplegate, who bequeathed *librum meum vocatum peres plowman* to a woman called Agnes Eggesfield on St Margaret's Day, 1400).[11]

There is some truth in R. W. V. Elliott's observation that

> If the argument of Langland's poem is often riddling, his diction is remarkable for its simplicity, remarkable not solely because he is

---

8 Cf. Wittig, 'Long Will's Pilgrimage' (see n. 7 above) 261.
9 See P. Ziegler, *The Black Death* (Pelican repr. 1971) 270.
10 For a careful account of *PP* in relation to contemporary radical thought see
    P. Gradon, 'Langland and the Ideology of Dissent', *PBA* 66 (1980) 179–205.
11 See Introduction, note 9.

often probing profound spiritual problems, but also because the alliterative tradition throve on ornamentation.[12]

The term 'simplicity' may be allowed to stand, given certain important qualifications, only if we exclude from consideration those lines of the poem (nearly one in every thirty) that include Latin words or phrases as integral parts of their structure, and additionally if we leave out of account the Latin *quotations* (over 300 in number) which are not 'enclosed' within the verse but 'appended' to it. Many of these lines and passages are far from simple, a few of them are decidedly riddling, and several are offered without translation and require to be 'construed' before they can be 'kenned'. Therefore while I agree with Elliott (following Burrow) that Langland's audience 'included many people not familiar with the rich vocabulary of other alliterative poets' I cannot go on with him to assume

> that it was also an audience of to no small extent unlettered, 'lewed' people, whose familiarity with the techniques and diction of contemporary sermons would have provided some equipment towards an understanding of Langland's thought. (ibid.)

A proper understanding of Langland's *thought* necessitates an ability to construe his *words*; but since many of these are in Latin, that presupposes in turn a real, and quite literal, familiarity with *grammatica*. It presupposes, in other words, an audience of *clerks*. It is to Langland's development and exploitation of Latin – remarkable, indeed, for its richness and complexity more than for its simplicity – that I now turn in the next two sections of this chapter.

II. APPENDED LATIN

In her pioneering study of Latin in *Piers Plowman*, Sr Carmeline Sullivan distinguished between three main forms in which it appears. The first is that of 'extraneous Latin quotations', inessential to the sense, and having the character of marginal glosses or footnotes. The second is that of quotations which are syntactically articulated with the text; these it is customary for modern editions to number as lines of verse (e.g. Pr 132–8, XV 118) whether or not the original is in verse. The third form is that of the macaronic line proper. These three categories seem to me generally valid, although it should not be suggested that the first group are in some sense expendable. They are surely more integral to Langland's text than, say,

12 R. W. V. Elliott, 'The Langland Country' in Hussey, ed., *Critical Approaches*, 234–5.

the marginal glosses in such Chaucer manuscripts as Ellesmere, or the (more certainly authorial) marginal comments (in prose) and summarising head-notes (in verse) of Gower's *Confessio Amantis*, which have an editorial character. Moreover, even when syntactically unarticulated with the text, they cannot really be regarded as 'extraneous' in many cases, since as well as serving 'to bolster up the thought expressed in the text',[13] they may become the object of further comment in the text, as in this instance from Will's angry interchange with his friar confessor:

> 'Ac a barn withouten bapteme may noght so be saved –
> *Nisi quis renatus fuerit.*
> Loke, ye lettred men, wheither I lye or do noght' (XI 82–3).

Here the quotation, while syntactically free-standing, forms part both of Will's diatribe against the friar for failing to baptize and also part of the written 'text' of the poem in a wider sense, referred to the clerks among his readers for their judgement as to its intrinsic truth and its argumentative weight.

The thematic and structural role of the quotations has been illuminatingly explored by John Alford;[14] but the richness and density of their stylistic functioning deserves much fuller investigation. I single out here, once again from the 'battle of quotations' between Piers and the Priest in the Pardon Scene, one example which Sullivan classifies among those 'syntactically articulated with the text' (*op. cit.* p. 29), though strictly it may be regarded as 'appended' or 'extraneous'. Piers has just been saying that he will turn from his preoccupation with material labour to a penitential regime, weeping instead of sleeping, even if this results in loss of 'wheat bread' (*sc.* through omitting some of his necessary tasks as a ploughman):

> 'The prophete his payn eet in penaunce and in sorwe,
> By that the Sauter seith – so dide othere manye.
> That loveth God lelly, his liflode is ful esy:
> *Fuerunt michi lacrime mee panes die ac nocte.'* (VII 122–124a).

Here the quotation from Psalm 41:4, though syntactically *un*articulated with the text, is semantically embedded *in* the text in a thoroughly 'organic' way (cf. Sullivan, p. 1), forming part of an intricate pattern of translinguistic paronomasia. The French word *payn*, as the *MED* quotations show virtually conclusively, was first used by Langland here to mean simply 'bread': in its other appearances (themselves later than *Piers*

13 Sr Carmeline Sullivan, *The Latin Insertions and the Macaronic Verse in Piers Plowman* (Washington: Catholic University of America, 1932) 1.
14 J. A. Alford, 'The Role of the Quotations in *PP*', *Speculum* 52 (1977) 80–99.

Plowman) it is still a French term from the language of *haute cuisine* (more common is the compound *paindemain*, a fine white bread similar to the *coket and clermatyn*, also first instanced in Langland, of VI 304).[15] Its use seems contextually justified since the 'prophete' in question is King David, for whom fine 'whete breed' (121) might be appropriate, and appropriately referred to as 'payn'. The cross-caesural pararhyme of *payn* with pen-*aunce* would then be seen as pointing up the ironic contrast between what David is in the eyes of the world and what he *really* is (i.e. in the eyes of God) – a great sinner 'that Uries deeth conspired' (X 420): even as he eats *payn* (a 'mete of moore cost', XIII 41) he eats with *pain*, having made himself 'wel at ese' with what he has 'myswonne' (XIII 42).

The 'pain' felt in 'penaunce' – the *poena* from which *poenitentia* derives – is primarily, of course, remorse, the ever-renewed bite or pang of conscience; but for Langland, as a medieval Christian poet with a powerful *sense* of the relation between outward sign and inward reality, this pang is properly experienced in a way accessible to the *senses*: in tears, the sign of remorse, and in fasting, the sign of repentance. The deep spiritual *connection* between the two parts of Piers' declaration at 121 – 'And *wepen* whan I sholde slepe, though *whete* breed me faille', highlighted by the assonance of the italicised lifts of this 'minimal'-type line, is paradoxically affirmed despite the disjunctive *though*: for it is in the context of repentance that a negative act (omission of his ploughman's work) will become a positive means to grace (fasting with sorrow is beneficial for the soul). Now what occurs in 'conversion' is not simply a change of attitude towards God and oneself, but also a change of attitude towards the 'things of this world' – in the broadest sense, creation *tout court*.[16] The tears of the fasting penitent do not merely replace his bread, they *become* bread: pain becomes *payn*. But while a passage such as this reveals a measure of affinity with that 'view of the intimate and necessary relationship between words and things' which Jill Mann (following Jean Jolivet) calls '(primitive) grammatical Platonism',[17] the more important point to be noticed, I believe, is not the supposed referential affinities of the homophonic lexemes but rather the location of the *key* to the passage's sacramental meaning in the *Latin* line quoted. This, above all, needs to be 'construed' before it can be 'kenned': for it is here that the religious act of 'converting' tears into 'bread' is actually *stated*:

Fuerunt michi lacrime mee panes die ac nocte (VII 124a).

15 See *MED* s.vv. *pain* n., *pain-demeine* n., *coket* n. (2) and *cler-matin* n.
16 See Vernet, op. cit., 117–20 (on conversion).
17 Mann, art. cit., 68; Jolivet's study of 'platonisme grammatical' is in P. Gallais & Y.-J. Riou, eds., *Mélanges offerts à René Crozet* (Poitiers, 1962), II, 93–9.

Paradoxical as it may sound, the *Latin* is needed to 'gloss' the English: properly to understand *payn* we must first construe *panes*, in the double sense of 'translation' – rendering one language into another, and interpreting one thing as we say, 'in terms of another': *translatio* is both the literal transfer of a sense (*res*) from one linguistic form (*nomen*) to another *and* the transposition of a *denotatum* from one category of reference to another.

In Langland's thought, which is sacramental not Platonistic, the spiritual reality does not underlie material actuality (including human speech) as a substance underlies a shadow, but more as a form underlies (and determines) that which it informs. Form is that which is grasped by the intellect: it is not the substance of things but their meaning.[18] And since that meaning finds its fullest manifestation in Scripture, a unique status belongs to the language of the Bible, the Fathers, and the sacred liturgy that is drawn from both. This is why Anima, who traces the decay of culture to the decline of the Church, calls 'Grammer, *the ground of al*' (XV 370).

It will have emerged, then, that I disagree with Sr Sullivan about the 'inorganic' character of Langland's free-standing Latin quotations: 'appended' they may be, but 'extraneous' they are not. Indeed there is very little essential difference between them and those of the second and third type, which are integrated at the syntactical and at the syntactical and metrical levels respectively. This can be brought out by discussing a second example, in which the 'appended' quotation (untranslated as is customary) is preceded and followed by macaronic lines containing fully-integrated Latin phrases (one of them at least a quotation proper). It comes from a passage already cited in examining VII 122–124*a*, that describing the gluttonous Doctor of Divinity and his man at Clergie's dinner:

> Ac hir sauce was over sour and unsavourly grounde
> In a morter, *Post mortem*, of many bitter peyne –
> But if thei synge for tho soules and wepe salte teris:
> *Vos qui peccata hominum comeditis, nisi pro eis lacrimas et*
> *oraciones effuderitis, ea que in deliciis comeditis, in*
> *tormentis evometis.*
> Conscience ful curteisly tho commaunded Scripture
> Bifore Pacience breed to brynge and me that was his mette.

18 Cf. Aquinas: '. . . res visibiles sacramentorum dicuntur verba per similitudinem quandam, inquantum scilicet participant quandam vim significandi, quae principaliter est in ipsis verbis' (*ST*, 3. qu. 60, a. 7, ad 1). Though Langland's thought seems to me better described in Aristotelean than in Platonic categories, the sacramental (as in Aquinas) tends to bridge the gap between two apparently contradictory types of metaphysic.

> He sette a sour loof toforn us and seide, *'Agite penitenciam'*,
> And siththe he drough us drynke: *'Dia perseverans –*
> As longe', quod he, 'as lif and lycame may dure' (XIII 43–50).

I have not space here to do adequate justice to this remarkable allegory, in which the ill-gotten gains 'eaten' by the Friar will after death turn from 'sour' to 'bitter' unless purged by 'salt' tears, and in which the *payn* of this life (*peccata/deliciae*) becomes the *peyne* of the next (*tormenta*) unless subjected, before it is too late, to a radical 'conversion' into penitential 'mete of moore cost' (cf. 41), in which suffering not pleasure is the end (*lacrimae et oraciones*). My main contention is that, as in the earlier passage (the *lacrimae/panes* imagery of which it echoes), the 'appended quotation' – of unknown origin – serves as the proper 'gloss' on the eating and tasting ideas of the preceding and following English lines, while going beyond the function of 'gloss' or 'footnote' to become the fruitful source of the new and unexpected metaphors of lines 48–9. For the *meaning* of 'sour' in *sour loof* 48 becomes 'converted' from that of 'sour' in *sour and unsavourly grounde* 43, but only, I maintain, in the light of 45*a* properly construed: the *translatio* of metaphor depends on and presupposes the *translatio* of translation. The key to finding in the unknown quotation's *lacrimas* an allusion to the *lacrimae* of Psalm 41:4 is the conjunction of *sour loof* with the injunction *'Agite penitenciam'*, the *nomen* conferred by Scripture which serves to expose the true *res* denoted: or, put another way, the Latin communicates the form or inner essence (penitence) of the outward visible sign (tears).

In a sense, then, we may speak of Langland as engaged in *exploiting* 'grammatical Platonism': the word *diu* 'long' that annominatively 'underlies' the (more probably) original *Dia* receives literal translation in line 50 'As longe . . . dure', but the very form of the actual lexeme ('form' *here* meaning 'phonetic/graphetic configuration') points to the true or 'Platonic' form of *diu* 'long' as being *Dia* 'healing drug': at a higher level, the proper *translatio* ('spiritual signification') of *diu perseverans* is 'earning salvation' through a repentance which converts, preserves ('salte teris' 45) and, through abstinence, miraculously heals and feeds:

> And thanne he broughte us forth a mees of oother mete, of
> *Miserere mei, Deus*
>
> *Et quorum tecta sunt peccata*
> In a dissh of derne shrifte, *Dixi et confitebor tibi.* (XIII 53–4).

If we 'lift the lid' of the Latin words which cover the sense, using the secret (*derne*) rite of sacramental confession, what we will find is the mercy of God and the assurance of salvation: the 'true' meaning of our actions disclosed, and then *en*closed again (through absolution), as Patience explains to Haukyn:

'*Per confessionem* to a preest *peccata occiduntur* –

As David seith in the Sauter, *et quorum tecta sunt peccata*.

And as it nevere [n]adde ybe, to noghte bryngeth dedly synne,
That it nevere eft is sene ne soor, but semeth a wounde yheeled'
(XIV 91, 93, 95–6).

The full force of that heavily-stressed stave *sunt* in the 'enclosed' Latin of line 93 is of 'are, in reality, in the eyes of God', and it has enough residual momentum virtually to 'convert' the normal sense of *semeth* 'seems *as opposed to* is'.

Langland achieves some remarkable effects through his manipulation of Latin and English in the same line; and it is even arguable that his 'formal inditing', if by that we understand his mastery of learned *ratio* in the *locutio vulgaris*, here reaches its apogee, in poetry which is at once utterly 'clerkly' and uniquely English. But first it is necessary to describe what appear to be the underlying principles of Langland's macaronic craftsmanship.

III.   ENCLOSED LATIN

A.   *Macaronic Making*

The macaronic technique, as Sr Sullivan observes in her Introduction, existed before the name was invented, apparently by Folengo in 1517 (see *OED* s.v. *macaronic*), and was especially popular with medieval Latin poets of a broadly 'Goliardic' type for use in satires and complaints. It is, then, a 'clerkly' form, though one favoured by those on the fringes of the clerical establishment, not by sober figures like Alanus, who enjoyed the status of modern *auctores*. It may occur as a sporadic, occasional feature designed to give vividness and bite to the opening or close of an otherwise wholly Latin piece, as in Walter of Châtillon's verses on the Feast of Fools ('*A la feste sui venuz* et ostendam, quare / singulorum singulos mores explicare')[19] or in the archetypal 'Goliardic' invective from the *Carmina Burana* associated with Walter's school, *Utar contra vitia*, where the

19 *Moralisch-satirische Gedichte Walters von Chatillon*, ed. K. Strecker, (Heidelberg, 1929) no. 13.

venality of the papacy is cleverly attacked by a piece of translinguistic verbal play ('vel si verbum gallicum vis apocopare / *"paies paies!"* dist li mot, si vis impetrare').[20] In these and similar cases the vernacular phrases 'enclosed' within the Latin have something of the effect if not the exact form of the 'appended' or free-standing quotation. But in the best examples rich 'harmonic' effects can be obtained by simultaneously 'articulating' the two languages at the syntactic level and 'disjoining' them at the metrical level, so that the sense runs on uninterruptedly but the Latin and the English lines both rhyme only with themselves.

Two fairly straightforward examples from English poems contemporary with Langland are 'On the Rebellion of Jack Straw' (in eight-line stanzas of alternate Latin and English) and 'On the Times', dated by Wright *c.* 1388 (in alternate Latin and English arranged in loose quatrains),[21] a poem with a version of Langland's *Dum 'rex' a 'regere'* couplet tacked on at the end in the manner of the Goliardic measure *cum auctoritate* (ending in a free-standing quotation from a real or invented *auctoritas*). 'On the Times' combines racy colloquial idiom with alliterative patterns that counter the metrical disjunction between the two languages:

> Women lo! with here brestes
> *procedunt arte profana;*
> Prechers ne pristes
> *non possunt haec pellere vana* (p. 276)

and in one instance weaves in a French phrase (possibly mimicking the toper's incoherence) reminiscent of the tavern-cry *Dieu save Dame Emme* (Pr 225):

> 'Wyv sa belle',[22] thei cry,
> *fragrantia vina bibentes,*
> Thei drynke tyl they be dry,
> *lingua sensuque carentes.* (p. 277).

This stanza recalls Langland's one line of tri-lingual macaronic verse ('For *"quant OPORTET vient en place il ny ad que PATI"'*, X 436: Type IIIc with the macaronic staves crossed chiastically). It also suggests what hints he might have found in the tradition of *rhythmus* for his unique method of integrating Latin words and phrases into alliterative long lines so as to preserve the integrity of both and yet create a more intimate unity than the usual 'disjunctive' approach permitted.

In addition to satirical pieces, there existed moral and religious poems

20 *Carmina Burana*, ed. A. Hilka and O. Schumann (Heidelberg, 1930), I, no. 42.
21 *Political Poems and Songs*, ed. T. Wright (1859), I, nos 15 and 22 (unlineated).
22 The reading of MS Harl. 536 (*Vive la belle*), printed in Wright's textual note, may either be the original or, more probably, a deliberate correction.

like *Esto Memor Mortis* (from CUL MS Ee. 6. 29), which is prefaced by a characteristically 'Goliardic' Leonine *auctoritas*, and not only alternates its (disjunctively rhymed) macaronic half-lines in successive stanzas but also, in two of its refrain-couplets, crosses them chiastically with an effect of dramatic unexpectedness, as here:

> *Nam nulli vult parcere* Dethe þat is vn-dere,
> *Pro argenti munere*, Ne for noon fayre prayere;
> *Sed cum rapit propere*, He chaunges eche mannys chere,
> *In peccati scelere* Yif he be fownden here.
>   *Set cum dampnatis* Helle to þy mede þou wynnes,
>   þat neuyr blynnes *Pro peccatis sceleratis*   (ll. 19–24).[23]

A number of devices here (internal half-line alliteration and rhyme: 19, 21; 20; verbal variation: 22a, 24b; skilful control of stress after and before the caesura: 23b, 24a) call Langland to mind, though there is no question of indebtedness either way. In the right hands, the macaronic form is capable of a poetic seriousness, even solemnity belied by its jocose Renaissance label. Although Langland differs from such writers as this nameless lyric composer, whose 'pleasing contrast of directness and sonorousness' was noted by Carleton Brown,[24] in employing phrases from various *auctores* instead of himself versifying in Latin, he shares with him a capacity to bring together, through juxtaposing *grammatica* and the *vulgaris locutio*, the transcendent and empirical domains of human thought and action, the tower and ditch on the one hand, and the field of folk on the other.[25] This is nowhere more strikingly exemplified than in the lines from XIII 43ff discussed on pp. 91–2 above:

> Ac hir sauce was over sour and unsavourly grounde
> In a morter, *Post mortem*, of many bitter peyne.

Superficially nothing could seem less proportional to the chastisement incurred by an incompetent cook than the pains of hell; yet the lines convey, under the pressure of 'grammatical Platonism', a sense that immense consequences may follow from our trifling deeds, the 'mortal' from the 'venial', just as in the verbal form[26] of the prosaic *morter* lies hidden *mortem*, 'Dethe þat is vn-dere'.

---

23 *Religious Lyrics of the XIVth Century*, ed. Carleton Brown (Oxford, 1924), 135.
24 Ed. cit., p. xxii. The piece is not noticed in standard discussions of Death lyrics such as those of Douglas Gray, Rosemary Woolf and Philippa Tristram.
25 I have already made this point in the Introduction to my edition of *PP*, xxxi.
26 'Form' here = 'phonetic-graphetic configuration' (cf. p. 92 above) *as opposed to* 'meaning'; in another terminology, one might speak of 'substance' (or 'matter') as opposed to 'significance' (or 'form'). I follow the former, in accord with common usage.

B. *Macaronic Structure*

Langland's 242 macaronic lines (a total exceeding the lines in Passus II) occur in all parts of the poem, but are especially concentrated in the long passus V and XV (the Confessions; Anima) and in Passus XVIII (the Harrowing of Hell). It is useful to classify them as precisely as possible and with an eye on their metrical features, since it seems *a priori* probable that one reason for Langland's resort to Latin stave-words was his renunciation of much of the restricted vocabulary of the traditional alliterative maker.[27] In this we see coming together two aspects of his 'clerkliness' which it is important not to dissociate: a concern for his primary audience of fellow clerks, and an awareness of a wider readership of the *commune*, not all of whom would have been, in Elliott's words, 'to no small extent unlettered, "lewed" people'. The *MED* entry under *leued* 1(a) alone contains eight separate senses, and it is not at all clear whether, for instance, in Lewte's 'It is *licitum* for lewed men to [l]egge the sothe' (XI 96) a contrast is intended with those Will has just appealed to (XI 83): 'Loke, ye lettred men, wheither I lye or do noght', or with the category of ordained and higher clergy alone: 'persons and preestes and prelates of Holy Chirche' (XI 97). Will's own ambiguous status (intended for higher orders but now confined to a lower one) is thus aptly figured in the amphibian medium he favours: both are 'licit' for him, though his claim upon *grammatica* is not that of an *auctor*. Yet it is a real claim, as the very Latinity of the *licitum*-stave attests.

Langland's macaronic lines fall into three main classes, which may be described as the isolate, the conjugate and the composite types. In addition, there are a number of quasi-macaronic, mongrel and pure Latin verse lines. In most cases the Latin is not original but consists of words or phrases derived from the Bible, the Liturgy and common prayers; names and titles; and quotations from certain other authors such as Bernard and Cato. Although there are a few lines enclosing Latin which apparently do not conform to the regular patterns described in Chapter 2, section II above, displaying, for example, a blank first lift[28] (perhaps a 'licit' anomaly here, though avoided in all-English lines), the majority are regular and all varieties, except Types Ic and Id, appear, as does

---

27 On this see further below pp. 104–6, also Oakden, *Alliterative Poetry*, II, 175–93 and Turville-Petre, *Alliterative Revival* 69–92, esp. 71, also the acute comments of Burrow, *Ricardian Poetry* 32–5, esp. on Langland's 'ironic use of the diction of alliterative poetry'.
28 E.g. III 339 (on which see further p. 101 below), with mute second stave (or possible *p/b* stave-rhyme), giving 'anomalous' *ab/ba*, and III 343 (also mute second stave).

muting.[29] While 'concentrations' of enclosed Latin occur in particular sections,[30] translinear and running macaronics are rare (see below). What follows is a brief description of the formal *ratio* of Langland's macaronic practice.

In the *single isolate* line, only one lift in each line is Latin (or, in a few cases, French):

> Ex. 1.i   The *culorum* of this cas kepe I noght to shewe   III 280.

(Here, the pronunciation is presumed to be *clorum*, so this is not one of the 'licensed' irregular lines).

> Ex. 1.ii   Preestes and persons with *Placebo* to hunte   III 311.
> 1.iii   'Yet I preie yow', quod Piers, '*pur charite*, and ye konne'
> VI 253.

(1. iii has a muted stave *pur*).[31] This line is called isolate because the Latin stave word stands isolated against the English ones. In the *double isolate*, the balance is exact, with one Latin and one English stave in each Standard half-line:

> Ex. 2.i   For '*Nullum malum* the man mette with *inpunitum*'   IV 143
> 2.ii   And he broughte us of *Beati quorum* of *Beatus vir*res makyng
> XIII 52.

In 2,i the second Latin lift is a blank stave and in the first metre and phrase-structure are in tension, with *Nullum* forming part of the 'onset' dip, unless this line is read as 'licensed', with first-lift unalliterating. In 2.ii the Latin stave-word in each isolate lift is a variant of the same word, while the phrasal unity of the *b*-lift is boldly ruptured by treating *vir* as a 'mongrel' *stave*, half-Latin, half-English, a 'miniature' manifestation of the structural principle instantiated in this type of line.[32]

The effect of naturalness in 2.ii, as of an easy transition from one language to another (as easy as register-switching, which in a sense it is), is paralleled in another of Langland's most felicitous examples:

> Ex. 3.   'Ye – *quis est ille*?' quod Pacience, 'quik – *laudabimus eum*!'
> XIV 103.

---

29 Type I*a* (Latin stave in positions 1, 2 and 3 respectively): III 280, III 259, II 181; I*b*: XIII 137, XV 609, XVI 30, XVII 228; I*c*: none, but cf. C IV 190; I*d*: none; I*e*: XIV 306 (possibly Type III*b*); II*a*: XIII 151, XV 608; II*b*: XI 114, XII 279 (with mute second and liaisonal third stave); III*a*: I 52, VII 72, XV 268; III*b*:? XIV 306 (or I*e*); III*c*: XV 269.

30 So do passages entirely *without* Latin, e.g. XII 217–77, XX 34–256, XI 320–80, XIII 255–312, or with only one Latin stave, e.g. XIII 198–249.

31 This stock phrase is regularly mute (e.g. VIII 11, XIII 30); cf. also VII 163.

32 Also a double isolate in structure is the dazzling Latin-French line X 436.

This illustrates how skilfully Langland combines the conversational (*Ye, quik*) with the homiletic, splitting into two halves a quotation from Scripture (Ecclus 31:5) that seems discreetly veiled in Latin as if to conceal its pessimistic doctrine (modified in the English that follows) from the ears of rich *lewed* men: English 'quik' seems to grow phonetically out of Latin *'quis'* almost as if to arrest it in the act of turning to thin air.[33]

In the second type of macaronic line, the *conjugate*, both Latin lifts are yoked together in one of the two half-lines, which thus form a balanced linguistic as well as metrical unit across the caesura from the English:

Ex. 4.i.	*Qui loquitur turpiloquium* is Luciferes hyne	Pr 39
4.ii.	And fecchen us vitailles at *fornicatores*	II 181
4.iii.	And Dives in deyntees lyvede and in *douce vie*	XIV 122
4.iv.	And leggen on longe with *Laboravi in gemitu meo*	XV 191
4.v.	*Presul* and *Pontifex* and *Metropolitanus*,	
	And othere names an heep, *Episcopus* and *Pastor*	
		XV 42–3.

In i, the simple copula *is* serves both to define the preceding Latin (*'this* is what it is to speak foul words') and to suggest an ontological link between word and reality.[34] The alliteration in ii helps to draw an abstract category of offenders against Canon Law into the tangible world of fetching food (Langland seems to sound *f* as /v/ in both Latin and English words).[35] The French in iii has an especially subtle effect, *douce vie* suggesting more immediately than would *dulci vita* the opulent court life of fourteenth century England where *deyntees* (itself a loan word from French) abounded for the *dives* (a Latin word-name that would be transparent to clerks as might, to some of them, the descent of *deynte* from *dignitatem*). In iv the muting of the key-stave *Lab-* graphically throws the stress upon the long vowel *a*, which enacts the sense of preceding *longe*. Finally, the two lines of v illustrate the unique double conjugate (42) and show that the clerkly style was by no means a foe to humour: in the 'T'-type line 43, despite muting of *Ep-*, the cross-caesural near-rhyme of *heep* and *Ep-*,

33 *Quyk*, here in the sense 'alive' as well as 'fast', is also used in another fine macaronic line (of single isolate type) in contrast both to native *quelt* and Latin *Quatriduanus* (a solemn word suggesting the awesome nature both of death and of Christ's deed) at XVI 114.
34 This may be called *'lexical* Platonism'; for the device of linking lexeme-segments translinguistically (*loq-* / *Luc-*) cf. *morter* / *mortem* and *Dia* / [*diu*] at XIII 44, 49 discussed above, p. 95.
35 In this example the Latin *form* both highlights the formally judicial aspect of the offence (cf. *transgressores* I 96, *infamis* V 166) and, through the according to the stave-sound of its native value /v/, affirms the *substance* of the sinful act underlying the 'clerkly' nomenclature.

followed by the bawdily sibilating -*piscopus*, produces an effect of authentically Goliardic mockery.

A few lines are *composites* of an isolate a-half and a conjugate b-half:

Ex. 5.i   Bettre than in *Beatus vir* or in *Beati omnes*   V 419
    5.ii   And bad *Nullum bonum* be *irremuneratum*   IV 144.

Here i, which has to be 'construed clausemele' before it can be 'kenned', reads somewhat prosaically out of context (as macaronics often do in Langland); but the power of ii, with its almost perfect syllabic balance between the phrasally unsymmetrical isolate and conjugate halves, is apparent in the way it poises and equates 'absence of good' with 'absence of reward', *No-meed* with *No-good*. This same line and its antecedent also illustrate the *running* macaronics[36] which may be of differing type (here isolate + composite):

Ex. 6.i   For '*Nullum malum* the man mette with *inpunitum*
           And bad *Nullum bonum* be *irremuneratum*'   IV 143–4

– with its fine shift of stress off the *Nullum* part of each parallel phrase to give equal weight to the ethical opposites. A particularly good example of this is

    6.ii   '*Reddite Cesari*', quod God, 'that *Cesari* bifalleth,
           Et que sunt Dei Deo, or ellis ye don ille'   I 52–3

where a double isolate is followed by a conjugate, preventing the repetition of *Caesari* and *Dei*/o from becoming mechanical. Here the potency of the contrast between the two languages is shown by the way in which both words (God, *Deus*) are used for the Creator and only one for the Emperor; *Cesares* at I 51 is too close to its original to do anything but confirm the accidental character of temporal rule hinted at in *bifalleth*, 'to fall to by lot' / 'to pertain to by right' (*MED* s.v. 3, 4a) in contrast with *sunt*, apodictically 'are' (this contrast is not in Vulgate Mt 22:21, which has *sunt* for both Caesar and God).

Translinear macaronics are very rare, but a particularly brilliant specimen is

    6.iii   For hir either is endited, and that of '*Ignorancia*
           Non excusat episcopos nec ydiotes preestes' XI 315–16

from Trajan's tirade, with its superbly ironic *ad hoc* adjectival form *ydiotes* indicating that this maker's *enditing* certainly cannot be indited of either ignorance or idiocy.[37]

---

36 Other examples are XIII 136–8 and XV 267–9.
37 See also XII 279–80 and XV 267–8.

C: Quasi-Macaronics

In addition to perfect macaronic structures of varying degrees of complexity, Langland writes lines which are *intermediate* between the latter and lines of appended Latin, in that they both contain English and yet are metrically irregular:

Ex. 7.i Thanne hénte Hópe an hórn of *Deus tu convérsus vivificábis nos*
     ii And bléw it with *Beáti / quorum remísse sunt iniquitátes,*

(V 507–8)

Here i can be scanned easily as Type IIb, with the prose quotation of the b-half being treated as verse and the second /v/ stave being mute; but ii can only be seen as irregular (*aa/xy*, with caesura after *Beati*). These lines may be classified as 'quasi-macaronic', but sometimes they verge on becoming mongrel mixtures of English verse and Latin prose, and readers must follow their ears in deciding whether to agree with Skeat and Kane-Donaldson, for example, that

Ex. 7.iii And thanne hadde Pácience a pítaunce, *Pro hác orabit ád te*
       Ómnis sánctus in tempore óportúno (XIII 56–56*a*)

is a mongrel line with a verse a-half followed by a line of prose (as in the MSS) or divide it as I have done, scanning 56 as a 'T'-type line and 56*a* as a versified line, of the same type as 69 ('*Periculum est in falsis fratribus*'), with anomalous scansions (*ax/ax can* be achieved in 56*a*, but 69 is clearly *xy/aa*).

On the whole, it seems to me preferable to regard intermediate lines as quasi-macaronic and 'hung-over' Latin lines like XIII 56*a* or 53*a* (which Kane-Donaldson also print as a verse-line) as 'versified' prose, and to accept that some mongrel lines represent an only partially successful attempt to versify a prose original, as in:

Ex. 7.iv Than Zácheus for he séide, / '*Dimidíum bonórum / dó paupéribus*'
(XIII 195)

which seems to require wrenched stress in the third lift and a second caesura before *do*. More often than not, Langland's transposition of Latin prose (often psalm-verse prose) into regular alliterating long lines is brilliantly accomplished and represents a wittily apt and clerkly tribute to the poet of the original:

Ex. 8.i And seide, '*Si ámbulavéro / in medio úmbre mórtis*
     ii *Non timébo mála, quoniam tu mécum és.* (VII 116–17).

The caesura-mark in 8.i is conjectural, but even if put before *umbre* (giving *ab/ab* instead of *ax/àx*, both variants of Type III), it still leaves the English phrase as part of the *dip*.[38] The line is thus 'quasi-macaronic' not mongrel, while 8.ii is Standard, like

> Ex 8.iii   *Libenter súffertis insípientes / cum sítis ipsi sápientes*
> (VIII 93)

with its cross-caesural pararhyme and *similiter desinens*, a line 'versified' from 2 Cor 11:19 by the omission of *enim* before *suffertis*.[39]

In a few cases, Langland seems to have produced macaronic lines of apparently anomalous pattern, when with minor alteration of word-order and without affecting the sense he could have achieved perfect regularity.

> Ex. 9.i   Was *omnia probate*, and that plesed hire herte IV 339
>
>   ii   *Quod bonum est tenete* – Truthe that text made IV 343.

Here, even if wrenching of stress and *p/b* alliteration could regularise i, no such resort is possible in ii, in spite of the presence of a *t* stave in *tenete*, and the line is 'mongrelised' under the pressure of a celebrated maxim of unalterable verbal shape: *probate omnia* and *tenete quod est bonum* would have jarred on the ears of clerks even if *sonus bene cohaereat* (cf. Chap. 2, I above). But since 'Truth that text made', and it was *his* 'heart' that Langland's conscience was concerned to please, the maker, having tried all, hangs on to the good. This constitutes a rejection of the specious which is wholly intelligible, and the same holds good in

> Ex. 9.iii   *Qui cum Patre et Filio* – that faire hem bifalle   (V 58)

where transposing the order of the Persons would have been excluded. In all three cases there is some small element of *sonus*, however, to 'compensate' as it were, the *artist's* conscience – the *b* of *probate* that is heard stavally when the word is *not* wrenched, the enriched fourth lift of IV 343 and V 58 (with its pararhyme echo of *Filio* in the Latin a-half).

No such formal compensation, however, and likewise no evident constraint of sense, appear to account for the irregularity of

> Ex. 9.iv   *Piger pro frigore* no feeld nolde tilie   (VI 236)

where retention of the Vulgate original *Propter frigus piger* (Prov 20:4) would have ensured a regular Type IIIa line. The extreme rarity of such metrically defective lines, however – something that would require more

---

38 This is also the case in III 350 and III 330 (which scans if we transpose *divicie multe*).

39 Langland's small verbal alterations of the Vulgate text in the interests of metre rarely affect matters of substance. Cf. examples 9.ii and iii.

space for demonstration than is possible here – points to the generally very high level of care taken by Langland to reconcile the demands of 'formal enditing' with those of a 'lif' devoted 'to [1]egge the sothe' (cf. XI 91, 96), the conscience of a clerk with the conscientiousness of a maker. To recall that 'Truthe that text *made*' (IV 343) was to be reminded that there was only one perfect Maker, that perfection of the 'work' was meaningless unless it truly helped the human maker 'the parfiter to ben' (XII 24), and that an acceptance or even deliberate choice of (occasional) artistic imperfection was a proper mark of humility, a *felix culpa* to be vindicated (in the *Winner and Waster*-poet's words) 'never the lattere at the laste, when ledys bene knawen' (*WW* 29) and (in the *Morte Arthure*-poet's) 'nothyre voyde . . . ne vayne, bot wyrchip tille hymselvyne' (*MA* 10).

IV. FRENCHE MEN AND FRE MEN

Towards the end of his speech 'arating' Will for rebellious impatience, Reason appeals to the authority of Scripture (quoting I Pet 2:13) and then to a proverb in rhyming verse:

> Frenche men and fre men[40] affaiteth thus hire children:
> *Bele vertue est suffraunce; mal dire est petite vengeance.*
> *Bien dire et bien suffrir fait lui suffrant a bien venir*   (XI 383–4).

Langland no more translates the French than the Latin, making no concession to the ignorance of the 'newe clerkes' of whom Anima later complains that there is

> naught oon among an hundred that an auctour can construwe,
> Ne rede a lettre in any langage but in Latyn or in Englissh
>
> (XV 373–4).

In the C-text revision of this passage, to be dated c. 1385,[41] Langland translates the proverb in part, before quoting the French: 'Is no vertue so fair, ne of valewe ne profit, / So is soffrance . . .' (C XIII 199–200). It is as if he had come to recognise the fact, also recorded by John Trevisa in his famous addition of 1385 to his translation of Higden, that 'in al þe gramerscoles of Engelond childern leueþ Frensch, and construeþ and lurneþ an Englysch . . . þat now childern of gramerscole conneþ no more Frensch þan can here lift heele'.[42] Trevisa goes on fair-mindedly to

---

40 There is probably some play here on *frank* (*MED* s.v. adj) 'free' and *fraunchise* n. 1 (a) 'freedom'.
41 See the Introduction to my edition, p. xvi.
42 K. Sisam, ed.: *C14th Verse and Prose*, p. 149.

balance a gain (learning Latin faster than hitherto, when they had first to learn French before commencing *grammatica*) against a loss (lack of a useful accomplishment when travelling abroad – French being indeed *lingua franca* – 'and in meny caas also'). For Langland, however, there is only loss: because 'fre men' no longer 'affaiteth'[43] their children formally, in a *language* which occupies a unique middle ground between *vulgaris locutio* and *grammatica* (as it did in the traditional grammar school), they are also unable to 'wisse' them (C XIII 201) in the substantial moral values of patient *suffraunce* that are learned at least in part through disciplines of languages.

Langland's own easy familiarity with French is shown not, as with Gower, in the writing of lyric or moral poems in the language nor, as with Chaucer, in a repeated frequentation of its literary masterpieces. It seems to reflect, rather, some experience of the 'meny caas' of which Trevisa speaks – the world of law, politics, business and church affairs in which an unbeneficed clerk could find supplementary income from work akin to that of his modern name-sake: the copying of letters and documents. It is this world that provides the striking analogy used by Trajan in his attack on 'ydiotes preestes' 'that lewed men bitrayen' (XI 316, 302), a speech anticipating that of Anima:

> A chartre is chalangeable bifore a chief justice:
> If fals Latyn be in that lettre, the lawe it impugneth,
> Or peynted parentrelynarie, parcelles overskipped.
> The gome that gloseth so chartres for a goky is holden
>
> (XI 303–6).

Langland's example is drawn from a Latin charter, such as he had doubtless drawn up himself, but his point gains its force from the extreme precision with which the French legal terminology is deployed. *Parentrelynarie* and quite possibly *chalangeable*[44] are first recorded here, and the linguistic status of at least the former is unsure: should it be italicised like *douce vie* in XIV 122, the line then being classified as a single isolate macaronic? Certainly the choice of the technical term in 305 is itself an illustration of how 'Werke wittnesse will bere who wirche kane beste' (*Winner and Waster* 30): for it proves that he, the critic of *lewed* clerks, is not open to the charge of being thought a *goky*. Here the style may be said to be 'formal enditing' in another sense of that phrase – the articulation of a moral truth and the assertion of a moral judgement ('arating', 'legging the sothe') – the validity of both of which derives from the *konnynge* (cf. XI 297, 300) of the expression (just as that of a document depends on the integrity

43 See *MED* s.v.2(a) 'to educate a child / discipline the heart' and compare 3 'to overcome (the flesh)' illustrated from B V 66.
44 See *MED* s.vv. *par* prep. (c) and *chalangeable*. The former may involve wordplay on *paraunter*, with sense 'haphazardly'.

of its form, and the form on the conscientiousness of its scribe). Unscrupulous bishop and unlettered chaplain are both guilty:

> For hir either is endited, and that of '*Ignorancia*
> *Non excusat episcopos* nec ydiotes preestes'   (XI 315–16).

Here there is an evident stylistic correlation between the two indictments – that of the bishop (whose ignorance is a culpable 'overskipping' of ordinands' qualifications, but who can read the Latin in which the charge is couched), and that of the 'idiot priest' himself, an ungrammatical *goky* who needs to have *his* charge expressed in plain English (even if the French plural *ydiotes*, unique to Langland,[45] serves, in its macaronic mischievousness, as a last twist of the clerkly knife.

Langland's awareness of the tongue of 'Frenche men' helps to make him 'fre' in a literary world where loyalty to 'letters' could all too easily have led to imprisonment in an inappropriate vocabulary and style. Thus his Envy's *sorwe* ('gnawing anxiety' not 'remorse') makes him *megre* (V 127), a word taken from French and first recorded here,[46] and possibly echoed in the *Purity*-poet's *megre þay wexen* (1198).[47] The term exactly conveys the psycho-physical aspects of this vicious disposition, originating in the soul but inescapably embodied in the face and form. In the case of another word which makes some of its earliest appearances in Langland, *exciten*, a comparison of the B and C texts usefully brings out the subtlety of his response to overtone and suggestion and his awareness of the fluid and shifting relationship between French and native English. Expanding the description of Lechery in C with material from the Haukyn passage in B, he takes over the vividly concrete account of how Actyf

> gan taste
> Aboute the mouth or bynethe bigynneth to grope,
> Til eitheres wille wexeth kene, and to the werke yeden
> (XIII 345–7)

but extends it, with great psychological insight, to show the role of 'tales' and 'speche' in partnership with physical contact as they

> *Exited* either other till oure olde synne (C VI 185, 186, 188).

Langland here seems to be playing on *MED* senses 5 and 6 (respectively to stimulate physically and to arouse an emotion / thought), but there are also suggestions of sense 3(a) 'to incite to vice' and, by ironic contrast,

---

45 See *MED* s.v. *idiotes*; the singular itself is not found before Langland.
46 See *MED* s.v.; in most uses the sense is simply a physical one.
47 For evidence that the *Purity*-poet had read Langland see my '*Kynde Craft* and the *Play of Paramorez*' in *From the 14th to the 15th Century*, ed. P. Boitani and A. Torti (Cambridge and Tübingen, 1987).

of 4(a) 'to exhort to devotion or virtuous behaviour', the only other sense in which he uses the word ('exciteth us by the Evangelie . . .' XI 189). It is not simply that the loan-word bears much the same range of signification as the native *stir*; rather, the former, with its stronger overtones of purely *mental* action, functions to demonstrate the inward and *willed* character of lechery as a *sin*, not just an appetite gone out of control, 'a freletee of flessh' and 'a cours of kynde' as Mede had earlier wished to have it, and therefore 'synne of the sevene sonnest relessed' (III 55, 56, 58). Just as the words of the Gospel 'excite' us to virtue, so our own words can be deliberately used to 'excite' to evil. But there may be some indirect evidence that Langland had come to see *exciten* as a tainted word, too ambiguous to be usable indifferently in contexts of virtue and sin: for in the C-text revision of B XI 189 he changes 'exciteth us by the Evangelie' to 'as þe euaungelie witnesseth' (XII 100).

Langland's making free with the language of 'fre men' is demonstrated by his witty (and well-known) exposure of the ignorance of Coveitise, who 'wende riflynge were restitucion' because he 'lerned nevere rede on boke' and 'kan no Frenssh' (V 234–5).[48] The point here is not simply ignorance of a language, ignorance *tout court*; rather, not knowing French is as emblematic of moral *lewednesse* as Piers' apparent 'knowing' Latin in the Pardon Scene (discussed above p. 87) is symbolic of moral and religious understanding and wisdom. But Langland saw also a literal basis for the symbolic malcomprehension. For in reply to Repentance's question 'Repentedestow evere . . . or restitucion madest?' (V 228) Coveitise offers an emphatic affirmative 'Yis . . . / I roos whan thei were *a-reste* and riflede hire males!' (V 230). Coveitise has, in a sense, some basis for his error: the word *rest* is, after all, contained in *restitucion*, and if *ydiotes preestes* abound who 'in masse or in matyns maketh . . . defaute' (XI 308), sinning by omission, can the formally *lewed* be endited for misconstruing if this is all the 'kenning' they get? For:

> . . . if gold ruste, what shal iren do?
> For if a preest be foul, on whom we truste,
> No wonder is a lewed man to ruste   (*GP* 500–2).

The implication is less that the *lewed* need to learn French than that they need to be taught morality through the precept and example of their pastors, whose own education, therefore, becomes a matter of vital import. Langland removed this joke, which could conceivably foster too indulgent an attitude towards the avaricious laity, from the C-text (cf. C VI 237–8), but he returned to the wordplay that had originally attracted him in a new passage added to the Minorite Friar's exhortation in X 54–5:

48 See the interesting 'Note on "Riflynge"' by C. Wilcockson, *MÆ* 52 (1983) 302–5.

For rather haue we no *reste* til we *restitue*
Oure lyf to oure lord god for oure lycames gultes.

Here the restitution is the final one a man can make, and the rest the
eternal one of heaven; but the new lines reveal the same underlying
affinities with 'grammatical realism' that have been remarked before (see
pp. 89–91 above).

The word *restitue*, whether a direct loan from OF *restituer* or a back-
formation from *restitucion*, seems to have been introduced by Langland as
early as B V 274 (see *MED* s.v.). It is one of a number, such as *marchaunden*
(XIII 393), also a coinage, or *regratrie* (III 83), from the world of trade,
mitigacion (V 470) and *amercy* (VI 39), from the sphere of law, and
nounpower (XVII 313), from that of philosophy,[49] that help both to furnish
stave-words and to impart to the poetry its characteristically clerkly tone
of gritty intellectuality and polylingual breadth. Langland's English
blends fluidly into French in the manner of the colours in a spectrum: at
one end there are clearly foreign phrases like *douce vie* (XIV 122), at the
other more fully assimilated expressions like *paraventure* in XI 420 ('Pryde
now and presumpcion paraventure wol thee appele'), a line in which only
one lexical word is of native origin and which reverberates with the tolling
majesty of the 'heighe doom'. But perhaps his most individual lines – and
they are many – are those in which French-derived words are combined
with the 'rude speche' (Ymaginatif's phrase, XI 418), the *vulgaris locutio* at
its earthiest, of which Nevill Coghill wrote so sensitively in 'God's
Wenches and the Light that Spoke':[50]

Adam, whiles he spak noght, hadde paradis at wille;
Ac whan he mame*lede* aboute *mete* and entre*meted* to knowe
The wisedom and the wit of God, he was put fram blisse
(XI 415–17).

Worth noting here is not only the clerkly play on native *mete* and French
entremete, which 'Platonically' hints at a link between feeding and in-
terfering via the allusion to *entermes* (<Fr. *entre-mes* 'a dish between main
courses' (see *MED* s.v.)), but also the colloquial bluntness of *mamelede*,[51]
which serves to bring the awesome event of the Fall down to the level of
our lowest need, as in more celebrated lines like these on the Incarnation:

And in the wombe of that wenche was he fourty woukes,
Til he weex a faunt thorugh hir flessh . . .   (XVI 100–1).

49 See *MED* svv. Langland's contribution to the vocabulary deserves investi-
gation.
50 In N. Davis and C. L. Wrenn, *Studies presented to J. R. R. Tolkien* (1962) 200–18.
51 This word is our *mumble* (see *OED* s.v.). Cf. V 21, and see *MED* s.v.

It is not so much here that *faunt* is *sermo altus* or *wenche sermo humilis* in its essential nature: against the deceiving linguistic conventionalism of such as Chaucer's May ('I am a gentil womman and no wenche' E 2202) we should set the 'Platonic' realism of the Manciple's

> And *for that oother is a povre womman,*
> She shal be cleped his wenche or his lemman   (H 219–20).

Rather, it is the deft collocation of the two registers that functions to activate our sense of the mystery underlying both language and the reality it mediates and creates: the lexeme *wenche* undergoes 'ennoblement' through its juxtaposition with *faunt*, just as the 'pure povre maide' Mary (cf. XI 247) becomes miraculously exalted through 'the wisedom and the wit of God' (XI 417) manifested in the 'good sleighte' of the Incarnation (XVIII 161).

The topics examined in this section require (and deserve) a far more extended consideration than is possible here. John Burrow's remark that 'discussion of Chaucer's poetic language, lacking a regular diet of detailed word-studies, suffers from chronic malnutrition'[52] is *a fortiori* applicable in the case of Langland. But enough has perhaps been said to support the claim that Langland's *vulgaris*, like Dante's, fed on both *grammatica* and *franca*, is to be regarded as *nobilior* not *licet* but *quia* 'in diversas prolationes et vocabula sit divisa'.[53]

---

52 *Essays on Medieval Literature* (Oxford, 1984) p. 61.
53 *De Vulgari Eloquio*, ed. cit., p. 379.

Chapter Four

Reding in Retorik

It is *licitum* for lewed men to [1] egge the sothe
If hem liketh and lest – ech a lawe it graunteth;

Thyng that al the world woot, wherfore sholdestow spare
To reden it in retorik to arate dedly synne?   (XI 96–7, 101–2).

I.   WORDS, WORTS AND WILL: LANGLAND'S SERIOUS WORDPLAY

Langland's handling of rhetoric is too large a subject for a single chapter of
a study of his poetic art, and I have accordingly concentrated on a detailed
(but even so, selective) discussion of a single *figura verborum*, the pun. But
I wish to preface my analysis of a handful of examples with some account
of what I take to be Langland's view of language as a whole, by way of
justifying my choice of this particular figure. For it hardly needs saying
that puns are still commonly regarded as unserious, and this is not
surprising as their main purpose in conversation (like that of their
equivalent figure at the level of the whole utterance, irony) is to amuse.
But there is plenty of evidence that wordplay was much favoured by
clerkly writers in Latin, who, especially if they were Englishmen, could
have defended the serious value of the trope by pointing to Pope
Gregory's celebrated *Non Angli sed Angeli* (reported in more extended
form by Bede), on which so momentous an event as the conversion of
England had hung.[1] This instance seems to hint at the almost divinely-
ordained character of the figures of *retorik*: what on the surface may seem
a fault (the propensity of some words to look and sound alike) can be
turned to a source of strength and salvation through the *maistrie* of God (a

---

1 Leech, *Linguistic Guide*, 214, notes this case. For the original, where Gregory
follows on with more puns on *de ira* and *alleluia*, see Bede's *Historia Ecclesiastica*,
II i, in Plummer, ed., *Opera*, p. 80.

theme I discuss in section IV. D. below). Just as in Lewtee's words, quoted as epigraph to this chapter, *retorik* is closely allied with both cognitive and moral values (telling *sothe*, rebuking *synne*), so I would argue, Langland's interest in language generally, as in the specific figures of the art of rhetoric, is indissolubly linked with his belief that words are a divine gift and the divinely-chosen means to bring about man's salvation.[2]

To spell out this last point in more detail: grace, the means to virtuous or *leel* living, comes through the words of God, given in Scripture and ritually embodied in the Liturgy, *lele wordes* which are the *lawe of Holy Chirche* (XVI 6). The *divine* 'use' of words[3] may be regarded as its norm or absolute standard: according to it, words operate sacramentally, enacting that which they signify, as in the miracle at Cana ('He wroghte that by no wit but thorugh word oone', XIX 122), where only material elements undergo transformation, or in the Eucharist, where the full power of the sacrament is revealed only in the transformation of the recipient's soul.[4] Langland, without being in any sense a 'Wycliffite', places a remarkable stress on the spiritual value of the *word*, which Patience sees as essential for man's soul in the way that *wortes* can be for animals, which live

> by gras and by greyn and by grene rootes,
> In menynge that alle men myghte the same
> Lyve thorugh leel bileve and love . . .
>
>   . . .
>
>   . . . *Non in solo pane vivit homo, set in omni verbo,*
> *quod procedit de ore Dei*   (XIV 46–47a).

Not only is nature seen as having sacramental *menynge* for man's life, as in the famous poem of Alanus which calls *Omnis mundi creatura* a 'fidele signaculum' to man,[5] but the *actual verbum Dei* (scripture, sacrament) is envisaged as food, feeding man's soul almost as a bird feeds its young, by direct oral contact.

It is against some such background of thought that we should understand Patience's image of the Paternoster as able to be broken into 'pieces' (*verbum = panis*) and eaten, creating in the soul of the man who prays such

---

2 See esp. IX 101ff, and the discussion in Ch. 1, pp. 10–11 above.
3 On 'use' see further pp. 124–5 below.
4 Christ acts 'After the kynde that he cam of' (XIX 123), which recalls the potency of the divine Word at XIV 60–1. Langland's relating of 'the word of Christ' to 'that . . . whereby all things are made' suggests indebtedness to the teaching of St Ambrose on the sacraments, who sees 'the heavenly word' as that which is 'effectual in the heavenly sacraments' (*On the Sacraments*, ed. J. H. Srawley (1950) 86–90), Botte, ed., *Ambroise*, p. 110, for the original.
5 For the text see Raby, *Oxford Book of Medieval Latin Verse*, no. 242, st.1.

spiritual virtues as patience, which enable him to endure the lack of actual *physical* food (XIV 48–59*a*), on the model of the hermit saints whose sustenance was 'mynde of God Almyghty' (XV 295). There is a special emblematic significance, therefore, in the fact that Patience offers Haukyn the Waferer 'food' made up of words that are both exemplarily *de ore Dei* ('the *Lord's* prayer') and become man's own as he utters or 'eats' them in his action of praying. For it is through God's creative 'breeth' that 'men and beestes *lyven*' (XIV 61) – each at their appropriate level in the scale of being – even though most people, like Haukyn, are too 'buxom and busy aboute breed and drynke' (*solo pane*) to apprehend the sinful and sterile character of their 'unbuxom speche' (XIII 251, 275).[6] Valuable as is the bread that this 'type of the common man' (Eliot's phrase)[7] brings forth, it is a bread that feeds only the beast in man, and is insufficient for a spiritual being to *live* by.

Haukyn's neglect of prayer, then – that 'word' which *is* 'bread' – is revealed in his lack of 'spiritual helthe' (XIV 284). Stained by 'wrathe and wikkede wille', he has a 'fals tonge' that utters 'yvel speche', and a 'leve tonge' only to 'chide' (XIII 320, 327, 321, 322). For all this, 'Actif' *is* on a higher plane than his precursor in the Field of Folk, Wrath, who made 'wortes' out of 'wikkede wordes' (V 160) – was not merely preoccupied with *panis* and indifferent to *verbum Dei*, but 'actively' disgorged his spiritual venom as a food for others to consume and be corrupted by. Wrath corrupts speech into sinful action: for just as *wortes* is an easy auditory deformation of *wordes*, it is also visually very close to *workes*, the *anti*-sacramental 'enactment', so to speak, of *wikkede wille*. Angry words, Langland indicates, are at the opposite pole from that responsible *retorik* that relies on *sothe* as the 'leel' and *licitum* basis for rebuking sin: untruth or lying is the first stage to actual violence, as in the simultaneously comic and disturbing scene of the fighting nuns:

> Of wikkede wordes I Wrathe hire wortes made,
> Til 'Thow lixt!' and 'Thow lixt!' lopen out at ones
> And either hitte oother under the cheke   (V 160–2).

The relationship and the contrast between Haukyn and Wrathe is very plainly brought out in the matter of their attitude to punishment. Wrath can learn only by being 'baleised on the bare ers' like a 'child' (V 173), whereas Haukyn, though impressed by the utility of *payn defaute* as a divine chastisement, has a potentially *adult* moral sense that 'may no blessynge doon us boote but if we wile *amende*' (XIII 257). It is this that

6 See further my study of 'Langland's Structural Imagery', 320ff, and the article by Jill Mann, 'Eating and Drinking in *PP*' in D. Mehl, ed., *Essays and Studies* (1979) 26–43.
7 *Murder in the Cathedral*, final chorus; *Complete Poems and Plays*, p. 282.

enables him to receive Patience's 'kenning' and so reach an authentic sense of sinfulness from which true conversion can grow. Thus his lines

> 'So hard it is . . . to lyve and to do synne.
> Synne seweth us evere' . . . and sory gan wexe(XIV 322–3)

not only echo, they also contrast with, the 'unbuxom' words of another of his precursors from the Field, Envy: 'I am evere sory . . . I am but selde oother' (V 126); for through them glimmers real understanding of the difference between *hard* as 'harsh' and its inadmissible anti-pun[8] 'difficult' (sinning is all *too* easy).

The hardness of *Patience*'s task, as Haukyn's teacher, is that of finding words that will adequately explain what virtue and the values of a more spiritual existence are 'proprely to mene' (XIV 274), a task which I discussed at the beginning of Chapter Three. On the face of it, there is something almost perverse in the way he goes about instructing his *lewed* interlocutor by breaking up bits of his Latin text on the virtue of Poverty and feeding them to Haukyn as if he were a 'beest'. But the apparent perversity can, I think, be explained if we recall the other structural relationship in which Haukyn stands – his relationship with Will. For insofar as Will is not himself a 'person' or 'preest', one of the clergy bound by the silence of the confessional, he is (though formally a clerk) close to such *lewed men* as Actif, and authorised to 'arate dedly synne' because he recognises in it all men's sin, including his own. To put it another way, in the person of Haukyn he is himself undergoing instruction in the *leel* signification of that virtue which he can, as a clerk, define: he is allowing the *verbum* to become *panis* for the sake of his own spiritual health. Thus when Patience calls poverty both *cura animarum* 'that which takes care of souls' and *remocio curarum* 'the removal of cares from the soul' (XIV 285, 289a) he is saying something which goes beyond the immediate comprehension of Haukyn the *lewed man* to appeal to that of Will the *clerk* (and, of course, the clerkly audience for whom he is writing). The two *Latin* phrases (one enclosed, one appended) need to be 'construed' in response to the challenge posed by their apparent formal identity (English 'cure' and 'care' are the same word, *cura*,[9] in the tongue of clerks): only then can their lesson be 'kenned'.

---

8 The 'anti-pun' is Christopher Ricks's name for the kind of pun 'which creates its double meaning by evoking but excluding' (*The Force of Poetry*, p. 174): A sense of a word is called up 'which the sense positively precludes'; 'that other sense is thereby surmised and then ruled out' (ibid. p. 100).

9 The two senses of *cura* given in Lewis and Short, *A Latin Dictionary*, s.v. I. A.2(c) and II are *co-polysemes* (separate senses of the same lexical item) for which ME has two distinct *lexemes*, respectively *cure* (*MED* s.v. 5(e)) and *care*, n.

Now on the face of it, Langland's procedure here would seem to imply the inherent insufficiency of the vernacular for the purpose of 'expouning' what a crucial idea is 'proprely to mene', and the plausible corollary that direct access to scriptural knowledge must be kept from those who speak only, in Auden's phrase, 'the vulgar lingo / Of armed cities'.[10] But while it is true that Langland exhibits no marked preoccupation with the tendency of words to strain and sometimes break under the burden of meaning (Eliot, *Burnt Norton* V), let alone a quasi-mystical longing for the silence into which 'Words, after speech, reach' (ibid), he does, through his Latin wordplay, succeed in unsettling rather than in re-assuring. For such wordplay suggests that ambiguity, the chief (if not the sole) difficulty in 'expouning' proper meanings, is not a feature of the 'vulgar lingo' only but of language as such. What Langland's use of rhetorical wordplay serves to underline is the need for us to sharpen our awareness of and sensitivity to *all* forms of linguistic expression. If *speche* is, as Wit affirms, 'spire of grace' (IX 101), and if the responsible maker who is also a clerk tempers his 'fithele' (IX 103) 'the parfiter to ben' (XII 24), then his wordplay must also be a responsible exercise of *retorik*: a special and justifiable way of making words *work*.

Langland's attitude to the pun is one which captures *in parvo* his attitude to language as a whole: as something at once to be trusted in (because the Word revealed itself through words) and to be held suspect (because human, all too human). When a pun is 'made', whether in conversation or in poetry, an unusual degree of alertness is required from the hearer. Langland's unusual fondness for wordplay (it is not found amongst the other alliterative makers, except the *Pearl*-poet, to any extent) is suggestive of the kind and degree of attentiveness his poetry demands. Langland has his certainties, but they are certainties of faith, not certainties about the words in which, perforce, beliefs must find expression. Contrasting two very different kinds of writer, Samuel Johnson and Geoffrey Hill, Christopher Ricks remarks:

> Clearly there is an art, an allegiance, a strong choice of life, which will distrust any amalgam of the forthright and the tentative, or of the forthright and the treacherous . . . But there is need for an art of dubiety as well as the art of indubitability.[11]

I agree with this, but think that Ricks's dichotomy does not cover an art such as Langland's. He has Johnson's certainty about faith, but not his certainty about language. And he has Hill's dubiety about speech, but not his dubiety about faith. His puns always create a sense of insecurity, even

10 *The Age of Anxiety*, in E. Mendelson, ed., *Collected Poems* (1976), p. 373.
11 *The Force of Poetry*, p. 315.

in those cases where a certain route out of the ambiguity is finally indicated. I believe this to be intentional: man must not live by the word alone any more than by bread alone, unless it is to be the *verbum quod procedit de ore Dei*, a 'word' which is not construed by the intellect but grasped 'thorugh wil oone' (XV 210). The discussion which follows, concentrating as it does on the detailed working of Langland's *verbal* art, should be read not only in the context of these ideas but with a recognition that an 'amalgam of the forthright and the tentative' accurately describes his view of how the language of religious poetry necessarily functions.

II.   ANNOMINATIVE CHIME AND ANTI-CHIME

There are over 180 examples of punning wordplay in the B-text,[12] and about 200 in C, such as the revised passage on *restitue / rest* in C X 54–5 (discussed p. 106 above) or the following, which will serve to introduce this section. Revising Piers' words to the Knight about the levelling power of death:

> For in charnel at chirche cherles ben yvel to knowe,
> Or a knyght from a knave there – knowe this in thyn herte
>
> (VI 48–9)

he replaces the somewhat slack final b-half with 'or a quene fram a queene' (C VIII 46). Here the gap between the two vowel-sounds in *quene* and *queene* (slack and tense *e* respectively),[13] though so slight that Chaucer was willing to rhyme words containing them,[14] is nonetheless phonemic in English, generating senses for the lexemes as distinct, though not as distant, as those in *creatour* and *creature* at XVI 215.[15] But the importance of the revision is that it concentrates attention on the form ('phonetic/graphetic configuration') of the two lexemes so as to engender more dubieties than can be certainly resolved. The bones of common

---

12 The pioneering study is B. F. Huppé, '*Petrus id est Christus*: Word Play in *PP*, B' (*ELH* 17 (1950) 163–91) which covers chime ('vowel harmony') as well as homophony and polysemy. See also J. Lawlor, *PP: an Essay in Criticism* 265–77, W. W. Ryan, 'Word-Play in some OE Homilies and a Late ME Poem' in Atwood and Hill, eds, *Studies . . .* , and J. Dillon, '*PP*: Word-Play and its Structural Significance', *MÆ* 50 (1981) 40–9 (this last unconvincing in many examples). Huppé notes acutely that the various rhetorical devices 'represent a deliberate conscious use of identity and difference in the sound of words. They approximate the pun in enforcing meaning through sound' (art. cit. 164).

13 See *MED* s.v. *quene* n(1) and *quen(e* n(2). The relevant sense of *quene* (1) here is 'a lowborn woman . . . a harlot'.

14 Contrast *Troilus* V 1026–7, *nede: brede* (/e:/) with II 671–2, *nede: drede* (/ɛ:/).

15 For discussion of this see my 'Speech, Silence, Words and Voices', 21–2.

woman and royal lady cannot certainly (or rather, certainly cannot) be told apart, even if their names can (though not always indubitably, since identical spellings for both exist): so is there any real, essential difference between them? In the world, the answer may be given, there is an actual, if not a real difference: for death, and what follows death – divine judgement – will alone finally settle what is really real for us (obliterating the transitory distinction between real and actual). And in the next life, even *queen* may not mean what it means here (we may remember in this regard the Dreamer's perplexity in *Pearl* 492).

Now what this example illustrates is not the polysemantic *or* the homonymic pun, but what may be called the *quasi-pun* or chime,[16] in the language of the rhetoricians *annominatio* or *paronomasia*.[17] In the *chime* we have, to quote Isidore of Seville, 'almost the same word in a different sense' or, in Alexander of Villedieu's formulation, 'words almost identical, signifying different things'.[18] Isidore's example, *abire an obire te convenit*, with its pararhyme on the opposed morpheme prefixes, illustrates exactly the same figure of words that we find in the *quene / queene* example or in Conscience's description of Mede as 'tikel of hire tail, talewis of tonge' (III 131). Here *tail* and *tale* chime together, and their annominative collocation helps to associate *tail* also with *tonge*. But the pun proper (or improper) is located not in the nouns but in the first adjective, which here combines *OED* senses 3b 'easily affected . . . loose . . . with reference to incontinency' (quoting this line), in reference to the *tail*, with sense 5, 'uncertain, unreliable', in secondary reference to *tonge*, to which it is attracted both by the alliteration of first and fourth lifts and by the cross-caesural annominative pararhyme *tail / tale-*[19] (there may also be a

16 Leech, *Linguistic Guide* 209–12, discusses chime under 'jingles' or approximate homonymic puns but follows Empson in applying the *term* 'chiming' to words phonetically bonded by links as diverse as alliteration and pararhyme (*foul/fair*; *big/beg*gar'd, p. 95). Despite *OED*'s 'mere rhyme, *jingle*' under *chime* 6b I prefer that term as more susceptible of non-pejorative use today than *jingle* and apply it to both Leech's 'jingles' and his pararhyming (but not simply alliterating) cases of 'chiming'.

17 Despite some differences in usage, the overlap between these two terms is extensive, and I see no advantage in distinguishing between them here.

18 *Etym.* I xxxvi 12: 'in significatione diversa dictio *paene* ipsa'; *Doctrinale* 2474: 'voces, *paene* pares quae sunt, diversa notantes'. Both definitions exclude the strict pun but include additionally to Gervase of Melkley's 'similitudo literarum vel sillabarum' (*Ars Poetica* p. 16) an explicit reference to the difference of meaning accompanying similarity of form. In the definition of Donatus (*Ars Grammatica* III 5) paronomasia is 'veluti quaedam denominatio' (ed. Keil, p. 398) but his example (*amentium/amantium*) tacitly suggests that difference of sense as well as likeness of form is a relevant feature of this figure.

19 In Leech's terms both illustrate 'chiming', but in mine only the pararhyme example counts.

proper pun on *tail* 'pudendum' and 'score or account', the latter under *OED* sb.² sense 4).

In the next example, there is no chime, so the polysemantic wordplay dominates, and there seems to be no significant subsidiary pun on *tail*, when Anima enjoins clerks to be 'Trewe of youre tonge and of youre tail bothe' (XV 105). Here *trewe* first means 'telling the truth' and then 'living a chaste life', both given under *OED* sense 3 (the latter a special sense of the general 'virtuous'). There is 'doubleness of sense', that *duplex sensus ex verbis* which Alexander of Villedieu calls *amphibologia*.[20] But amphibology here does not entail ambiguity[21] in the common sense of that word in prose contexts – uncertainty as to which of two possible meanings is intended; for the qualifying *tonge* and *tail* phrases serve to specify that speech and sex respectively are intended, while at the same time the use of a single adjective with reference to both underlines what verbal and sexual integrity are deemed to have in common – 'truth'. Elsewhere, however, there is genuine ambiguity, with its characteristic uncertainty or dubiety, as in these lines, already discussed in Chapter II section vii under pararhyme:

> For blood may suffre blood bothe hungry and acale,
> Ac blood may noght se blood blede, but hym rewe
>
> (XVIII 395–6).

The first three appearances of *blood* carry the single clear sense 'one who is related to another by blood' (*MED* s.v. 6c), but the fourth acquires a real ambiguity through its abrupt juxtaposition with the gradational *blede*, which partially 'retro-activates' the co-polyseme[22] 'blood' (*MED* s.v. 1). The shock remains even when the ambiguity is satisfactorily resolved, as it easily may be: for Langland has powerfully reminded us, in an image fraught with deep theological meaning, of the inescapably literal basis of what we casually call 'blood-relationship'.[23] It is not least among those *archana verba* which he goes on to say *non licet homini loqui*.

The distinction I have drawn between pun and chime is a clear one, but it should not come as a surprise to discover that actual examples reveal on analysis a complex structure that resists too rigid a separation of the two. Alexander of Villedieu's definition of *paronomasia* as 'voces, paene pares quae sunt, diversa notantes', which he illustrates with the example 'non curas vera, sed aera' (*Doctrinale* 2474–5) usefully covers the following, from Anima's criticism of the endowed clergy:

---

20 'Sive duplex sensus ex verbis possit haberi' (*Doctrinale* 2403). See Section IV.
21 As in *Troilus* IV 1406, the only recorded use in ME, where 'duplicity' is implied.
22 The separate senses of a word with multiple meaning are its co-polysemes.
23 Langland sees Christ's 'kinship' *with* man (through the Incarnation) as ratified by his shedding of blood *for* man (in the Passion).

A medicyne moot therto that may amende prelates,
That sholden preie for the pees; possession hem *letteth*.
Taketh hire landes, ye lordes, and *leteth* hem lyve by dymes
(XV 560–2).

Now the contrast or opposition here between the two italicised words is even smaller than that between *quene* and *queene* in C VIII 46 (discussed above p. 113), a matter not of quality but of quantity in the vowels, and it is reduced still further by the unstress on *leteth* as against *queene*, which carries equal stress with its partner in chime. But it is real enough nonetheless, and partly, I think, because a semantic as well as a purely formal relationship is set up between the two lexemes, their very similarity in form (*voces paene pares*) ironically highlighting their difference in sense (*diversa notantes*). Thus some of the force of *letteth* 'prevents' is communicated to *leteth* 'allow', so that Anima's injunction to the lords adds up to the statement 'Prevent them from living on endowments by making them live on tithes' (or, 'Make them live on tithes by preventing them from living on endowments', which is much the same). Lack of 'possession' will then *let* them pray.

The next example illustrates what may be described as an 'anti-chime', an expression I model on Christopher Ricks' 'anti-pun, by which another sense of a word is called up only to be fended off' and in which 'there is only one sense admitted but there is another sense denied admission':[24]

They dorste noght loke on Oure Lord, the [lothli]este of hem alle,
But *leten* hym lede forth what hym liked and *lete* what hym liste
(XVIII 406–7).

In this scene from the Harrowing of Hell, the devils' inability to prevent Christ from freeing the patriarchs is further emphasised, I believe, by the anti-chime on *letten* 'prevent'. By its very absence, this verb takes on a shadowy or phantasmal 'presence' (though 'denied admission', in Ricks' phrase, more effectively than Christ!), through the double stress on the co-polysemes with which it pararhymes (*MED* senses 1 and 5a of *leten*, 'allow' and 'leave'). The line belongs to the rare type Id, the 'enriched extended', like Pr 126, and coming after another *l*-alliterating line, it sums up with slow, hollowly-echoing finality, the final failure of Satan's attempt to 'let' the divine purpose and plan.

A second example of an anti-chime or, more precisely, of an anti-pun (if the two lexemes do not differ in quantity) occurs in this passage of direct exhortation to 'lords' not to seek worldly recognition for their charitable actions:

---

24 *The Force of Poetry*, pp 142, 265. Ricks does not distinguish chime from pun.

Reding in Retorik

On aventure ye *have[n]* youre hire here and youre *hevene* als

(III 72).

Like XVIII 407, this is a Type Id line, scanning on vowels, with internal a-half pararhyme (*hire/here*) and cross-caesural chime on lifts 1 and 4 (*haven/hevene*).[25] A small emendation to MS W's *have* seems justified on the presumption that Langland generally favoured the older full forms,[26] but it is inevitably bound to make this example less 'indubitable' than the previous one. Accepting *haven* with long vowel – the quantity was variable – we see generated a powerful opposition between the materialistic conception of divine *mede* (as a 'hire' paid here on earth) and the more spiritual one, the true heaven which the lords are in danger of bringing down to earth.[27] But *haven* also evokes its anti-pun (or, if its vowel is short, its anti-chime) *haven* (*MED* n. 1) 'a port or harbour' which had the figurative sense of 'salvation, eternal life' (ibid. under (c)): evokes, only to deny admission, for *haven* (s.v. n. 2, 'possession') is no 'haven' of salvation in reality, because only the *rejection* of material values can ensure the final winning of eternal 'treasure'.

III. FROM CHIME TO HOMOPHONE

'Heaven' is so central, so pivotal an idea in *Piers Plowman*, from the moment we see it imaged in the 'tour on a toft' of Pr 14 and its dominant role in the speech of Holy Church (I 111–59) as the sublime dwelling-place of God, that it not surprisingly figures more than once in various types of wordplay. One of the examples least open to dubiety occurs in Patience's speech on the degrees of love, which quotes from the teaching of his *lemman* of that name:

'With wordes and with werkes', quod she, 'and wil of thyn herte
Thow love leelly thi soule al thi lif tyme.
And so thow lere the to lovye, for the Lordes love of *hevene*,
Thyn enemy in alle wise *evene*forth with thiselve'   (XIII 140–3).

---

25 The homophonic play on aven*ture* and *haven*, suggesting a link between notions of transience and possession, though present, is diminished in force by the first homophone's appearance in the anacrusis.
26 On the probably conservative character of his linguistic forms, see M. L. Samuels, 'Langland's Dialect' (*MÆ* LIV (1985)) 238, 244.
27 This example and several like it are sensitively discussed by James Simpson in 'The Transformation of Meaning: a Figure of Thought in *PP*' (*RES* 37 (1986)).

Here the running alliteration of 141–2 terminates in a 'translinear key-stave' that rhymes identically (or else chimes, depending on the quantity of the vowel in *evene*) with the structural key-stave of 143. The result is both to give greater prominence to the staves themselves and to draw them into the closest association, with important semantic consequences. What we realise is that to love 'for the love of Heaven's lord' (the literal sense of the idiom) but also 'with the heavenly-love typical of that Lord – viz. charity' (a phrasal rather than a verbal *amphibologia*) *is* to love one's enemy 'equally with' oneself, for it is to love as God loves and so to make 'all even'.

In the second example of this pun, a more cerebral and less spiritual aspect of the *heaven* / *even* nexus is exploited. In attacking the unregulated multiplication of friars, a common complaint of the time, Conscience evokes the medieval normative concept of number as something finished, perfect, rounded and complete,[28] a notion integral to the view of celestial form that underlies the structure of the *Divine Comedy* or *Pearl*:

> kynde wit me telleth
> It is wikked to wage yow – ye wexen out of noumbre!
> *Hevene* hath *evene* noumbre, and helle is withoute noumbre
>
> (XX 268–70).

Now for this passage to make sense it must be noted that *evene* does not simply denote (as *MED* s.v. 5 has it) 'of numbers, even not odd' – that is, divisible by 2 as opposed to having 'one left over', *impair*. Rather it implies 'fixed, finished, incapable of being added to by one without becoming *in*complete', and the contrast is with a state in which the occupants are in chaos, not orderly and harmonious, as well as one of indefinite quantitative extent. The lines need to be read in conjunction with XIII 142–3, since the 'numerical' nature of heaven is plainly connected with the moral and spiritual quality of its Lord – who, loving *eveneforth* with himself, must be deemed to love without limit, *withoute noumbre* in the sense of 'without quantitative limit to his love – *sc.* since he is infinite'. The dizzying element of paradox latent here is very characteristic of Langland, who may well have been supposing an etymological link between (the apparently unrelated) *heaven* and *heavy* in Holy Church's startling image of divine love as a sort of Titanic fish that cannot be restrained in the celestial net:

> For *hevene* myghte nat holden it, so was it *hevy* of hymself
>
> (I 153).

---

28 Commenting on 'quantum mysterium [numeri] habent' Isidore remarks: 'Tolle numerum in rebus omnibus, et omnia pereunt' (*Etym.* III.iv).

Langland might have found small grounds for such speculations in the paragraph of Isidore's *Etymologies* devoted to *caelum* 'heaven' (III. xxxi), but he may well have found inspiration in the section 'De Paganis' (VIII. x) for his brilliantly inventive piece of oppositive chiming in Anima's words about baptism:

> And so it fareth by a barn that born is of wombe:
> Til it be cristned in Cristes name and confermed of the bisshop,
> It is *hethene* as to *hevene*ward, and helplees to the soule.
> 'Hethen' is to mene after heeth and untiled erthe . . .
>
> (XV 454–7).

The 'barn' born merely 'of wombe', of the natural order, belongs merely to 'erthe'; but the child 'cristned in Cristes name' leaves earth for heaven, since the Incarnate Word has 'of the erthe eten his fille' (I 154). However, the inexplicable affinity between God and Man, heaven and earth, seems miraculously and almost magically reflected in that indubitable anno-minative nexus between *hethene* and *hevene* (a perfect homophony if the latter's vowel is long, as it was in some usages). There is of course no hint of this wordplay in Isidore, but the example illustrates Langland's mind at its most clerkly, while also testifying to that real element of childlike pleasure in the properties of words which Lewis Carroll captures in the absurd etymologies of Alice (not more absurd than some of Isidore's) and which underlies the pleasure that the unsophisticated have always taken in the pun. For a pun always implies pattern; and even as it 'defam-iliarises' (who would have thought 'heathen' and 'heaven' could be connected?) it suggests a mysterious order in reality,[29] *archana que licet homini loqui* – if only he can find the right *verba*.

IV.   CLERKLY POLYSEMY[30]

A.   *Cardinals and Commons*

This quasi-magical approach to etymological wordplay may seem close to the 'primitive grammatical Platonism' discussed in Chapter Three (see p.

29 Lawlor notes how wordplay serves 'to bring before us the riddling complex-ities of a universe which both reveals and hides itself' (op. cit. 271).
30 Lack of space prevents any discussion here of an important subject that deserves study – Langland's debt to medieval Latin religious poets of the 12th and 13th centuries. On John of Hoveden see my 'Treatment of the Crucifixion in *PP*' (*Anal. Cart.* 33 (1983) esp. 180–1) and generally W. J. Ong, 'Wit and Mystery', *Spec.* 22 (1947), esp. 315.

90 above); but in addition to a spontaneous and *lewed* delight like that the simplest feel on connecting 'heathen' with 'heath' and then with 'heaven', there is the more rigorously 'clerkly' attitude which we find in the (not unironically named) 'lewed vicory' of XIX 412. This 'curatour of Holy Kirke', unlike his predecessor whom Piers had called a 'lewed lorel' (VII 137), wishes Piers well (XIX 429ff); yet he seems highly sceptical of that Conscience which Piers claimed had 'kenned' him (with VII 134 compare XIX 414, 454). It is not difficult to feel that there is no real 'dubiety' in his position: what he is attacking is not the cardinal virtues *per se* but rather what they have become in the usage of a corrupt clergy and a disillusioned laity. For in the actual world of his experience

> alle tho faire vertues, as vices thei semeth,
> Ech man subtileth a sleighte synne to hide,
> And coloureth it for a konnynge   (XIX 459–61)

so that the *peccata* of Ps 50 are no longer *tecta* 'In a dissh of derne shrifte', (XIII 54) but only under *ypocrisie*, that 'wal . . . whitlymed and . . . foul withinne' of which Anima speaks (XV 113). For the *vicory*, 'Cardinal Vertues' is just an implausible character whose very name sounds like an oxymoron.

Now the attitude we observe in what I have called the vicory's 'clerkly scepticism' is one of a refusal to endorse the privileged status of a purely etymological account of language. It may well be that 'cardinal' comes from *cardo* 'a hinge' and that the divine authority resides

> Amonges foure vertues, most vertuous of alle vertues,
> That cardinals ben called and closynge yates[31]   (Pr 103–4)

but experience shows that when the actual cardinals 'that kaughte of that name' (Pr 107) 'coome among the comune peple' (XIX 423) they bring with them only lechery and greed. What prevents the corrupt actuality from totally undermining the credibility of the divine ideal (which to faith must also be the real) is Langland's own 'clerkly' awareness, already anticipated in the glowing lines of the Prologue passage quoted above, that even *lele wordes* can become mere *bele paroles* when they grow on a tree whose 'roote is roten' (XV 101).[32] This is illustrated by the play on the two senses of *vertues* (*OED* s.v. 1 and 2) 'powers' and 'moral excellence' in the phrase 'most vertuous of alle vertues' (Pr 103), which requires that the 'power' left to Peter in Pr 100 should be an authority based on spiritual

---

31 The gates in question are those of heaven (see Pr 105–6) and Langland may be playing on the secondary sense of 'cardines caeli . . . extremae partes . . . axis . . . dictae . . . eo, quod per eos vertitur caelum' (*Etym.* III.xxxviii).
32 On this theme see my '*Lele Wordes* . . .', *RES* 34 (1983) esp. 139–41.

goodness and not be confused with, or degenerate into, the 'power' that the Cardinals at court 'presumed' in themselves (Pr 108), however legitimate in theory their procedure and action was. In other words, although Langland affirms the objective character of religious order and the legitimacy of its institutional embodiments, he does not simply equate authority with office, or confound virtue in power. This means that he can recognise the truth in the vicory's criticism without necessarily committing himself to either radical heterodoxy (equating authority only with virtue) or to total cynicism (denying that there is any need to distinguish between virtue and power).[33]

If it seems fair to say that the cynical attitude is voiced by the 'unblessed' brewer on whom Conscience rounds so fiercely (XIX 407) it is nonetheless not correct to identify the vicory's position as the radical one *tout court*. This is shown by the way in which Conscience's cry

> But Conscience be the *comune fode*, and Cardinale Vertues,
> Leve it wel, thei ben lost, bothe lif and soule   (XIX 410–11)

is taken up by the vicory in his protest that when the only cardinals he meets arrive – from the Pope –

> . . . we clerkes, whan thei come, for hir *comunes* paieth

and

> The comune *clamat cotidie*, ech a man til oother,
> 'The contree is the corseder that cardinals come inne'
> (XIX 416–17, 419).

Now properly understood this passage does not constitute a formal rejection of Conscience's stipulation, so much as a realistic assessment of its likely chances of being realised. The vicory does not deny the need of spiritual food for the people in stressing the compulsion to provide literal food for the 'powers' – the 'Cardinal Vertues' that conceal from the *commune* any sustaining experience of the cardinal *virtues*. The commons' quotidian cry is a heartfelt call for *panem quotidianum*, that 'pece of the Paternoster' on which Patience himself relied for his name and nature – *Fiat voluntas tua* (XIV 48–9). Langland's own 'position' – if it may be judged wise to express it so – can only be 'construed' by setting the ideal language of Conscience in dialectical relationship with the 'actual' speech of the vicory: for the 'real' is only to be constituted thus, in the visionary blindness and dark clarity of a troubled but unbroken faith.[34] The truth about words is that, like the sacraments, they belong to man's pilgrim life

---

33 See on this P. Gradon, 'Langland and the Ideology of Dissent', 197–200.
34 See further 'Langland's Structural Imagery' 322–4 and 'Dominant Ideology', a review in *EC* 33 (1983) esp. 240–2.

on earth, to the existence of those who are called but not yet safe in their true *haven*, where there will be no need for either sacraments or for language.

As I see it, the vicory's *lewednesse* is no more literal than the 'learning' displayed by Piers in his quoting of Latin; it is not that he is unable through ignorance to recognise the spiritual significance of cardinals as much as of cardinal virtues, but rather that he voices the testimony of experience as against authority, and his 'lewdness' as a clerk, far from condemning him, lends substance to his charge, which is a 'leggyng the sothe' concerning 'Thyng that al the world woot' (XI 96, 101) and would doubtless be regarded as *licitum* by Lewtee. He speaks not only for 'we clerkes' but also for the *comune*, those who in the Prologue 'crye in vers of Latyn' (143) but cannot construe the reality of power – and the potential danger – concealed in the maxim they mouth. The *comune* who find the cardinals a 'curse' upon the land could, under the leadership of a John Ball,[35] prove a threat to both authority and office in the Church, and one may well doubt whether Langland would have left these lines unrevised in C had he lived. But there is no need to speculate as to whether Langland would have presented the *comune* in a more critical light after witnessing the events of the Peasants' Revolt of 1381, for there is evidence already in B that he sensed the tension between two key meanings of the word that were important to him – 'general or universal' and 'low, inferior' (respectively *MED* senses 7 and 8).

In the Prologue, the *commune* may be seen as one estate, contrasted with the other two, who have a directive role over the lowest order:

> The Kyng and Knyghthod and Clergie bothe
> Casten that the Commune sholde hem [communes] fynde
>
> (Pr 116–7).

Even if the emendation from C[36] replacing the B-archetype's *self* is not accepted, it remains the case that the referent is an inclusive one, as l. 119 makes clear: the common people in their representative role are to provide for *all* through furnishing – from among their number, of course – the basic productive class of the ploughmen: a hierarchy of roles is envisaged, but not a conflict of interests. And in Passus I Holy Church gives a reason for presuming that a just social order will indeed be

---

35 On Ball's teaching see Berners' *Froissart* (ed. Macaulay, 1913) ch. CCCLXXXI, p. 251, and M. H. Keen, *England in the Later Middle Ages* (1973) 271–3. I question Keen's point that Langland's 'conservative social philosophy' is 'naive' (p. 273), though agreeing that it is too idealistic to constitute a specific social programme.

36 Kane-Donaldson (*B-Text*, p. 92) here rightly discern 'elimination of the pun' as a sign of archetypal corruption of the B-original (taken to read as in C).

possible if it is based on the law of God, who 'comaunded of his curteisie in commune three thynges' (I 20). The stress on the first lift here brings it into collocation with *commune* (whether or not this stave is muted to give a 'T'-type line) so as to suggest how the *common* good is the object of a divine *command*: individual goods are not 'nedfulle' (= strictly necessary) and are not the result of an ordinance of the Creator. The word *curteisie* is also important here:[37] God's act is one of generous service and something deserving of imitation by the members of all the estates, each in his own way, as is shown in the interchange of services between Piers and the Knight who 'curteisly' utters his (or understands Piers') words (VI 33). Because men have common needs and a common end (in the sense of both 'purpose in life' and 'mortal nature'), they must do their work not separately (even the *lif-holy* hermits Anima mentions need their frugal requirements to be met by the 'curteisie' of *lawefulle men* – members of the *commune*; see XV 308, 303) but *in commune* 'together'. In the ideal Christendom ordained by Grace in Passus XIX all are to be 'lele, and ech a craft love oother' (XIX 251); though some must inevitably be lower than others, this does not make them 'lower' in an absolute sense, and amongst the 'higher' orders, 'who that moost maistries kan, be myldest of berynge' (XIX 257).

This is the ideal order of things, a social system in which 'curteisie' will prevail between the classes, being not a specifically 'class' quality but a spiritual one that should be 'common' to all. But *Piers Plowman*, although it both envisions and urgently presses for a restoration of original Christian values as the only solution to social collapse, also reflects faithfully the actualities of contemporary England, and not least of the common people. Thus while he may see one degraded institution, the brothel, as sustained in existence by the rich and not the poor (XIV 251–2) Langland is aware that the usual euphemism for prostitute, *commune womman*, points to a reality that does little credit to the *commune* itself. For the majority of the *commune*, if they were not rich, were not poor either, but rather *mene* 'ordinary', 'commonplace'[38] (cf. *MED* s.v. 2(d)); in addition to the Lady Medes there were those like the *commune womman* who keeps *compaignie* with the Pardoner in VI 641. Thus while it is true that in the trial at Westminster, Mede is condemned by 'the mooste peple' (IV 159) as well as the authoritative 'rightfulle' (157), we cannot feel secure in equating these two. So when we are told that

---

37 For discussion of this phrase in context see my note in *NQ* 31 (1984) 153–6.
38 When Haukyn, the representative 'common man', asks Patience 'What is poverte . . . proprely to mene?' (XIV 274) it is not his own condition he wishes to have explained to him.

Mede mornede tho, and made hevy chere,
For the mooste *commune* of that court called hire an hore
(IV 165–6)

it is difficult to avoid sensing the phantasmal presence of the phrase *commune hore* and to wonder whether the point is that the 'mooste commune' see Mede for what she is, despite her finery, because they have first-hand knowledge of 'common' *commune wommen* and know the type whenever they see it. (In C IV 161 this line removes *mooste* and *of that court* and replaces *hore* by (as I have argued elsewhere)[39] the compound phrase *queynte-comune hore*. The revision makes *commune* itself even less susceptible of a commendatory sense than in B).

B.   Right Use and the Righteous

Langland's great strength as a poet, it seems to me (and this is a product of his being a clerk as well as a maker), is that he does not in fact confuse the 'right' *use* of a word with its 'true' *meaning*. His practice shows him aware that 'the meaning of a word is its use in the language';[40] there is, after all, no way of regulating meaning (in the sense of 'the way people use words'): words will be words because people are only people – fallen creatures using a fallen speech marked by provisionality and imperfection. But even if there is no 'true' *meaning* to which a word like *commune* can be compelled to conform, there may be a 'right' *use*, a use that makes for life in accordance with Truth (Truth having here a moral sense, as generally in Middle English, when the 'neutral' term is the now obsolete *sooth*). This 'right' use may be called the *lele* use of language, though Langland of course speaks of *lele* 'words' (XVI 6) not of *lele* uses, just as the *Gawain*-poet, too, speaks of 'lel letteres loken' (*SGGK* 35) and not 'letteres lelly loken': both predicate the quality of the thing used rather than of the manner of use or the user's attitude. Anima describes the leaves of the Tree of Charity as being 'lele wordes, the lawe of Holy Chirche' and the blossoms as 'buxom speche and benigne lokynge' (XVI 6–7) where, once again, the *buxumnesse* is a quality of the speaker (such as the Knight who proffers himself 'so faire' to Piers at VI 24) which will be reflected in his choice of words, rather than an intrinsic property of the words themselves. Conversely, the 'foule wordes' of such passages as X 40 are not individual lexical items as such (Langland, strikingly, does not shirk the 'broadness' of *ers-wynnynge* or *queynte-comune* at C VI 306 and IV 161) but words used in a way that corrupts instead of edifying, that rots the roots of the Christian community instead of encouraging the vigorous growth

39 See '*Lele Wordes* and *Bele Paroles*' p. 149.
40 Ludwig Wittgenstein, *Philosophical Investigations* (tr. Anscombe) I.43.

of the virtues – leaves, blossoms and 'the fruyt Charite' (XVI 9). The 'true meaning' of words for Langland, then, *is* their 'right use'.

Langland's alert awareness of how words will 'slip, slide . . . will not stay in place' can be illustrated from some examples of the words *right* and *rightful*, which reveal a salutary scepticism in the face of the supposed certainties they are used to embody. Ymaginatif, speaking in boldly figurative language of how the Incarnation was first revealed to *clannesse* (the shepherds) and *clerkes* (the Magi), observes that the Evangelist

> speketh there of riche men *right* noght, ne of *right* witty
>
> (XII 143).

On the face of it, this is the 'neutral' use of the intensifying adverb (*MED* s.v. adv. 3 (c) and (a)); but at least in the second the 'neutrality' of *right* begins to slide and perish: for if the Magi are both 'clerkes' and 'the hyeste lettred oute' (XII 144) then those who are merely 'witty' cannot be wise or clever *in the right way*, although *very* wise / clever. The underlying cause of the 'slippage' of sense is the 'pull' of *two* relevant anti-puns, *MED* senses 7(a) 'correctly' and 9(a) 'virtuously': for it is to men who were *right witty* in just those senses that the mysteries *were* revealed. The momentary certainty we will – quite understandably – have felt in *right noght* crumbles into dubiety as we reflect more closely upon the apparent repetition of the same word in *right witty*. But as there is a doubt which corrodes, so there is also a doubt which cleanses. Langland's verbal technique has as its aim to sharpen our attentiveness both to the thought and to the words available to express the thought.

This becomes clear in a second example, from Patience's attempt to 'expounen' Poverty in English to Haukyn:

> Selde is poore *right* riche but of *rightful* heritage   (XIV 291)

where it is the heavy first-stave stress engendered by the long onset that draws attention to (and nearly grants 'admission' to) the anti-pun 'correctly' (*MED* s.v. *right* 7(a)). The suggestion is, paradoxically, that the poor only become (the text actually has *are*) rich through a lawfully acquired inheritance; since they rarely become very (*right*) rich *save* in this way (and since, it is implied, those who *are* rich are rarely rightfully so), to become rich in any *other* way is to become rich un*righteously* (*MED* s,v. 9(a)). The effect here is one of what may be called 'retrospective toning', the moral senses of the adverb being drawn out only after we have encountered the succeeding adjective and absorbed the sense of the line as a whole.

A final, more emotionally charged and less elliptical case is that of Longeus' cry after he has pierced Christ's side and been cured of blindness by the blood from His wound:

'Have on me ruthe, *right*ful Jesu!' – and *right* with that he wepte
(XVIII 91).

On the surface, this only differs from XIV 291 in the order of the adjective
and the adverb, the latter here having the sense 'straight away' (*MED* s.v.
1c); but something of the 'moral' sense of *rightful* spills over into the
'neutral-intensive' adverb, so that the conjoint anti-pun 'correctly/piously'
(*MED* s.v. 7(a), 9(a)) so thrusts on, so throngs the ear that it virtually
(but not unvirtuously) gains admission as a real, and deeply serious
duplex sensus, double without duplicity. Langland shows how Longeus,
by appealing to the compassion (*ruthe*) of Jesus but simultaneously
acknowledging his justice (*rightful*) experiences in one miraculous mo-
ment both salvation and healing.[41] His weeping is both immediate and of
the proper kind, *right*, tears of conversion, from eyes opened by the
'portatif and persaunt' love of Christ (cf. I 157), tangibly and then visibly
present to him through his own act of 'foule vileynye' (XVIII 94):

The blood sprong doun by the spere and unspered the knyghtes eighen
(XVIII 86).

Since Longeus' *spere* proves a *spire of grace* to him (IX 101) he has not spilt
speech but has spoken *lele worde*s that have become part of the lore of Holy
Church.[42] The whole astonishing scene, one of the greatest moments in
the poem's greatest passus, pivots upon the deep duality of *ruthe* and
right, divine pity and that human conception of justice which performs a
'caytyves' deed while deeming it 'knyghthood' (XVIII 96).[43] The word
right, like the human construct it anti-puns into existence, perishes only
to be reconstituted under the 'sacramental' sign of repentance – tears.[44]

C. To Bid or not to Bid

The amphibologies so far examined occur in words which exact in specific
contexts an unusually high attentiveness; but there are others which ask a
more general vigilance, since they feature prominently not just in com-
mon speech but in the discussion of a major theme of the poem (as it was a
major issue of the time) – the relationship between mendicancy and

41 For the close link between these ideas, see '*Lele Wordes* . . .' 141–7 and cf.
Haukyn's comment at XIII 248–59.
42 In the *Legenda Aurea* (ed. Graesse) ch. 47 Longinus himself cures his blind
slayer posthumously; see further Peebles, *Legend of Longinus* (1911).
43 For valuable clarification of the idea of pity, see J. D. Burnley, *Chaucer's
Language and the Philosophers' Tradition* (1979) esp. 138–48.
44 For a celebrated instance of sacramental tears see *St Erkenwald* (ed. Morse)
309–40, esp. 314 (on which see Morse's note *ad loc*), 329–30. Burnley's remarks
on this scene (*Philosophers' Tradition*, 146) are slightly misleading.

holiness, prayer and poverty. The verb *bidden* had among its senses two
which are closely linked – 'to pray to God' (*MED* s.v. 2) and 'to ask or beg
for something' (s.v. 1) (the former act often being constituted of the
latter). These two senses do not appear to have been hierarchically related
as are the religious and non-religious uses of PDE 'pray'; and the difficulty
of keeping the uses distinct was increased by the existence of the sense
'beg (for alms)' (*MED* s.v. 3, a specialisation of 1). Langland seems to have
given a good deal of thought to the problem of begging, not only because
of the number of 'ordinary' beggars in his society but because of the
widespread activity of the mendicant orders[45] and, more immediately
perhaps, his own marginal position as an unordained, non-religious clerk
whose *biddynge* 'praying (for others)' was perforce accompanied by
'asking (from others)'. His ideal vision of things, expressed in Anima's
account of the early hermits, is one in which both prayer and provision are
gratuitous acts of 'curteisie': the *rightfulle* should *fynde . . . lyflode* for the
lif-holy (XV 307–8), not on the basis of a sordid *quid pro quo* arrangement
(such as Mede and her friar-confessor contrive, III 43–63), but as a way of
giving back to God what belongs rightfully to him alone as the universal
creator and provider:

> For we ben Goddes foles and *abiden* alwey,
> Til briddes brynge us that we sholde [by lyve]   (XV 313–4).

Man's properest prayer, Langland seems to be saying, is endurance not
supplication, on the model of Christ, who

> suffrede in ensample that we sholde suffren also,
> And seide to swiche that suffre wolde that *Pacientes vincunt*
> (XV 266–7).

The tension between *biden* and its anti-chime *bidden* becomes acute in a
passage, to be discussed below, which has become a major interpretative
crux. But it is already there between senses of co-polysemes that require
(as they provoke) especial vigilance from the reader or hearer of the
poetry, as in Mede's assertion that

> Beggeres for hir *biddynge bidden* men mede   (III 219).

It is not sufficient to find a 'safe' way of reading this line in relying on our
antecedent suspicion of the speaker, based as that is on Holy Church's
explicit attack and warning. For the whole point is that Mede is appealing
to the criteria of actuality, not that of ideal essences, and the institutional
church of common experience where everyone seems to 'sing for simony'

---

45 'The failed exemplars of *poverte*' as M. Godden calls them in 'Plowmen and
Hermits in Langland's *PP*', *RES* 34 (1984) p. 152.

has undeniably been shown to have taken Mede to its bosom.[46] Her argument cannot therefore be rejected *a priori* because it is Mede who voices it: on the contrary, it needs to be carefully understood before it can be refuted as specious. Mede has said in the previous line that servants 'take' meed, and in the next declares that minstrels 'ask for' meed; it is between these two neutral statements that the dangerous line appears, the danger lying partly in the temptation to treat its amphibology as illusory. The abrupt cross-caesural juxtaposition of the two words causes a blurring of the distinction between them. *Biddynge* ought to mean 'the prayers they (undertake to) say (for their benefactors' good)' (*MED* s.v. 2) but it becomes retroactively toned by *bidden* 'ask for money, beg' (*MED* s.v. 3) while the latter, in turn, takes on some of the morally approbative colouration of the former. The problem for interpretation, as I see it, is, 'How can we keep asunder what Mede has so cunningly put together?' Langland will not do our work for us; but clearly he indicates that there is work to be done: wordplay is really one of the most strenuous forms of *word-work*, for poet and readers alike.

A similar challenge is offered in a passage where Dame Studie, who is distinguishing between the worldly ('Catonian') and spiritual ways of dealing with 'fals folk and feithlees' (X 193) says that Theologie ('Christian moral teaching')

> . . . *biddeth* us be as bretheren, and *bidde* for oure enemys
>
> (X 197).

The wordplay here did not occasion any difficulty for the B-text scribes as is the case in the third example I shall discuss; but this does not prevent Kane and Donaldson from suspecting the line and emending *bidde* with the A-text's *blissen* – a totally unnecessary decision founded on a strange failure to grasp Langland's *procédé* here.[47] In this case, the operative senses are *MED* 4 'command' and 2 'pray', Studie's implication being that our prayer for ourselves will only be efficacious if we pray for (and forgive) others: the allusion is to the fifth petition of the Lord's Prayer. Behaving as bretheren (for Langland a model image of Christian communal existence)[48] is not an option but something God commands (*biddeth*) and the force of this sense flows over and 'benignly' expands in *bidde*: we must not think that prayer can be Christian if unaccompanied by a change in our relationship with our fellow men. Now Langland in this instance does not leave us to do all the work, since the moral point he is

---

46 Crucial passages like XV 103–43 (echoing I 190–99) show that *pace* Yunck (*The Lineage of Lady Meed* (Notre Dame, 1963)) Langland *is* especially concerned with 'clerkes that ben avarouse' (XV 136) since they are 'the roote of the right feith to rule the peple' (XV 100) and their example crucial.
47 See Kane-Donaldson, *B-Text*, X 202, Kane, *A-Text*, XI 151.
48 Cf. e.g. Trajan at XI 198–201, Christ at XVIII 376–9; and also X 297–302.

making is so fundamental and serious that its communication cannot be left to the 'right witty' alone but must be boldly highlighted for the *lewed*. Thus Studie insists that we should not only '*bidde* for oure enemys' (that in itself might not prove *too* much of an effort) but also 'lene hem whan hem nedeth' and 'gyven men that asked' (X 198, 201). In a word, she is encouraging us deliberately to *mis*construe the meaning of certain actions, such as deceitful *biddynge* 'begging' and in doing so exert a divine cunning, something which from a worldly viewpoint is 'folye' but from an eternal perspective proves to be the highest form of 'wit'. In rejecting the Catonian 'sic ars deluditur arte' (X 191*a*), Studie requires her audience to awake their faith and *biden* patiently so that 'Ars . . . artem falleret' (XVIII 161*a*).

In my final example, the textual evidence shows that scribes in both the B and C traditions (the latter here perhaps to be understood as a supplementary branch of B, if the text is unrevised)[49] were responding to the apparently ambiguous character of the speaker and creating a reading which irretrievably comprises him, in the eyes of several modern critics. It is certainly true that the speech of *Nede* in XX 35–50, which plays 'traductively' on the word a dozen times, does so in a way recalling *Mede* in the speech from which my first example came.[50] It is nonetheless unmistakable that the doctrine Nede teaches Will is one of *taking* when one is in direst need, not one of *begging*. What Nede urges upon Will is Anima's hard task of 'abiden alwey' and 'suffren also' (XV 313, 266, discussed above) in a manner recalling that of Christ, to whom these words are boldly ascribed as he is dying on the cross:

> . . . nede hath ynome me, that I moot nede *abide*
> And *suffre* sorwes ful soure   (XX 46–7).

It is on the basis of that *abide* that Nede urges Will to

> . . . be noght abasshed to *bide* and to be nedy,
> Sith he that wroghte al the world was wilfulliche nedy
> (XX 48–9).[51]

The reference to the creation is no accident here, for Nede has already, in speaking of man's right to 'thre thynges . . . his lif for to save' (XX 11) echoed Holy Church's seminal instruction to Will at the outset of his life's journey, that God

49 Full certainty here is impossible in the absence of a critical edition of C.
50 See pp. 127–8 above; in *traductio* the same word is re-introduced several times in a passage.
51 I have argued against the hostile view of Nede as 'meridian demon' (in R. Adams' 'The Nature of Need in *PP* XX', (1978, p. 299)) and 'harbinger of Antichrist' (P. Gradon, 'Ideology of Dissent', p. 203) in my 'Treatment of the Crucifixion in *PP* . . .' (1983) pp. 191–2.

> . . . comaunded of his curteisie in commune three thynges:
> Are none nedfulle but tho . . .   (I 20–1).

Here both the alpha-group of B-MSS (and the *g* sub-group) and the C-MS Skeat used read *bidde*, and this led Skeat to emend his base-MS L, here a faithful witness of the beta-original, which is supported by the x-group reading of C (as in the text of Pearsall) in XX 48.[52] But what Langland is actually doing is exercising one of his most potent pieces of annominative wordplay: *biden* summons up the anti-chime *bidden* only to deny it admission, while at the same time beckoning in its salutary co-polyseme (= 'pray') because the latter is founded on the authority of its homophone (*bidde* = 'command'). We should pray (*bidde*) through suffering (*bide*) because that is what God, in his unfathomably unsparing 'curteisie', commands (*biddeth*).

D.   Taxing Mercy and Beguiling Grace

No more striking instances of the difficulty of using words *lelly* appear than the strange cases of mercy the taxman and grace the beguiler. The first of these occurs in Piers' speech to the Knight setting out a programme aimed to alter the way in which Knyghthod conducts itself toward the Commune in the matter of rights:

> Loke ye tene no tenaunt but Truthe wole assente:
> · And though ye mowe *amercy* hem, lat *mercy* be taxour
> And mekenesse thi maister, maugree Medes chekes
>   (VI 38–40).

Though well-disposed to the Knight who has 'proffered himself so fair' (VI 24), Piers shows the seriousness of his warning in the tense paradox of the *tene/tenaunt* anti-pun of line 38, which amounts to saying 'These words are *not* related, and if you relate them by your behaviour, then Truth will *not* assent' and the reverberating antithesis between *meke* and *Medes chekes* (the idea, too, looks forward to Grace's injunction, already discussed, that 'who that moost maistries kan, be myldest of berynge' (XIX 257) – i.e. make meekness his master). But he shows it above all in the play on *amercy* and *mercy* (the former is spelled *mersyen* in parallel C VIII 37, perhaps the original spelling)[53] which, despite their shared derivation, have quite different implications for the administration of justice at all levels, from the manor court to the high court of heaven. *Amercien* is a legal phrase coming from the AF *a merci* 'at the mercy (of the court)' (see

52 See my text and K-D *ad loc*, Skeat, *C-text* XXIII 48 (= Pearsall XXII 48).
53 Cf. Samuels, 'Langland's Dialect' p. 244 on the value of C-MS X as a basis for reconstructing Langland's dialect; it is the apocopation, not *s* for *c*, that is significant.

MED s.v. *amercen*); but in telling the Knight to let meekness be *his* master, Piers is urging him effectively to remember that he will one day stand himself at the divine judgement seat and need mercy for his misdeeds. Thus, whereas Truth would lose its nature by assenting to the 'tening' of a tenant, justice assumes its true nature by relinquishing a right (to impose a fine): if mercy is *taxour* no 'merciment' will be imposed. Langland is not, of course, suggesting that all formal justice is really just licensed extortion (though a good deal of it was) but rather that the 'brotherly' way of exercising power (what one *mowe* or *kan*) is to refrain from doing so, remembering the injunction of the Angel in the Prologue: *Nudum ius a te vestiri vult pietate* (Pr 135).

Langland, I am arguing, believed that since all men depend on the mercy of God, their proper attitude to their 'rights' in this world is one that sees them as graces granted by God, not in consideration of men's merits but as part of a mysterious divine plan which cannot be fully grasped by reason but must be endured and 'suffered' in faith:

> 'Thynketh [that alle craftes', quod Grace], 'cometh of my yifte;
> Loketh that noon lakke oother, but loveth alle as bretheren'
> > (XIX 255–6).

And in praising the divine love, which sought self-extinction and 'need' in order to 'know' its own creation from within, he writes:

> Right so is love a ledere and the lawe shapeth:
> Upon man for his mysdedes the mercyment he taxeth
> > (I 161–2).

For Love to 'shape' the law ('mould' as well as 'create') is to make it possible for a *mercyment* 'fine' to become an act of mercy: to acquire a divine character in losing its purely and merely human one. This is not to claim that Langland was indifferent to justice or underestimated the utility of law; but he is very far from the positivism which identifies the two.[54] Just as there is a 'natural' law which gives man the right to take food and clothing by force or stealth 'whan men hym werneth, and he no moneye weldeth' (XX 12), so there is a divine law, enunciated by Holy Church, which says:

> Though ye be myghty to mote, beeth meke in youre werkes,
> For the same mesure that ye mete, amys outher ellis,
> Ye shulle ben weyen therwith whan ye wenden hennes
> > (I 176–8).

---

54 See discussion of these passages and of the theme generally in M. Stokes, *Justice and Mercy in PP* (and cf. my qualifications of Stokes' argument in *NQ* 33 (1986)). Simpson ('Transformation of Meaning', p. 164) comments on I 161–2 in a similar sense to mine, as does Bennett, *PP: Pr & I–VII*, 115.

Paradoxically, then, the 'lele' *use* of a word such as *mercyment* – the use that is in accord with 'the lawe of Holy Chirche', charity and humility – is a kind of benign *mis*use, a 'misconstruing' through which God 'kennes' man 'in herte' (I 165).

Now a paradox may affront reason, but it is not in itself incompatible with it, as I have argued elsewhere.[55] Langland is aware that meekness is impossible without grace, yet grace tends to be found only among the meek, as in Ymaginatif's warning to Will against the two kinds of abundance, wit and wealth, which serve to 'swell a man's soul' with pride:

> Sapience, seith the Bok, swelleth a mannes soule . . .
>
>   . . .   . . .
>
> And richesse right so, but if the roote be trewe.
>   Ac grace is a gras therfore, tho grevaunces to abate.
> Ac grace ne groweth noght but amonges [gomes] lowe:
> Pacience and poverte the place is ther it groweth,
> And in lele lyvynge men and in lif holy,
> And thorugh the gifte of the Holy Goost . . .   (XII 57–63).

This passage brings together a number of important ideas and images central to Langland's whole vision of man's destiny: it is the same doctrine that Anima is to teach at the beginning of Passus XVI, when he develops his symbol of the Tree of Patience (as it should perhaps be properly called), whose *more* 'root' is mercy and *myddul stok* 'trunk' is *ruthe* (XVI 5). The two passages together furnish room for a doctrine of society that will allow some to be richer than others and still attain salvation – that is, a doctrine which does not necessitate bringing all to one dead level, with either all goods in common or else a universal impoverishment. A just knightly class needs a 'true root' as much as the class of clerks about whose rotten root Anima complains in XV 100–2; but it must not seek to purge its own rottenness by tearing up its roots, for example by alienating its property to religious orders (and thereby poisoning *them* at the root) or by seeking to take on the habiliments of the ploughman, however fair such a proffer may seem. Property obtained by extortion (as in 'teneful' *amerciment*) is no more 'graithly geten' than the hoard of human apples stolen from God's orchard by the Devil, for 'ther gile is the roote' (XVIII 291).

It is one of Langland's greatest triumphs in his handling of polysemy that he does not turn his eyes from the ways in which even the language

55 See my 'Inner Dreams in *PP*', *MÆ* LV (1986) p. 36; and for a general account of the background to such a 'paradoxical injunction' as loving one's enemies, see J. Simpson, 'From Reason to Affective Knowledge', ibid., 1–23, esp. 15 (on X 195–7).

of religion can be abused, generating a diabolical simulacrum which corrupts faith and feeling in a supposedly religious society and culture. At one of the most exalted moments in Passus XIX, when the Holy Spirit 'In liknesse of a lightnynge . . . lighte on hem alle' (XIX 203), Conscience and the whole community greet 'Cristes messager' with the exultant cry 'Help us, God of grace!' (213). By the end of Passus XX the jubilation has become untuned, and the cry is more like one of despair:

> And siththe he gradde after Grace, til I gan awake
>
> (XX 387).

One of the grimmest and most testing experiences that these last passūs afford is that of the good being corrupted into its opposite, or rather, into an opposite which goes disguised as the reality – covered under 'pryvee speche and peyntede wordes' (XX 115). No word is exempt from that 'painting', not even the word *grace*, which bore in addition to its 'lele' uses the dangerously neutral one recorded by *MED* s.v. 4: 'good will; favouritism, bias; an act of favour; a gift, boon.' The true Grace may truly claim that 'alle . . . cometh of my yifte' (XIX 255), but Gile (the false grace) is also at work, 'privy speech and painted words' being among the most potent 'wiles' through which Coveitise in Passus XX 'giled the peple' (XX 124–5) just as did, earlier, his grosser avatar in the Field of Folk:

> Ne hadde the grace of gyle ygo amonges my ware,
> It hadde ben unsold this seven yer, so me God helpe!
>
> (V 203–4).

It is doubtless a chilling thought that we could replace the lower case of *gyle* by a capital without any difficulty; yet if the mere existence of such a phrase as 'the grace of Guile' concedes a shadowy actuality to the Satanic kingdom, it is also true that Langland does not allow this *bele parole* to achieve the hallowed status of a *lele word*: its impudence is eventually exposed as impotence also.

The proof that this is so is given us not at the conclusion of the poem but in what may be described as its metaphysical as much as its dramatic *climax*. This is the debate between Christ and Satan that takes place in Passus XVIII. Here, in a very remarkable way, Christ's *maistrie* is demonstrated not in the exercise of (irresistible) power, as in the raising of Lazarus (XVI 115), an event so troublingly present to Satan's mind as he hears Christ's 'vois loude in that light' (XVIII 262, 266), but in mastery of *truth*, the reality which confounds pretence, strips hypocrisy and lets in the light upon 'fair biheste and . . . fals truthe' (XX 118). This is *maistrie* in *MED*'s sense 4: 'mastery of a subject or an art'. Not for nothing is Grace 'gyour of alle clerkes', in the Lewed Vicory's words (XIX 428), for he is 'Cristes messager', and Christ, in Ymaginatif's words, 'of clergie is roote'

(XII 71). Such a 'trewe roote' shows its nature through the argument in the course of which Christ proclaims the defeat of Satan's mimicry of God's work by a truly masterly display of amphibology:

> Thus ylik a lusard with a lady visage,
> Thefliche thow me robbedest; the Olde Lawe graunteth
> That gilours be bigiled – and that is good reson: . . .
>
> . . .   . . .
>
> And that grace gile destruye, good feith it asketh
>
> (XVIII 338–40, 348).

Both *reson* and *feith* come triumphantly together in Christ's case as, with scintillating clerkly relish, he confounds the 'lusard' Lucifer whose *lesynges* are now unmasked.

In spite of the ambiguous syntax of 348a, it is clear that *grace* quite literally 'comes first', is, that is to say, the prime reality of which Guile's 'grace', however actual, is only an insubstantial parody, a *lesynge* through faith in which men fall into 'fals truthe'. It only *appears*, therefore, that Guile *mowe* or *kan* ('is able' or 'knows how to') destroy Grace: for such is the serpentine duplicity of our forked human tongues and our divided *humana natura*. Sinful man is able and, through sin, learns how to, corrupt good reason, good faith, and good itself.

E. Gathering the Good

No word in the language, it would seem, should be less susceptible of being 'coloured queyntely and covered under sophistrie' (XIX 349) than *good* itself, with its 'Platonically' apt annominative affinity to God. Yet none, Langland shows, needs greater protection if it is to remain 'in place', *lele*. The problem is greater in ME than in Present Day English, for whereas the ethical and property senses do not overlap now, in ME the singular could mean 'material goods' (*MED* s.v. 11 and 12, in contrast with 1 and 6). Langland attempts to enforce the *lele* use of *good* by connecting these two senses with each other and with God, the author of both the things of the world and those of the spirit, in the admonitory conclusion of Holy Church's instruction to Will:

> But if ye loven leelly and lene the povere
> Of swich *good* as God sent, *goodliche* parteth,
> Ye have na moore merite . . .
>
> than Malkyn . . .   (I 181–4).

Here the phrase *as God sent* has a partly retro-active effect upon *good* (*MED* s.v. 11), evoking its co-polyseme (*MED* 1, 6), an effect re-inforced by following *goodliche*: if we recognise that it *is* God who sends what we possess, by dividing our own goods generously, then goods will indeed be good for us and accurately reflect their divine origin without distortion in the 'mirour that highte Middelerthe' (XI 9). The passage is especially noteworthy in the way that it contrasts *leelly* with *treweliche*, a word, as hardly needs saying, of substantial moral import in *Piers Plowman*; for only two lines before Langland has written

> For though ye be trew of youre tonge and treweliche wynne
>
> · · ·   · · ·
>
> But if ye loven leelly . . .   (I 179, 181)

and it seems that for *trewthe* (of speech and life) to become spiritually meritorious it must develop into active charity: *treweliche wynne* becoming *goodliche parten* via *loven leelly*. It is not 'trewe' but 'leel' that is unquali-fiedly criterial: it is not conformity between thought and utterance but between word and action that is the *unum necessarium* and also the *sine qua non* for salvation. Any possible 'Platonic' equation of 'right knowledge' with 'righteousness' is firmly ruled out.[56]

Almost the opposte process to that of retro-active toning described above occurs in the description of Haukyn:

> . . . of pointes his cote
> Was colomy thorugh coveitise and unkynde desiryng.
> Moore to *good* than to *God* the gome his love caste
>   (XIII 354–6).

Here there is momentary surprise – a state that stimulates attention – as the anti-pun *good* (*MED* 1 'goodness' and 6 'righteous conduct') dis-quietingly engendered by the chiming *God* is 'denied admission' (in the second half of the line *love*, conversely, yields up its 'leel' ghost under the throttling pressure of *unkynde desiryng*). Even more emphatic is the line a little later in which Haukyn confesses his continual efforts

> Thorugh gile to gaderen the *good* that ich have (XIII 369)

and his mourning more

> For losse of *good*, leve me, than for likames giltes
>   (XIII 386).[57]

---

56 The key passage for this doctrine is Trajan's speech, esp. XI 140–65. His statement that 'leel love and lyvyng in truthe / Pulte out of pyne a paynym . . .' is followed by 'Yblissed be truthe that so brak helle yates' (XI 161–3) which refers immediately to his own release from hell but also looks forward to Christ's release of the patriarchs in XVIII through his *maistrye* of *truthe* (see p. 133 above).

57 The line scans as Type Ie with 'inverse counterpoint' (*aba/ab*).

Here the tension built up from the *duplex sensus ex verbis* almost reaches breaking-point: not only can *good* in the excluded anti-pun's sense *not* be 'gathered' through guile, such gathering actually contributes to the exclusion of that value from life, as does mourning for the loss of a 'good' loved with *unkynde desiryng*. For the good Haukyn has and loses does him no good, and neither – such is his tragic plight – can the *good* ('baptismal grace') whose loss through misdirected love he *fails* to mourn: it is no more his by right than the 'hoord' of holy men 'gadrede togideres' by Satan (XVI 80) and later relinquished to its rightful owner is *his* (arguably *gile* here as in V 203 should be personified).

To Langland *unkynde desiryng* and the closely-related *coveitise* (discussed below) are forces which corrode and corrupt the good in 'goods'; but they can go further and menace good itself. An example of this is the sacrament of marriage, which the poem shows as currently declining into a mere commercial transaction.[58] Thus Wit foresees disaster 'For some' who

> For coveitise of catel unkyndely ben wedded.
> . . .   . . .
> For *goode* sholde wedde *goode*, though thei no *good* hadde
> > (IX 157, 160).

Just as *coveitise* is *unkynde* because the author of 'things', God, is generous, and has made man in his image to 'goodliche parten' as he does, so marriage 'Moore for *coveitise of good* than kynde love of bothe' (XIV 269) is a crime against the author of the sacrament, of love, of *kynde* and of 'good'. Read with a *lewed* rather than a clerkly eye, line IX 160 may seem innocent of a *duplex sensus*, especially since the inflected nominal adjective signals a distinction not possible today between the ethical and material senses (we for our part would say 'goods' for *good*). But the alert reader becomes conscious of fending-off the anti-pun that clutches and clings to the line, suggesting the sense that 'wealth should wed wealth even in the absence of virtue'. For that is nothing less than the *unkynde* way of regarding marriage – as 'brocage' (XIV 267): corruption of the sacrament, not surprisingly, is accompanied by, and accompanies, corruption of language;[59] for a sacramental like a linguistic system is a living structure of efficacious signs.

58 Significant signs of a contemporary reaction against this trend appear in all the major 'Ricardian' poets – in Chaucer's *Franklin's Tale*, in Gower's *Traitié pour essampler les Amantz Marietz* (in *French Works*, ed. Macaulay (Oxford, 1899) 381) esp. IV.2) and in *Purity*, where the association of avarice with unnatural love, though more oblique, seems to be present (see my '*Kynde Craft* and the *Play of Paramorez*' in the *Bennett Memorial Lectures*, ed. P. Boitani (1987)).
59 Examples are the Friar-Confessors' 'soft' absolutions of Mede and Contricion at I 37–47 and XX 363–9 respectively.

To diagnose acutely the symptoms of linguistic and spiritual decay is not, however, to despair of good meanings any more than of good marriages. The effect of the perilously unstable line I have analysed is not simply to deny that goods can ever be good, and to assert therefore one or other of the two radical doctrines (communism; destitution) which it seems clear Langland was resolutely active to avoid.[60] As God's creation, the goods of the world must be at least potentially 'good': 'Viditque Deus cuncta quae fecerat, et erant valde bona' (Gen 1:31). Yet they are not absolutely but only relatively and provisionally good, whereas the virtues, gathered not through guile but through grace, are good *simpliciter*, and so genuinely self-sufficing.[61] Thus Langland holds that virtuous people can achieve happiness in the absence of wealth, whereas the possession of wealth will not guarantee happiness, let alone aid salvation, and its doubling through the union of the rich 'by assent of sondry parties and silver to boote' (XIV 268) will *decrease* the chances of obtaining either in inverse proportion. Langland's hope is not a mere ideal but a trust founded in faith that the sacraments are truly efficacious, and have the power to bring about that which they signify – to validate, for example, the hard and high words of the marriage vows: and it is because he believes in the *reality* of grace that he is not abandoned to *wanhope* by the *actuality* of sin.

It is in the light of this argument that Langland's plainly evident *preference* for poverty as a condition predisposing to the operation of grace must be seen in order to be properly understood. Experience and imaginative reflection as much as (and, in the sequence of the poem, before) the authority of ascetic fathers like 'lered . . . Austyn' (XIV 316) bring this home to Will and to the reader, for is it not Ymaginatif who first declares that 'grace ne groweth noght but amonges [gomes] lowe' and that 'Pacience and poverte the place is ther it groweth' (XII 60–1)? The correlative of this is to be found in Wit's earlier assurance that those who reject *coveitise* will indeed receive the help they need to endure the privation of material *good*:

> For no londes, but for love, loke ye be wedded,
> And thanne gete ye the grace of *God*, and *good* ynough to live with
> (IX 177–8).

---

60 Langland's consistent doctrine that 'lawefulle men' should provide for 'religious', taught by Anima at XV 306–8, is re-stated by Conscience in promising the friars 'breed and clothes / And othere necessaries ynowe' (XX 248–9), thus excluding the 'radical' alternatives.

61 This is what makes the corruption of such crucial ethical and religious *words* as *virtues* and *grace* so potentially dangerous to the Christian *commune* at large.

To the *lewed* reader this is a promise that the sacramental grace of marriage will be accompanied by a guaranteed minimum wage, so to speak; but Langland was not so naive as to believe that material injustice is always remedied *in via* as it was for 'Job the gentile', who avouched how 'wikked men, thei welden the welthe of this worlde' (X 23–4) and his own 'joye deere aboughte' (XII 42). The clerks in Langland's audience, by contrast, are invited to see in that *good* a benignly guileful admission of the anti-pun sense 'goodness': the hard message is that the grace of God is 'good enough to live with' – even if that means dying, in the worst case, for lack of the 'three things needful' like Christ, than whom 'nevere noon so nedy ne poverer deide' (XX 50). Langland is sadly (in both the medieval and modern senses) resigned to accepting that those who live as 'goddes foles and abiden alwey' (XV 313) must be prepared to become 'fooles . . . wel gladdere to deye / Than to lyve lenger' (XX 62–3) in a world where even a friar confessor 'gadereth . . . there he shryveth' (XX 369)

F.   The Couplings of Coveitise

Although the siege against Unity in the Last Passus of *Piers Plowman* is led by the lord Antichrist, with his banner-bearer Pride, a special significance seems to attach to Coveitise, which deserves examination here before I conclude my discussion of Langland's polysemy. Although the word denotes one of the Deadly Sins and is so employed most commonly in Middle English, it is also capable of a 'neutral' use to which Langland seems to have been especially sensitive, a use which he struggles to transform into something *lele*, honest, trustworthy and ultimately capable of good.[62] Thus when Coveitise approaches, 'His wepne . . . al wiles, to wynnen and to hiden' (XX 124), Conscience cries out

> wolde Crist of his grace
> That Coveitise were Cristene, that is so kene to fighte
>
> (XX 140–1).

He seems to be treating Coveitise almost as if he were Mede, capable of being either good or bad, although the Conscience of the Eighth Vision lacks the categorical severity of his earlier First Vision self. Now this is made possible, I believe, not simply because, as the *Ayenbite of Inwit* has it, 'Þer is an holy coueytise and an holy enuye'[63] – metaphorical senses of a very overt kind – but because this is one of the Deadly Sins whose name is actually neutral in itself, referring to 'strong desire' (*MED* s.v. 3(a)) which

---

62 *Coveitise* is illuminatingly discussed by James Simpson ('Transformation of Meaning', p. 167) in terms very similar to mine.
63 The *Ayenbite* example (ed. Morris, p. 137/4) is quoted in *MED* under sense 3(a).

first has to be defined by its object before it can be adequately evaluated. Conscience could not wish Lecherie or Sleuthe 'Cristene' in the same way without sounding decidedly odd in doing so.

Now Langland brings out the strange duplicity of this word in such a passage as this from Wit's exhortation on marriage, already quoted in part and discussed above:

> Forthi I counseille alle Cristene *coveite* noght be wedded
> For *coveitise* of catel ne of kynrede riche   (IX 173–4).

The rhythm here would require a pause at the caesura in 174, yet the meaning suggests the need for a slighter secondary pause after *coveitise*, so that the warning can be correctly apprehended as directed not just against 'desire for wealth' (not, in itself, an evil) but against the sin of *coveitise* proper, 'immoderate desire for acquiring worldly goods or estate; greed' (*MED* s.v. 1). It is not desire (*cupido*) that is wrong but *unkynde desiryng* (*cupiditas*). The neutral sense is present in the verbal form of line 173, which is of course in serious danger of adverse retroactive toning from the following noun.

The potency of this vicious quality is never more aptly communicated by Langland than under the figure of sexual temptation and desire, especially in connection with the clergy, a class vowed to celibacy but all too often engaged to avarice, their soul's invisible concubine:

> Manye curatours kepen hem clene of hire bodies;
> Thei ben acombred with *coveitise*, thei konne noght out crepe,
> So harde hath avarice yhasped hem togideres.
> And that is no truthe of the Trinite   (I 195–8).

Although the primary reference of the images is to a bag and a chest (standard figures in the iconography of this vice)[64] there is an unmistakable secondary overtone of a suffocating sexual embrace. The speaker here is Holy Church, but her point is expanded further and made explicit in Conscience's attack on Mede, which shows him already using that 'neutral' sense noted in the first example I gave in this section:

> Barons and burgeises she bryngeth in sorwe,
> And al the comune in care that *coveiten* lyve in truthe,
> For clergie and *coveitise* she coupleth togideres   (III 163–5).

Here the neutral 'strong desire' (*cupido*) of the people becomes perverted because they see their spiritual leaders and teachers, the clergy, locked in an unholy concubinage with greed: 'that is no truthe of the Trinite', as Holy Church has it, and so the *comune* fail in their desire, and once again

---

64 Cf. 'Avarice hath almaries and yren-bounden cofres' at XIV 246.

the neutral verb is fatally compromised, drawn helplessly into the sphere of its potent and minatory neighbour. Finally, the testimony of Holy Church and Conscience is ratified by Reason, here addressing not solely the clergy but all in positions of power, including the prelates of the Church:

> And ye that han lawes to kepe, lat Truthe be youre *coveitise*
> Moore than gold outher giftes if ye wol God plese
>
> (V 52–3).

Here, as in IX 173–4, the rhythm and sense pull in different directions: first the line-end pause at 52 suggests a 'metaphoricisation' of *MED* sense 1 'covetousness', but then reflection inclines the reader rather towards the sense 'strong desire' – something which can have for its object spiritual or material wealth or gain.

Langland is keenly aware of the presence of the anti-pun in the line in which Haukyn, a man especially prey to the vice, states how he was given penances by his priest

> Al for *coveitise* of my Cristendom in clennesse to kepen it
>
> (XIV 11).

This is virtually untranslatable into modern English, and is only doubtfully idiomatic in the original, for it involves bringing to bear an unusual mental pressure upon the word, which strains and struggles to escape from meaningful collocation with its alliterating partner *Cristendom*, as in my opening example:

> wolde Crist of his grace
> That Coveitise were Cristene   (XX 140–1)

– but even more so here. For one of the main things that is preventing Haukyn from keeping his baptismal garment (emblem of his soul in a state of grace) 'clene an houre' (XIV 12) is that he has 'love' for *good* while being 'looth to do truthe' (XIII 356, 359). The force of the anti-pun is also felt in another line, this time on the clergy rather than the 'representative' layman Haukyn, from Reason's list of the *impossibilia* that will need to be fulfilled before he will recommend the King to have 'ruthe' on Mede:

> Til clerkene *coveitise* be to clothe the povere and fede   (IV 119).

Are we to follow the mad Lear's advice here and look with our ears? Change places, and, handy-dandy, which is the *lele* word and which its thievish simulacrum? We may either find the reference to be to *MED* sense 1, 'covetousness', giving the meaning 'Let clerkly greed be transformed in nature and become charity', or else to *MED* sense 3 'strong desire', giving then, 'Let clerkly ambition be directed only towards the things of God ("good", "truth", "grace" and "love") and thereby avoid being *de*formed into the horrid image of true (that is, 'fals') *Coveitise* and *unkynde desiryng.*'

It is to Langland's great credit that he does not allow his readers to *believe* in the impossible, however much he may urge them to hope and pray for it. As a maker, his standing temptation must always have been, as it is for all makers, to be content if his work is 'enblaunched with *bele paroles*'; but as a clerk he seems never to have forgotten Theologie's warning that

>   witty is Truthe,
> And Conscience is of his counseil and knoweth yow echone,
> And if he fynde yow in defaute and with the false holde,
> It shal bisitte youre soules ful soure at the laste   (II 137–41).

Whatever 'defaute' appears in Langland, it has been my contention that his work exhibits a passionate effort to reconcile his artistic with his moral conscience. The evidence lies in the text, in the examples I have given and in many others I have been unable to give for lack of space, but which are there for the finding. In studying the art of Langland we are 'involved', to quote Geoffrey Hill, 'with something other than a "conceptual elaboration of the similarity between literary and moral judgment". It is rather a recognition that in the act of "making" we are necessarily delivered up to judgment'.[65]

---

65 *The Lords of Limit*, p. 14. The quotation in Hill is from Adrian Cunningham.

Conclusion

> . . . because there is no end
> To the vanity of our calling, make intercession
> For the treason of all clerks.[1]

> . . . at times a bore, but,
> while knowing Speech can at best, a shadow echoing
> the silent light, bear witness
> to the Truth it is not, he wished it were . . .[2]

Commenting recently on the Dreamer's *apologia* to Ymaginatif (discussed in the third section of Chapter One) Malcolm Godden remarks:

> The narrator's proper role is prayer, the role which he eventually lays claim to in the C text; but his actual work is poetry, *makynges*, which for him involves discovery as well as teaching. The making of poetry holds him back from the life of prayer . . .[3]

In the B-text *apologia*, it will be recalled, Will actually accepts Ymaginatif's challenge to justify his activity and sets out 'somwhat me to *excuse*' (XII 20).[4] This passage was excised from the version of the encounter in Passus XIV of C, but Langland seems to have been remembering it when he composed the 'autobiographical' scene that opens Passus V in C, the scene to which Godden's comment is referring. For when Resoun challenges Will to explain why he seems 'an ydel man' (V 27) he asks him to give some grounds 'whereby thow myhte be *excused*' (V 34). We may speculate that some at least of Langland's readers would have recognised in the lines an abandonment of trust in the validity of the *former* 'excuse'; for it may be supposed that the most eager readers of the C-version would

1 W. H. Auden, *Collected Poems* (ed. Mendelson) p. 243 ('At the Grave of Henry James').
2 Ibid., pp. 522–3 ('The Cave of Making', from *Thanksgiving for a Habitat*).
3 'Plowmen and Hermits in Langland's *Piers Plowman*', *RES* 35 (1984) p. 161.
4 See ch. 1, section iii, pp. 14–19 above.

have been found amongst those who already knew the B-text, and to whom the troubled author's latest reflections would have been primarily addressed.

Godden's contrast between what Langland is prepared to 'claim' and what he actually does, between his 'role' and his 'work' is important and needs elaborating here, however briefly; for of course the C-text is itself a work of poetry, and does not *exemplify* the 'role' to which Langland lays claim in the same way as does the B-text. And yet the autobiographical passage states quite clearly both what it was Langland continued to do and what its consequences for him were:

> . . . lytel ylet by, leueth me for sothe,
> Amonges lollares of Londone and lewede ermytes,
> For y *made* of tho men as *resoun* me tauhte   (C V 3–5).[5]

This passage recalls Lewtee's exhortation in B to '[l]egge the sothe' and to 'reden in retorik' those things 'that al the world woot' (XI 96, 101–2). And in place of Lewtee it even specifies the 'teaching' of *resoun*, the critical interlocutor who at C V 11 'arates' him (a word that cannot fail to bring to mind Lewtee's own view of the rationale of making – 'to arate dedly synne' (XI 102)).

Between them, the two passages – like the two 'versions' from which they come – may be thought to create an enigmatic 'inter-textual' space (or 'inter-face'). Despite his final refusal to 'excuse' himself by appealing to the necessity of 'solace' or to the potential utility of *retorik*, Langland appears to have continued to the end of his life to attempt to 'perfect the work'. Of all 'clerks' known to me, he seems to have been supremely aware of the 'vanity' and 'treason' of which Auden speaks in addressing the spirit of Henry James; and I know of none who bears better witness to the Truth that Speech is not, while wishing it were. My aim in this book has been both to affirm Langland's dedication to *leel lyvyng in truthe* and also to argue that he knew the 'mystery' of the Cave of Making, in Auden's phrase, 'from the inside'.[6]

---

5 Characteristically, perhaps, the authoritative ring of *resoun* is retroactively muted by the falling of the stress on *me*, which gives salience to the subjective element in all 'arating'.

6 *Collected Poems*, p. 523.

Appendix

Poet, Maker, Translator, Versifier

It is interesting to note how *poet* and *maker*, evidently not synonyms in Chaucer's and Langland's day, have become synonymous in sixteenth-century critical thought. 'A Poet', writes Puttenham, 'is as much to say as a maker'[1] and he ascribes the dignity of this 'high and incomparable title' (Sidney's phrase)[2] to the analogy between the poet and God as creators. It is of course the case that the 'very' poet will imitate nature, because 'Poesie [is] an art not only of making, but also of imitation',[3] but Puttenham contrasts him with the translator, who 'may well be sayd a versifier, but not a Poet'.[4] Versifying is not a sufficient and, for Sidney, not even a necessary condition of being a poet 'sith there haue beene most excellent Poets that neuer versified, and now swarme many versifiers that neede neuer aunswere to the name of Poets'.[5] 'Poet' and 'maker' are honorific, 'translator' and 'versifier' at best descriptive terms. By Shakespeare's time, despite the obsolescence of 'maker' and the plethora of distinguished translators, 'poet' retains unaltered its high sense of inspired creative artist. Theseus's claim (*MND* V.i.15–16) that the poet turns 'things unknown' to 'shapes' accords with Puttenham's that 'the very Poet makes and contriues out of his owne braine'.[6]

The *OED*'s sense 5 of *maker* 'a poet' is evidently a specialisation of sense 4, 'a creator or producer (of something – viz. a literary work)'. Chaucer's description of himself as the *makere* of his *litel bok* (*Troilus*, V 1786–7) hovers between senses 4 and 5. Contemporaries such as Usk and Gower

1 *'The Arte of English Poesie*, ch. 1, in G. G. Smith, ed.: *Elizabethan Critical Essays*, II, p. 3.
2 Sir Philip Sidney, *An Apologie for Poetrie*, in Smith, *Essays*, I, p. 155.
3 Puttenham, *Arte*, p. 3. Cf. also Sidney, *Apologie*, p. 158.
4 Puttenham, ibid.
5 Sidney, *Apologie*, p. 160; cf. also p. 182.
6 Puttenham, *Arte*, p. 3. For the positive sense of *contrive* in Langland, see C XIV 160; its normal overtones are of illicit or hostile designs (B XVI 137).

and followers such as Lydgate call him *poet*,[7] but Chaucer does not use the term of himself, and applies it to only two vernacular writers at all, Dante and Petrarch (*MkT*, B 3650; *ClPr*, E 31).[8] The same *Troilus* passage (V 1789–90) on the face of it seems to contradict the view that he distinguished poet from maker by its apparent equation of *makyng* and *poesye*. But it may be that there are actually *two* injunctions here – one, not to envy any vernacular poetry (?Boccaccio or Benoit), the other, to make obeisance to the classical writers (Virgile, etc). Langland's line 'Than pipede Pees of *poesie* a note' (B XVIII 410), written a few years earlier, quotes that 'note' from Alanus, not an ancient but certainly a non-vernacular writer, and this supports the notion that both he and Chaucer thought primarily of *poets* as *clerks*, who write *poetria* (in Latin), which only clerks can read (cf. Chaucer's Clerk calling Petrarch 'a worthy clerk', E 27). Further evidence that this is so is a C-text revision attacking the new clerks' inability to 'construe kyndeliche þat poetes made' (C XVII 110). The equivalent B-text line (XV 373) has *auctour*, implying that both poets and authors are creators, originators, who make 'out of their own brain'.

The last passage shows, however, that the distinction between the nouns 'poet' and 'maker' could not extend to the verbal forms, since English had only one verb for 'compose poetry' generally, namely *maken* (cf. the discussion of *endite* on p. 25 above). Yet since the writer of *Troilus* could not describe himself as *auctour* (and, presumably, as *poete*) he could hardly have recognised, as the Renaissance critics do, a distinction between 'maker' and 'translator'. While the God of Love's question (*LGW* Prol G 264) 'Hast thow nat *mad in Englysh* ek the bok [*sc.* of Troilus]' does not necessitate literal translation, that is the sense assumed by Alceste when she says Chaucer 'may translate a thyng in no malyce . . . / . . . for he useth bokes for to make' (G 341–2). Chaucer the 'grant translateur' is not distinct from Chaucer the maker, because when he makes books customarily, it is books that he uses to make them! At the time of *Troilus*, Chaucer could hardly have claimed to be a *poet* or *auctour*: all his *makyng* draws to some degree on what Puttenham calls the translator's 'foreine copie or example'.[9]

'Versify' is an altogether less common term in this period, occurring only once each in Chaucer and Langland. The Monk's statement that tragedies 'ben *versified* communely / Of six feet' (B 3168–9) clearly associates the word with classical metric, but does not totally exclude vernacular

7 Thomas Usk, *The Testament of Love*, III.iv, in Skeat, ed.: *Chaucerian and Other Pieces* (Oxford, 1897) p. 123; Gower, *Confessio Amantis*, ed. Macaulay, VIII 2942; Lydgate, *Troy Book* (*ed.* H. Bergen, EETS 97 (1906) II 4697.

8 For recent discussion see Spearing, *Medieval to Renaissance* (1986) esp. pp. 33–4.

9 Puttenham, *Arte*, p. 3.

composition. Anima's attack on the inability of new clerks to *'versifye* faire' (B XV 372), discussed more fully above (see pp. 21ff.), likewise implies Latin metrical composition, but without excluding use of the vernacular. At any rate, *versify* is totally without disparaging overtones, and on the contrary seems to suggest a learned and accomplished activity. In fourteenth as opposed to sixteenth century England versifiers, far from 'swarming', were probably somewhat thin on the ground.

Bibliography

The place of publication is London unless otherwise stated.

TEXTS

I   English

The Anglo-Saxon Minor Poems, ed. E. V. K. Dobbie (New York, 1942).

Beowulf and the Fight at Finnsburg, ed. Fr. Klaeber. 3rd edn (Boston 1950).

The Works of Geoffrey Chaucer, ed. F. N. Robinson. 2nd edn (1957).

Chaucerian and Other Pieces, ed. W. W. Skeat (Oxford, 1897).

Elizabethan Critical Essays, ed. G. Gregory Smith. 2 vols. (Oxford, 1904).

Fourteenth Century Verse and Prose, ed. Kenneth Sisam (Oxford, repr. 1955).

The Chronicles of Froissart, translated by Lord Berners. Ed. G. C. Macaulay (1913).

The Complete Works of John Gower: the French Works, ed. G. C. Macaulay (Oxford, 1899).

The English Works of John Gower, ed. G. C. Macaulay. EETS E.S. 81. 2 vols. (1900).

Geoffrey Hill. *Collected Poems* (Harmondsworth, 1985).

The Letters of G. M. Hopkins to Robert Bridges, ed. C. C. Abbott (Oxford, 1935).

Notebooks and Papers of G. M. Hopkins, ed. Humphry House (Oxford, 1937).

The Poems of G. M. Hopkins, ed. W. H. Gardner and N. H. MacKenzie. 4th edn. (Oxford, 1970).

Piers the Plowman in Three Parallel Texts, ed. W. W. Skeat. 2 vols. (Oxford, 1886).

Piers Plowman, ed. Elizabeth Salter and Derek Pearsall [C-text selections] (1967).

Langland: Piers Plowman (Pr and I–VII of B-text), ed. J. A. W. Bennett (Oxford, 1972).

Piers Plowman: the B Version, ed. George Kane and E. Talbot Donaldson (1975).

William Langland: The Vision of Piers Plowman, ed. A. V. C. Schmidt (repr. 1984).

Piers Plowman by William Langland: an Edition of the C-text, ed. Derek Pearsall (1978).

William Langland: Piers Plowman: the Z Version, ed. A. G. Rigg and Charlotte Brewer (Toronto, 1983).

John Lydgate: Troy Book, ed. H. Bergen, EETS ES 97, 103, 106, 126 (1906–20).

Medieval English Romances, ed. A. V. C. Schmidt and Nicolas Jacobs. 2 vols (1980).

Medieval Literature: Chaucer and the Alliterative Tradition, ed. Boris Ford. New Pelican Guide to English Literature (Harmondsworth, 1982).

Morte Arthure, ed. Edmund Brock. EETS 8 (2nd edn, 1871).

The Parlement of the Thre Ages, ed. M. Y. Offord. EETS 246 (1959).

The Poems of Alexander Pope, ed. John Butt (1963).

Religious Lyrics of the XIVth Century, ed. Carleton Brown (Oxford, 1924).

St Erkenwald, ed. Ruth Morse (Cambridge and New Jersey, 1975).

Sir Gawain and the Green Knight, ed. J. R. R. Tolkien and E. V. Gordon, 2nd edn. ed. Norman Davis (Oxford, 1968).

John Skelton: The Complete English Poems, ed. John Scattergood (Harmondsworth, 1983).

The Vercelli Book, ed. G. P. Krapp (Anglo-Saxon Poetic Records II) (New York, 1932).

The Poems of Wordsworth, ed. T. Hutchinson (Oxford, 1926).

William Wordsworth: The Prelude: 1799, 1805, 1850, ed. J. Wordsworth, M. H. Abrams and S. Gill (New York and London, 1979).

II Latin

Alanus de Insulis. *Alani de Insulis Opera Omnia*. PL 210 (1855).

Alexander of Villedieu. *Das Doctrinale des Alexander de Villa-Dei*, ed. D. Reichling (Berlin, 1893).

Ambrose. *Ambroise de Milan: Des Sacrements; Des Mystères*, ed. Bernard Botte. Sources Chrétiennes 25 (Paris, 1961).

Analecta Hymnica, ed. Dreves, G. M. and Blume, C. (Leipzig, 1886–1922).

Bede. See Keil, *Scriptores* for *De Arte Metrica* (*Grammatici Latini* VII).

—— *Venerabilis Baedae Opera Historica*, ed. C. Plummer (Oxford, 1896).

Biblia Vulgata, ed. A. Colunga and L. Turrado. 4th edn. (Madrid, 1965).

Carmina Burana, ed. A. Hilka and O. Schumann. 2 vols (Heidelberg, 1930).

Dante. *Tutte le Opere di Dante Alighieri*, ed. E. Moore (Oxford, 1897).

Donatus. See Keil, *Probi Donati Servi.*, in *Grammatici Latini*, IV.

Gervase of Melkley. *Gervais von Melkley: Ars Poetica*, ed. H. J. Gräbener (Leipzig, 1886).

Grammatici Latini, ed. H. Keil, vols. IV and VII (Leipzig, 1864, 1880).

Hildebert of Lavardin. *Hildeberti . . . Opera Omnia; Marbodi . . . Opuscula. PL* 171 (1893).

Isidore of Seville. *Etymologiarum sive Originum Libri XX*, ed. W. M. Lindsay. 2 vols. (Oxford, 1911).

Jerome. *Sancti Eusebii Hieronymi Epistulae, I*, ed. I. Hilberg. *CSEL* LIV. (Vienna, 1910).

Lateinische Sprichwörter und Sentenzen des Mittelalters, ed. H. Walther (Göttingen, 1963–9).

Legenda Aurea, ed. Th. Graesse. 2nd edn (Leipzig, 1850).

Marbod of Rennes. *Marbodi . . . Opuscula*; see Hildebert.

Medieval Latin Verse, The Oxford Book of, ed. by F. J. E. Raby (Oxford, repr. 1974).

Political Poems and Songs, ed. Thomas Wright. 2 vols (1859).

Summa Theologiae Sancti Thomae Aquinatis (Madrid, 1961).

Walter of Châtillon. *Die Lieder Walters von Chatillon*, ed. K. Strecker (Berlin, 1925). *Moralisch-satirische Gedichte Walters von Chatillon*, ed. K. Strecker (Heidelberg, 1929).

Walter Map. *The Latin Poems commonly attributed to Walter Mapes*, ed. Thomas Wright. Camden Society. (1841).

SECONDARY WORKS

Adams, R. 'The Nature of Need in *PP XX*', *Traditio* 34 (1978) 273–301.

Alford, J. A. 'The Role of the Quotations in *PP*', *Spec.* 52 (1977) 80–99.

Atwood, E. and Hill, A., eds. *Studies in the Language and Culture of the Middle Ages and Later.* Texas: University of Texas Press (1969).

Auerbach, E. (tr. W. R. Trask) *Mimesis* (Princeton, 1968).

—— 'Sermo humilis', *Romanische Forschungen* 64 (1952) 304–64.

Boitani, P. and Torti, A. eds. *From the 14th to the 15th Century* (Cambridge: Brewer, 1987).

Brewer, Charlotte. 'The Textual Implications of the "Z-Text" of *PP*'. Unpublished D. Phil. thesis (Oxford, 1986).

Burnley, J. D. *Chaucer's Language and the Philosophers' Tradition* (Cambridge: Brewer, 1979).

Burrow, J. A. 'Words, Works and Will: Theme and Structure in *PP*', in Hussey, ed. *PP: Critical Approaches* (1969) 111–24.

—— *Ricardian Poetry: Chaucer, Gower, Langland and the 'Gawain' Poet* (1971).

—— 'Langland *Nel Mezzo Del Cammin'*, in Heyworth, ed., *Bennett Studies* (1981) 21–41.

—— 'Autobiographical Poetry in the Middle Ages: the Case of Thomas Hoccleve'. Gollancz Memorial Lecture. *PBA* 68 (1982) 389–412.

—— *Essays on Medieval Literature* (Oxford, 1984).

Catto, J. I., ed. *The History of the University of Oxford, I: The Early Oxford Schools* (Oxford, 1984).

Coleman, Janet. *Piers Plowman and the 'Moderni'* (Rome, 1981).

Curtius, E. R. (tr. W. R. Trask). *European Literature and the Latin Middle Ages* (Princeton, 1953).

Davie, D. *Articulate Energy: An Inquiry into the Syntax of English Poetry* (1955).

Davis, N. and Wrenn, C. L., eds. *Studies Presented to J. R. R. Tolkien* (1962).

Dillon, Janette. '*PP*: A Particular Example of Wordplay and its Structural Significance', *MÆ* 50 (1981) 40–48.

Dronke, Peter. *Medieval Latin and the Rise of the European Love-Lyric*. 2 vols. (Oxford, 1965, 1966).

—— *The Medieval Poet and his World* (Rome, 1984).

Dunbabin, J. 'Careers and Vocations', in Catto, *History of University of Oxford*, 565–605.

Elliott, R. W. V. 'The Langland Country', in Hussey, *Critical Approaches*, 226–44.

Faral, E., ed. *Les Arts Poétiques du XIIe et du XIIIe Siècle* (Paris, 1924).

Fletcher, J. M. 'The Faculty of Arts', ch. 9 in Catto, ed. *History of University of Oxford*, 369–99.

Frank, R. W. *PP and the Scheme of Salvation*. New Haven: Yale University Press (1957).

Gallais, P. and Riou, Y.-J., eds. *Mélanges offerts à René Crozet*. 2 vols. (Poitiers, 1962).

Godden, M. 'Plowmen and Hermits in Langland's *PP*', *RES* 35 (1984) 129–63.

Gradon, Pamela. 'Langland and the Ideology of Dissent'. Gollancz Memorial Lecture. *PBA* 66 (1980) 179–205.

Gray, Douglas. *Themes and Images in the Medieval English Religious Lyric* (1972).

Haren, M. *Medieval Thought: the Western Intellectual Tradition from Antiquity to the 13th Century* (1985).

Harwood, Britton J. 'Imaginative in *PP*', *MÆ* 44 (1975) 49–63.

Heyworth, P. L., ed. *Medieval Studies for J. A. W. Bennett* (Oxford, 1981).

Hill, Geoffrey. *The Lords of Limit: Essays on Literature and Ideas*. (1984).

Huppé, B. F. '"*Petrus, id est, Christus*": Word Play in *PP*, B', *ELH* 17 (1950) 163–91.

Hussey, S. S., ed. *Piers Plowman: Critical Approaches* (1969).

Jacob, E. F. *Essays in the Conciliar Epoch.* Manchester: Manchester University Press (1963).

Jacobs, N. 'The Typology of Debate and the Interpretation of *Wynnere and Wastoure*', *RES* 36 (1985) 481–500.

Jolivet, Jean. 'Quelques cas de "platonisme grammatical" du VIIe au XIIe siècle', in Gallais and Riou, eds, *Mélanges . . . Crozet*, II, 93–9.

Kane, George. *The Autobiographical Fallacy in Chaucer and Langland Studies* (1965).

—— 'Music "Neither Unpleasant nor Monotonous' in Heyworth, ed. *Bennett Studies*, 43–63.

Keen, M. H. *England in the Later Middle Ages* (1973).

Lawlor, John. *Piers Plowman: An Essay in Criticism* (1962).

Lawrence, J. *Chapters on Alliterative Verse* (1893).

Lawton, D. A. 'Literary History and Scholarly Fancy: the Date of Two ME Alliterative Poems', *Parergon* 18 (Canberra, 1977) 17–25.

—— ed., *ME Alliterative Poetry and its Literary Background.* Cambridge: Brewer (1982).

Leach, A. F. *The Schools of Medieval England* (1915).

Leech, G. N. *A Linguistic Guide to English Poetry* (repr. 1979).

Levy, B. S. and Szarmach, P. E., eds., *The Alliterative Tradition in the Fourteenth Century.* Ohio: Kent State University Press (1981).

Lewis, C. S. *The Allegory of Love* (Oxford, 1936).

Lewry, P. O. 'Grammar, Logic and Rhetoric 1220–1320', ch. 10 in Catto, ed. *History of the University of Oxford* 401–33.

Mann, Jill. 'Satiric Subject and Satiric Object in Goliardic Literature', *Mittellateinisches Jahrbuch* 15 (1980) 63–86.

Middleton, Anne. 'The Audience and Public of *PP*', in Lawton, ed., *ME Alliterative Poetry* 101–123.

Minnis, A. J. 'Langland's Ymaginatif and late-medieval theories of imagination', *Comparative Criticism* 3 (1981) 71–103.

Murphy, James J. *Rhetoric in the Middle Ages.* University of California Press: Berkeley, Los Angeles and London (1974).

Oakden, J. P. *Alliterative Poetry in Middle English.* 2 vols. Manchester (1930).

Ong, Walter J. 'Wit and Mystery: a Revaluation in Medieval Hymnody', *Spec.* 22 (1947) 310–41.

Orme, N. *English Schools in the Middle Ages* (1973).

Palmer, R. 'Bede as a Textbook Writer: a Study of his *De Arte Metrica*', *Spec.* 34 (1959) 573–84.

Peebles, R. J. *The Legend of Longinus in Ecclesiastical Art and in English Literature.* Bryn Mawr Monographs 9 (1911).

Raby, F. J. E. *A History of Christian-Latin Poetry* (Oxford, 1927).

—— *A History of Secular Latin Poetry*. 2 vols. (Oxford, 1934).

Raw, Barbara. 'Piers and the Image of God in Man', in Hussey, ed. *Approaches* 143–79.

Ricks, Christopher. *The Force of Poetry* (Oxford, 1984).

Salter, Elizabeth. 'The Timeliness of *Wynnere and Wastoure*', *MÆ* 47 (1978) 40–65.

Schmidt, A. V. C. 'Langland and Scholastic Philosophy', *MÆ* 38 (1969) 134–56.

—— 'Langland's Structural Imagery', *EC* 30 (1980) 311–25.

—— '*Lele Wordes* and *Bele Paroles*: Some Aspects of Langland's Word-Play', *RES* 34 (1983) 137–50.

—— 'The Treatment of the Crucifixion in *PP* and in Rolle's *Meditations on the Passion*', *Analecta Cartusiana* 35 (1983) 174–96.

—— 'The Authenticity of the Z-Text of *PP*: a Metrical Examination', *MÆ* 53 (1984) 295–300.

—— 'Speech, Silence, Words and Voices in Eliot's Poetry', *UNISA English Studies* (Pretoria, S. Africa, (1983)) 17–22.

Schoeck, R. J. 'On Rhetoric in Fourteenth-Century Oxford', *Med. St.* 30 (1968) 214–25.

Schumacher, K. *Stüdien über den Stabreim in der mittelenglischen Alliterationsdichtung* (Bonn, 1914).

Simpson, James. 'The Transformation of Meaning: a Figure of Thought in *PP*', *RES* 37 (1986) 161–83.

—— 'From Reason to Affective Knowledge: Modes of Thought and Poetic Form in *PP*', *MÆ* 55 (1986) 1–23.

Spearing, A. C. 'Verbal Repetition in *PP* B and C', *JEGP* 62 (1963) 722–37. *Medieval to Renaissance in English Poetry* (Cambridge, 1985).

Stokes, Myra. *Justice and Mercy in 'Piers Plowman'. A Reading of the B Text Visio* (1984).

Strang, Barbara M. H. *Modern English Structure*. 2nd edn. (1968).

Sullivan, Sr Carmeline. *The Latin Insertions and the Macaronic Verse in 'PP'*. Washington: Catholic University of America (1932).

Tristram, Philippa. *Figures of Life and Death in Medieval English Literature.* (1976).

Turville-Petre, Thorlac. *The Alliterative Revival*. Cambridge: D. S. Brewer (1977).

Vernet, Felix. *Mediaeval Spirituality*. Tr. by the Benedictines of Talacre. (1930).

Walsh, P. G. '"Golias" and Goliardic Poetry', *MÆ* 52 (1983) 1–9.

Warton, Thomas. *The History of English Poetry* (1781). Repr. Ward, Lock, n.d.

White, Hugh. 'Langland's Ymaginatif, Kynde and the *Benjamin Major*', *MÆ* 55 (1986) 241–8.

Wilcockson, Colin. 'A Note on "Riflynge" in *PP* B. V. 234' *MÆ* 52 (1983) 302–5.

Wittgenstein, L. *Philosophical Investigations*. Tr. G. E. M. Anscombe. (Oxford, 1984).

Wittig, J. S. '*PP* B, Passus IX–XII: Elements in the Design of the Inward Journey', *Traditio* 28 (1972) 211–80.

—— 'The Dramatic and Rhetorical Development of Long Will's Pilgrimage', *NM* 76 (1975) 52–76.

Wood, R. A. 'A 14th Century London Owner of *PP*', *MÆ* 53 (1984) 83–90.

Woolf, Rosemary. *English Religious Lyric in the Middle Ages*. (Oxford, 1968).

Wrenn, C. L. *A Study of Old English Literature* (1967).

Yunck, J. A. *The Lineage of Lady Meed: The Development of Medieval Venality Satire*. Notre Dame, Indiana (1963).

Ziegler, Philip. *The Black Death*. (Harmondsworth, repr. 1971).

Index

Lif 64
Longinus (Longeus) 76, 125, 126
Lucifer 9, 71, 134
Lydgate, John 144

Magdalen, Mary 74
Makometh 65
Mann, Jill 81n, 90, 110n
Mannyng of Brunne, Robert 9n
Map, Walter 69n
Marbod of Rennes 68, 73, 74
Matthew, St 66
Mede, Lady 32, 60, 63, 72, 76, 78, 105,
   114, 123, 127, 128, 129, 130, 136n,
   139, 140
Middleton, Anne 34n
Milton, John 29
Minnis, A. J. 16n
Morse, Ruth 126n
Morte Arthure 7, 8, 10, 55, 56, 63n, 70,
   101, 102, 124
Moyses 37
Munde the Millere 9n
Murphy, J. J. 22n, 24, 25n

Nede 129

Oakden, J. P. 42n, 43n, 46n, 50n, 55n,
   62n, 63n, 96n
Offord, M. Y. 32n
Ong, W. J. 119n
Owen, Wilfred 67, 72

Palmer, R. 24n
Palmere, William 3
Parliament of the Three Ages, The 32, 33
Patience 64, 83, 84, 86, 91, 100, 110,
   111, 117, 121, 123n, 137
Paul, St 12, 75, 82
Pearsall, Derek 2n, 3n, 23, 75n, 130
Peter, St 12, 120
Petrarch 145
Piers 13, 51, 66, 77, 85, 86, 87, 90, 97,
   105, 113, 120, 122, 123, 124, 129, 130
Piers Plowman
   – A-text 33, 40, 53, 67, 76, 77, 78
   – C-text 10, 12, 15, 19, 33, 38, 40, 65,
   67, 77, 78, 87, 97, 102, 104, 105, 113,
   116, 122, 126, 129, 130
   – Z-text 19, 28, 29, 33, 36, 38, 67
Pope, Alexander 64n
Pride 14, 64, 138

Priscian 35n
Puttenham, George 2, 4, 42, 144, 145

Raby, F. J. E. 68, 74, 75n, 109
Raw, Barbara 82n
'On the Rebellion of Jack Straw' 94
Repentance 105
Reson 15, 32, 39, 83, 102, 140, 142
Ricks, Christopher 1n, 77n, 111n, 112,
   116n
Rolle, Richard 79n
Romaunt of the Rose 8
Ryan, W. W. 113n

Saint Erkenwald 63n, 126
Salter, Elizabeth 5
Samaritan 52, 70, 71
Samuels, M. L. 34n, 67n, 117n, 130n
Sarsens 73
Satan 9, 45, 47, 71, 133, 134, 136
Schoeck, R. J. 22n
Schumacher, K. 38n, 40n
Scripture 12, 48, 91, 92, 101, 102
Shakespeare, W. 144
Sidney, Sir Philip 144
Simpson, James 85n, 117n, 131n, 132n,
   138n
Sir Orfeo 8
Skeat, W. W. 2, 34, 35n, 46, 47n, 50n,
   66n, 100, 130
Skelton, John 13n
Sloth 11, 78, 139
Solomon 87
Spearing, A. C. 59n, 145n
Stokes, Myra 57n, 131n
Strang, B. M. H. 45n
Studie, Dame 5, 8, 10, 17, 82, 128, 129
Sullivan, Sr Carmeline 88, 89, 91, 93

Theologie 59, 60, 128, 141
Theseus 144
'On the Times' 94
Trajan 55, 57, 73n, 99, 103, 128n, 135n
Trevisa, John 22, 102, 103
Tristram, P. 95n
Truth, 8, 11, 40, 66, 77, 83, 101, 102,
   124, 130, 140, 141, 142, 143
Turville-Petre, T. 2n, 6, 7, 32n, 35n,
   96n

Unitee 138
Uriah 90